C000241309

Mies van der Rohe. Toronto-Dominion Centre, Toronto
Detlef Mertins, Photography Peter McCallum
Sept. 26, 1988, 6:30 a.m.

Sept. 26, 8:15 a.m.

Sept. 26, 10:15 a.m.

Sept. 26, 10:45 a.m.

Sept. 26, 5:30 p.m.

Sept. 26, 8:00 p.m.

# THE PRESENCE OF MIES

**Edited by Detlef Mertins**

*Contributors*:
George Baird
Brian Boigon
Beatriz Colomina
Rebecca Comay
K. Michael Hays
Dan Hoffman
Rosalind Krauss
Sanford Kwinter
Phyllis Lambert
Detlef Mertins
Fritz Neumeyer
Ben Nicholson
Ignasi de Solá-Morales Rubió

**Princeton Architectural Press  1994**

# The Presence of Mies

Published by
Princeton Architectural Press
37 East 7th Street  New York, New York 10003
1.800.722.6657   www.papress.com
© 1994 Detlef Mertins and Princeton Architectural Press
All rights reserved
04 03 02 01 00  5 4 3 2

Cover image taken from photograph of the Toronto-Dominion Centre at night, 1968.
Photo Panda. 68854-31.

Sponsored by The Canada Council and The Ontario Arts Council.

Library of Congress Cataloging-in-Publication Data
Mies van der Rohe, Ludwig, 1886–1969.
     The Presence of Mies / Detlef Mertins, editor ; George Baird. . .[et al., contributors].
          p.     cm.
     "This publication follows the symposium . . . held on September 26, 1992 in the
Council Chamber of Toronto City Hall to mark the twenty-fifth anniversary of the
Toronto-Dominion Centre"—T.p. verso.
     Includes bibliographical references.
     ISBN 1-56898-013-2
     1. Mies van der Rohe, Ludwig, 1886–1969—Criticism and interpretation—
Congresses.   2. Architecture, Modern—20th century—Congresses.
I. Mertins, Detlef.   II. Baird, George.   III. Title.
NA1088.M65A4     1994
720'.92—dc20                              94–16259
                                              CIP

## ACKNOWLEDGMENTS

*The Presence of Mies* began as a symposium held in 1992 to mark the twenty-fifth anniversary of the Toronto-Dominion Centre, designed by Ludwig Mies van der Rohe.

A project of the University of Toronto School of Architecture and Landscape Architecture, the symposium was sponsored by The Canada Council and the Toronto-Dominion Centre, as major sponsors, the Royal Architectural Institute of Canada, Knoll, the City of Toronto, the University of Toronto Architecture Students Union, the Steel Structures Education Foundation, the Goethe Institute (Toronto), Ballenford Architectural Books, the Toronto Society of Architects, and Artsweek. This publication has been generously funded by The Canada Council and the Ontario Arts Council.

Many thanks to Brigitte Shim for co-organizing the symposium, Brian Boigon for his critical insights, Anthony Eardley and Komala Prabhakar for their on-going support, Nigel Smith and Burton Hamfelt for graphic design, Donald Chong, Dathe Wong, and Elaine Dydik for their drawings, Kirsten Douglas for assisting in coordination, Mike Awad and John Howarth for photography, and Mark Thompson for copy editing. Special thanks to J. Robert S. Prichard (President, University of Toronto), Robert E. Millward (Commissioner of Planning and Development, City of Toronto) and Marc Baraness (Director of Architecture and Urban Design, City of Toronto) for their invaluable help in realizing the symposium, and to Kevin Lippert and Ann Urban for publishing the book. And finally, I am grateful to the authors whose enthusiasm and generosity have made this project a unique pleasure.
*Detlef Mertins*

# Contents

Introduction

**NEW MIES**
*Detlef Mertins*

The photographs of Mies van der Rohe's Toronto-Dominion Centre that
open this book register the transformations in its appearance over the
course of a day. Like other of Mies's prismatic and elemental projects of the
1950s and 1960s, the TDC has often been interpreted as exemplary of the
self-referential and transcendental modernist object. Yet the photographs
by Peter MacCallum reveal the identity of this apparently autonomous block
to be continually shifting under the play of light and weather, from total
opacity to total transparency, contingent on conditions in its surroundings
and on the perceptions of observers. What, then, might the notion of "presence" mean for such a building whose identity is both stable and unstable,
autonomous and contingent? Could it be that this seemingly familiar architecture is still in many ways unknown, and that the monolithic Miesian
edifice refracts the light of interpretation, multiplying its potential implications for contemporary architectural practices?

   This collection of essays taps the multiple resonances of Mies's work in
current thinking about architecture as it relates to issues of practice, technology, image culture, philosophy, art, and education. How is Mies being
opened up to new questions and reformulated problematics? How might
various branches of contemporary theory intersect with his work at a time
when historical research is excavating the prehistory of postmodernity
within the early twentieth century? And how might critical transformations
of Mies's architecture serve for new work appropriate to our own time? To
mark the twenty-fifth anniversary of the Toronto-Dominion Centre — which
Philip Johnson has called "the biggest Mies in the world" — a symposium
was convened in the Council Chamber of Viljo Revell's Toronto City Hall

(1964) to explore these questions. The mixture of contributors and disciplines produced a stimulating array of perspectives weaving in and out of common themes and articulating nuanced positions. Participants were grouped in pairs, each addressing a topic that was at once distinct from but related to the others, producing provocative convergences and a sense of compaction without suppressing tension and instability. This collection of essays flows from that event.

To begin, Phyllis Lambert and I reconsider aspects of Mies's research and practice. Lambert examines Mies's distinctive way of working, a process through which design ideas slowly assumed corporeal presence in refined structural typologies and tense groupings of buildings carefully calibrated to respond to given programs, means, and contexts. Focusing on the Berlin skyscraper projects of 1922 and the Toronto-Dominion Centre of 1967, my own contribution examines Mies's conception of the architectural "project" as critically mediating between the problematic material conditions of modernity and idealist longings for redemption and the return of origins.

Fritz Neumeyer, whose book on Mies's writings *The Artless Word* is a point of reference for many of the other papers, and Sanford Kwinter both address issues of architecture's relationship to technology. While Neumeyer stays close to Mies's own texts and projects to delineate his construction of the reciprocity of art and technology, subject and object, Kwinter places Mies's architectonic opposition between fixed structure and fluid space into the context of the modern episteme as evident in Germany during the Weimar period and its slippery slide into Fascism — in polymer science, chemical technology, dance notation, and the Autobahn program.

Dan Hoffman and Ben Nicholson discuss the pedagogical ambitions and work of their design studios, at the Cranbrook Academy of Art and the Illinois Institute of Technology respectively, where they have extended and transformed aspects of Mies's architecture and teaching. Hoffman's recent experimental work has been tied to Mies's investigations of grid, self-referential fabrication, and perceptual horizons. Nicholson's teaching has been part of the renewal of the curriculum at IIT, finally breaking from the ossified canonization of Miesian form to rework his curriculum while maintaining aspects of its initial spirit.

Rosalind Krauss and Ignasi de Solá-Morales Rubió stake out opposed interpretations of Minimalism and Mies. Krauss distances her reading of Mies from the recent rash of poststructuralist and anti-classical interpretations (citing Robin Evans, José Quetglas, and K. Michael Hays), preferring instead the modernist Mies of the grid, whose work she reads as analogous to the paintings of Agnes Martin, with their dialectical interplay of conceptual grid and perceptual effect. Krauss's return to the modernist Mies presents a challenge to rethink the idea of autonomy in dialectical terms, a challenge subsequently addressed by K. Michael Hays in his Afterword. Solá-Morales, on the other hand, insists on an anti-classical interpretation, one that takes as its points of departure sensations, perceptions, and materiality, rather than *a priori* conceptual categories such as the logic of vision represented by the grid. Solá-Morales continues here to elaborate his thinking towards an architecture of untimeliness.

Rebecca Comay and George Baird both test-drive Mies through philosophies that he never read. Comay's staging of an encounter between Mies and Martin Heidegger around the idea of the "almost nothing" challenges the easy alliance that has often been suggested and marks the profound differences between their thinking while recognizing the potential of ambiguous parallelisms. Baird's struggle to interpret the Toronto-Dominion Centre in relation to the idea of appearance in the public realm (as developed by Hannah Arendt, who had studied with Heidegger) is equally tentative, but contributes to understanding Mies's existentialist transformation of the historical civic plaza and public loggia. While both of these engagements remain tentative, they point to fruitful ways of thinking from Mies to contemporary philosophical and political concerns.

The final papers by Beatriz Colomina and Brian Boigon address the culture of images. Colomina begins by suggesting that Mies's careful self-construction through theoretical projects and texts in publications, exhibitions, and other media productions is at odds with the tectonic foundation myth of Mies as the son of a stonemason, and then goes on to suggest that Mies's architecture also bears the formal imprint of modern media such as photography. Boigon presents a clipped essay on modern jokery, stand-up comics, and curtain walls, drawing on verbal and visual images that move in and out of modern (Miesian) architecture, and up and down the ladder of (un)consciousness.

In his Afterword, K. Michael Hays draws on the preceding papers to put forward a new interpretation of Mies's abstraction, rereading the Seagram Building through Theodor Adorno's idea of the autonomous work of art as dialectically embodying and resisting the conditions of a totally reified society.

By sidestepping received interpretations of Mies as homotopic — to use the notion popularized by Demetri Porphyrios — these essays take stock of Mies's work critically and serve to open it — still so haunting and powerful — in surprising and unexpected directions. Just as the identity of the Toronto-Dominion Centre may be understood to fragment and multiply when placed into the field of context and reception — Sanford Kwinter asks the strategic question "To whom does Mies belong?" — so the identity of the architect may also remain contingent and profoundly mysterious. What, after all, might "presence" mean for a man who changed his name in such a way as to undermine the plausibility of designating a discrete and integrated unit of subjectivity.

It has often been noted that the year 1921 was decisive for the young Ludwig Mies and that a new man — a new Mies — was born in the convergence of several events at that time. This new identity was marked by both a new architecture and a new name. Historians have accounted for Mies's change of name — adding *van der Rohe* and an umlaut to the "e" in Mies — as an effort to muffle the disagreeable overtones of *mies*, which connotes something "rotting or foul" in German, by adding his mother's maiden name *Rohe* and joining it with the somewhat elegant and Dutch *van der.* While this explanation addresses Mies's cultivation of an aristocratic persona, it nevertheless fails to consider the complexity of the culture of pseudonyms and (re)constructed identities within which Mies circulated at the time, with its propensity for word-plays and the reduction of sense to non-sense. It also remains inadequate to the peculiar artificiality of the conjunction *van der* and ignores the connotation of "raw" (roh) in his mother's name, which would seem to reinforce the disagreeable *mies* rather than moderate it.

Mies's change of name occurred in the same period in which he launched a new direction in architecture by exploring the elemental properties of engineered materials and methods, had his records of the previous years destroyed, separated from his wife and children, transformed his Berlin apartment into a bachelor's atelier, moved his bed into the bathroom, and began sleeping with the plumbing fixtures. This rebirth was staged one year after Charles-Édouard Jeanneret assumed the name Le Corbusier and in the context of assumed names by both expressionists and Dadaists. (See Kurt Schwitters's playful transformation of *Mies* into *Nies,* which suggests "sneeze," in Colomina fig. 4.)

Having had their pre-war neo-classical work rejected for inclusion in the exhibition of unknown architects organized by Walter Gropius, Bruno Taut, and Adolf Behne for the Arbeitsrat für Kunst in 1919, Mies and his friend Ludwig Hilberseimer began to explore alternatives to the rising wave of expressionism. Hilberseimer warned of the misappropriations of Paul Scheerbart's vision of a fully technologized "glass architecture" by the expressionists (Taut's organicist utopianism was not the only fruit of Scheerbart's fantasies about technological society), and Mies began playing with light reflections on large sheets of thermally improved glass. And both Mies and Hilberseimer began to associate with the Berlin Dadaists and to participate in discussions that led to the formation of the magazine G, whose elementalist program succeeded Dada. Mies had met Hans Richter in late 1919, had attended the First International Dada Fair in the summer of 1920, and met the De Stijl Dadaist Theo van Doesburg that year and El Lissitzky in the following year.

While the expressionists had invested their hope for the renewal of organic wholeness in the figure of a New Man, a new humanist subject whose deep inwardness was to provide the strength to reconcile a troubled, fragmented, and uncertain modern world, the Dadaists rejected such transcendental and intoxicating subjectivity. As early as 1917, Richard Huelsenbeck had begun to rework the New Man into an inorganic, historically and materially contingent figure who "carries pandemonium within himself . . . for or against which no one can do anything." In photocollages, montages, and assemblages — constructive techniques developed in opposition to the media of painting and sculpture — they portrayed the new subjectivity as internalizing contradiction (rationality-fantasy, order-disorder) and living through the paradox of a technology born of nature but seemingly cast against it. And while most of Bruno Taut's Crystal Chain circle took inhuman names like Glas (Bruno Taut), Zacken (Wassili Luckhardt), Prometh (Hermann Finsterlin), Tancred (Paul Goesch), and Angkor (Hans Luckhardt) the Dadaists playfully recast themselves into a constellation of figures — with names such as Oberdada (Johannes Baader), Dadasoph (Raoul Hausmann), Weltdada (Richard Huelsenbeck), and Propagandada (Georg Grosz) — whose fictional personae provided new critical means for enacting the relationship of self to the structures of society and culture.

In the context of the Dadaists' reduction of language to the psychological level of pure articulation, formation, and sensation, Mies's assumed name suggests a more complex cultural project than has hitherto been suspected. Could it be that *van der* was also a play on *wandel* (transformation) or on *von der* (from the), in which case "Miës van der Rohe" might connote "something rotten or foul transformed from the raw"? Could it be that the seemingly sober and sternly elementalist Mies undermined his own aristocratic self-construction, making a joke at his own expense? Is it not suggestive that commentators and historians have had such a hard time coming to terms with the question "who was this man Mies?", this silent and mysterious figure who struggled to reinvent himself after 1921 as both autonomous *and* contingent on his field of perception — the historical conditions of modernity, technology and anonymity, and the playfully vicious irreverence of Dada?

Mies's opening up of architecture and himself to the rush of modern technological society played out an impulse to reconnect architecture and life that is being felt once again. At the turn of the century, this impulse had been expressed dramatically by the Viennese critic Hermann Bahr in his "Die Moderne" of 1890, and had been linked to the rethinking of subjectivity by the anti-metaphysical "new psychologies," including that of the Viennese scientist-philosopher Ernst Mach, whose *Analysis of Sensations* (1886) continued to be part of cultural and political debates into the 1920s. Mach's conception of reality as nothing more than a fluid combination of sensations and of the ego as a mass of sensations that changes its composition over time was of consequence for the telegraphic style of *Wortkunst* (word-art) poetry devised by the Cubists, Futurists, and expressionists. And Johannes Baader and Raoul Hausmann drew on Mach's interlocking of reality and fantasy in attempting to rebuild the myth of cultural progress within Dada as a practical, functional, even strategic fictionalizing. In reopening Mies — recontextualizing his work in both his time and ours — this anthology registers a similar impulse to reforge the links between architecture and changing conditions of life, recognizing that the theoretical framings and social issues have changed, but that architecture continues to participate in the reconstruction of social identities and, in that process, reconstructs itself.

# PRACTICE

1. Mies van der Rohe,
view of the Toronto banking district at
sunset showing the Toronto-Dominion
Centre, Toronto, Ontario.

## PUNCHING THROUGH THE CLOUDS:
## NOTES ON THE PLACE OF THE TORONTO-DOMINION CENTRE IN THE
## NORTH AMERICAN *OEUVRE* OF MIES

*Phyllis Lambert*

The Toronto-Dominion Centre (TDC), as its name indicates, is not one, but a number of buildings forming an urban complex, and the buildings that compose it are exemplary types in the *oeuvre* of Mies. I would like to explore these significant aspects of the TDC — Miesian urban space and building types — in the context of Mies's built work in North America. In doing so I will touch on the history of the commission and issues pertaining to the reception of Mies's work in the 1960s in Canada and in the United States.

### The Building Complex in Context
Mies van der Rohe was involved in the design of urban spaces in North America immediately on his arrival as Director of the Department of Architecture, Illinois Institute of Technology in 1938: from 1939 through 1958 he created the 110-acre campus for IIT. Most of Mies's built work prior to the design for the TDC in 1963 involved a complex of buildings forming urban spaces, notably complexes composed of two or more buildings. In Chicago the twin concrete and glass Promontory Apartments completed in 1949 were followed in 1951 by the seminal steel and glass 860 and 880 Lake Shore Drive Apartments, and shortly thereafter the paired buildings of Commonwealth Promenade and the 900 and 910 Lake Shore Drive Apartments, both completed in 1956. On another scale, Lafayette Park, the 78-acre urban renewal scheme in Detroit, was constructed between 1956 and 1963. Designed by Mies in association with Ludwig Hilberseimer, and largely following the latter's planning principles, the building groups were typically Miesian: paired slabs were

sited in tension, one with the other, either in a slipped parallel configuration or at right angles. Lafayette Park also involved the play of high-rise and low-rise structures. All of these complexes were composed of residential buildings at the edges of cities.

Mies's first interventions in the city center were the Seagram Building in New York (1954–58) and the Chicago Federal Center (1959–64). Both were designed for office use, and for both a well-defined open plaza space was integral to the design concept. The TDC therefore belongs to a powerful group of urban building complexes by Mies, which profoundly influenced both the form and architecture of the office building, open space in the city, and planning legislation in major North American cities. The extruded metal and glass curtain wall of Seagram and its use of tinted glass became, for better or for worse, widely replicated (figs. 2 & 3). And after the Seagram building was completed the planning legislation for New York City was revised in order to encourage street-level open space in association with high-rise buildings. In Chicago, the dense fabric of the downtown area known as the "Loop" was opened up by the Federal Center. While the history of the urban complex in the United States, including and beyond Rockefeller Center, still needs to be written, a successive series of designs for the TDC site itself shows that the concept of grouping buildings in order to create in-block open public spaces around high-rise buildings — and this despite Viljo Revell's Toronto City Hall (1956–65) — was anything but a standard design approach of the time. (See TDC, fig. 2.)

**History of the Commission**

Two projects for the site of the TDC were designed in the early 1960s prior to Mies's engagement, neither of which is recorded anywhere in the literature of architecture.[1] While the developer — the fledgling Fairview Corporation (before the merger with Cadillac) — had amassed the land, the Toronto-Dominion Bank — as principal user and part owner — designated the architect. The president of the bank, Alan Lambert, commissioned Skidmore Owings and Merrill (SOM) and its designer-in-chief, Gordon Bunshaft, the modernist bank architect *par excellence*. SOM had designed and built the glass-walled Manufacturers Trust Company (1953–54) and the pavilion-like branch of the Chase Manhattan Bank (1957–61), both in New York City.

For the TDC, Bunshaft proposed a single high-rise building with a banking hall subsumed within it, as had been normative since the 1930s. The building was indifferently placed on the site and Bunschaft was clearly more interested in designing a curving concrete structure, sweeping up without a break, without expansion joints, some sixty storeys above ground.

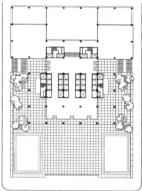

2. Mies van der Rohe,
Seagram Building. Daytime view, 1958.
Photo Ezra Stoller.

3. Mies van der Rohe,
Seagram Building, 1954–58, New York.
Plaza level plan.

Curved at the base, the external pier-columns allowed the extension of a larger floor plate on the lower floors for the banking hall, without differentiating base from tower. All expansion of the continuous 800-foot high concrete structure was to be resolved by hefty stainless steel piston-like slip joints placed at the top of the building — a daring and unproved solution, which the structural engineers in Toronto rejected. Bunshaft refused to change his design and lost the commission.

The design of the TDC was then given to the much less practiced Toronto firm that had been associated with SOM, John B. Parkin Associates. The Parkin firm again proposed a single building, but with a more conventional tower and the banking hall now located in a moat below ground level (figs. 4 & 5). Wary of Parkin's lack of experience in designing multi-storey buildings, the developer suggested hiring the New York firm of Harrison and Abromowitz as technical consultants. Wallace K. Harrison had been one of the architects of Rockefeller Center. However, Mies was invited for an interview on my insistent recommendation.[2] On the strength of the Seagram Building and the almost-completed Chicago Federal Center — and after Mies had asked Alan Lambert the question, "Do you want to have your bank in a *basement*?" — he was awarded the commission.

## TDC Building Types and Plaza

The TDC was late in Mies's practice. He was seventy-seven years old in 1963 and had been building in North America for almost twenty-five years. His compositional syntax of slipping planes dates back another quarter century to the Brick Country House of 1923. The spatial relationships of the TDC buildings, therefore, had a long lineage in his work. As an urban complex in a downtown business district, the Chicago Federal Center was a direct predecessor of the TDC. The urban design for both the Chicago and Toronto complexes involved two high-rise buildings of different height and length placed into a composition with a free-standing single-storey pavilion. The symbolism of a detached pavilion, signifying a special function — the post office at the Federal Center and the banking hall at the TDC — might well be a Miesian invention. But the association of a pavilion with high-rise buildings had a special significance in Mies's *oeuvre,* for each building type had been central to Mies's preoccupations since his arrival in North America. The association of these two building types — skeletal tower and free-span pavilion — and their formal relationships at the TDC constitutes a major synthesis of Mies's work after 1939.

The open urban spaces created by the placement of the buildings on the site form the most extensive and publicly-oriented plaza in Mies's *oeuvre.* The 4.6-acre site of the Federal Center in Chicago physically separates the post-office building and the eight-bay, forty-storey tower from the thirteen-bay, thirty-storey slab. (fig. 6) At Toronto no such separation exists (fig. 7); landscaping is therefore more extensive, and a large south-facing greensward was created as a place to sit or recline, distinct from the granite plaza to the north of the main tower, which forms the principal space of arrival and orientation.

### The Tall Building

In his archetypal studies of 1921–22 for the architectural expression of tall buildings, Mies was interested in exploring the reflective qualities of glass; hence the prismatic and curved forms of his proposals. These early towers were light-reflecting transparent shafts, the interior structure variably perceptible behind the glass skin. However, in the first of Mies's high-rises to be realized, the 1949 Promontory Apartments (fig. 8), the surface also represents the rational deep structure of the skeletal frame within, the enclosing skin of glass and brick being placed as infill aligned with the outer plane of column and slab. This preoccupation with an architecture of structural expression was evident in Mies's earliest American work, the two-storey buildings for the IIT campus, an attitude certainly related to the late nineteenth-century rationalist Chicago School buildings.

Mies continuously refined the architectural and constructional expression of the high-rise building. For his first project in steel and glass, 860–880 Lake Shore Drive (1948–51), the skin was still an infill between spandrel and column, and no ventilation unit was provided beyond the operable window. However, at 900–910 Lake Shore Drive (1953–56) Mies cantilevered the glass and aluminum skin past the concrete columns and slab, giving expression to the separation of the materials of structure and of enclosure. At the same time, the projected slab allowed ventilating units to be tucked within the depth of the column-space rather than protruding into the room. However, beyond these practicalities, and true to his startling studies of 1921–22, Mies found that the sheath created by an exoskeletal skin better expressed the essence of the tall building than did the infilled enclosure.[3] This principle was followed at the Toronto-Dominion Centre, as it had been at the Chicago Federal Center, but using steel rather than aluminum for the framing elements and wind-bracing I-beam stiffeners. Through the use of steel, all joints could be welded rather than mechanically attached as would be necessary for aluminum, achieving a water-tight skin and another level of refinement.

The Toronto-Dominion Bank Tower posed new design problems for Mies. Its fifty-four stories, making it then the tallest building in Canada, stretched the limits of conventional steel frame construction and required advanced

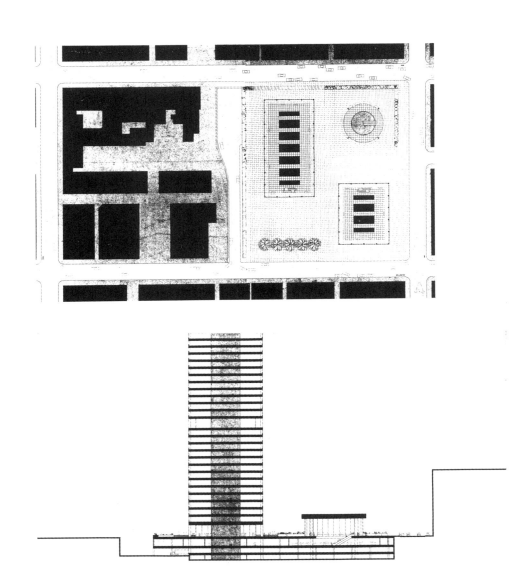

4 & 5. John B. Parkin Associates, architects,
Bregman + Hamann, engineers,
Skidmore Owings & Merrill, consultants.
Study for Toronto-Dominion Centre.
Site plan and east-west section.
Project no. 6266, 1963.

engineering, using high tensile steel for cross-bracing. The size of the structural bay was also a new development in Mies's office; the use of a rectangular bay of 30 feet by 40 feet, rather than the 30-foot square bay, developed from the reconsideration of the relationship of the core to useable floor space. In addition, the shopping concourse connecting various parts of the complex below the plaza level was a completely new problem for Mies's office.[4]

## The Free-Span Pavilion

Mies's interest in free-span buildings dates from the 1940s and evolved from the concert hall project of 1942, for which he made a collage showing spatial elements within a free-spanning factory structure, unobstructed by supporting elements. In discussing the architectural consequences of free-span roof structures, Mies likened the one-way roof span to the buttressed nave of Gothic cathedrals and the two-way span to the peripteral colonnade of classical Greek architecture. Investigations of one-way spanning systems began with the Farnsworth House (1945–50), Crown Hall at IIT (1952–56), and the unbuilt project for the Mannheim National Theater competition (1952–53).

The two-way system was first studied in Mies's office in 1950 by his former graduate student, Myron Goldsmith, in a theoretical study for a 50-foot by 50-foot house: the roof was supported by four columns, one in the middle of each side. A three-dimensional spanning system was studied in 1953 as a solution to the very long span of the 720-foot square roof for the Chicago Convention Hall, which Mies worked on with his graduate students at IIT. The study of a two-way structure for a specific commission was undertaken in 1959 for the unbuilt Bacardi building in Mexico. Gene Summers, also a former graduate student, was in charge of the project and immediately thereafter of the design for three built works involving two-way free-spans — the Federal Center Post Office (1959–64), the National Gallery in Berlin of 1962–68, and the bank pavilion of the Toronto-Dominion Centre (1963–69).

The structures for these three pavilions are different. The Federal Center Post Office does not have a free-span roof structure: overhead observation galleries required for the surveillance of the postal workers (a requirement for all U.S. Post offices, as it is for gambling halls in Las Vegas) were to be hung from the center of the roof, obviating a clear-span solution.[5] The four cross-shaped, intersecting I-beam steel columns, which support the gallery-loaded roof, divide the 197-foot square roof into nine bays. With its relatively shallow 4-foot 2-inch deep roof structure and the planar enclosing glass wall framed with bar stock between the cruciform columns at the

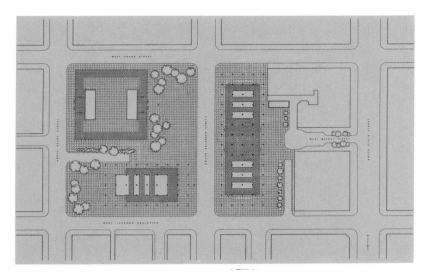

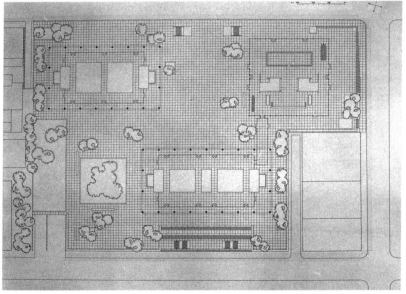

6. Mies van der Rohe,
Chicago Federal Center, 1959–64,
Chicago, Illinois. Site plan.

7. Mies van der Rohe, Toronto-Dominion
Centre, 1963–69, Toronto, Ontario.
Ground-floor plan.

8. Mies van der Rohe,
The Promontory Apartment Building,
1946–49, Chicago, Illinois.
Exterior perspective.

perimeter, the Post Office is a modest volume that interacts spatially and at plaza level with the free-standing columns and bar stock glazed enclosures of the two high-rise buildings that complete the Federal Center complex (fig. 9).

The structural system of the New National Gallery in Berlin, which was derived from the post-tensioned concrete roof of the unbuilt Bacardi building, is composed of massive two-way exposed steel plate girders forming a 5-foot 11-inch deep coffered roof plate that is the architecture of the building. The 214-foot square roof plate is supported at the perimeter by eight tapered cruciform steel columns, two on each side. The glass enclosure is pulled deeply back, emphasizing the roof plane by freeing it at the perimeter and creating a dramatic sculptural form set alone on a granite surfaced podium (fig. 10).

The Toronto-Dominion Bank pavilion spans 150 feet in both directions. The 5-foot deep beams of the pavilion are on 10-foot centers. Like the National Gallery in Berlin, these beams form a coffered-like roof plate; but rather than floating visually, a series of the intersecting I-beam columns at 10-foot intervals around the perimeter create continuity with the exposed steel roof beams, and visually as well as structurally create a supporting wall. Glazing at the center-line of the intersecting I-beam columns completes the enclosure (fig. 11). Because of the close rhythm of these members, the pavilion walls shift from solid to transparent as the viewer approaches and moves around it. This shift occurs in a similar way in all of Mies's tower structures and continues the ambiguous oscillation of transparency and reflectivity of the 1920s projects. The Toronto-Dominion Bank pavilion has a declamatory presence, sited tightly at the corner of a major commercial intersection, the locus of four major Canadian banks. It is a much more highly articulated and sophisticated building, inside and outside, than the Chicago Post Office pavilion.

This brief account of the development of a building type in Mies's office tells something of Mies's design process. Work on theoretical and practical design issues took place between school and office. Mies would often say that research must be engaged in periods of free time, for tight building schedules permitted little opportunity to do so. There were many thin years in his office when a few young architects, barely paid a living wage, felt privileged to be able to work there. Within his canon of a structural architecture, Mies encouraged particular research proposed by members of his staff if it was a logical development of a direction he had established. The office continuously undertook research which led to the refinement and development of certain problems: some architects investigated the architectural implications of mechanical and ventilating systems; some the skin for high-rise residential or commercial buildings; others — such as Goldsmith — researched structural issues. Gene Summers was the most active of Mies's collaborators in researching and developing different possibilities inherent in architectural/structural solutions for actual commissions, particularly for low-rise, free-span pavilions for Bacardi, the New National Gallery, the Federal Center, and the Toronto-Dominion Centre.

## Reception

I would like to end by posing a question. An interesting problem of reception is raised by the Toronto-Dominion Centre: why is it that the Seagram Building was instantly perceived as a master building while the TDC was ignored and reviled?

Comparing the number of articles on the Toronto-Dominion Centre with those on the Toronto City Hall is instructive and astounding. Only one article on the TDC was published in Canadian periodicals, and five in the United States and Europe from 1967 through 1972. (The Federal Center also attracted only nine — none in Canada). However, Viljo Revell's Toronto City Hall, built in the same period, generated a great deal of attention in Canada. The international competition generated twenty-six articles in three Canadian periodicals from 1956 through 1964. Almost an equal number of articles were devoted to the completed complex — twenty-one in five Canadian periodicals from 1965 through 1971. Outside Canada, interest in the Toronto City Hall was only moderate, equalling coverage of the TDC; a total of six articles were published in the United States and Europe during the 1960s.

The one article in Canada on the Toronto-Dominion Centre, written by the Toronto architect Macy DuBois for *Canadian Architect* in 1967, set out to discredit it in every way. We read in his first sentence: "Mies is struggling to teach the world the lesson of simplicity. If simplicity means the ignoring of parameters, so be it." DuBois continued: "The Toronto-Dominion Centre is twenty years too late because the lessons it teaches us were taught long ago. It is a building displaying the hand of one of the great architects of the twentieth century but it is not great architecture ... what was once a fresh and vital method of attack, has now become a style codified and listless. An approach that began by opening possibilities is now at a point where it is closing them."[6]

Only the tower building, not the complex, was discussed and to DuBois everything about it was disastrous. The entrance was bad, the flame-cut granite wall of the podium was unanimated and boring; office spaces, admittedly not designed by Mies, were pedestrian and the use of imitation plants in these spaces "an acknowledgment of the failure of design to

9. Mies van der Rohe,
Model for Chicago Federal Center.
View from northwest. 1960.
Photo Hedrich-Blessing.

10. Mies van der Rohe,
New National Gallery, 1962–68,
Berlin, Germany. Street-level view.
Photo Reinhard Friedrich.

11. Mies van der Rohe,
Toronto-Dominion Centre.
Interior view of banking pavilion. 1970.
Photo Ron Vickers.

provide a pleasant feeling." According to the critic, the lack of double glazing suggested that the design was misinformed about building science and building experience, as well as the severity of Toronto's climate relative to Chicago's. "We look for spatial variety. We look for the exploiting of light. We look for a sense of climate. We look for concern for orientation. We look for a sense of place and the numbers of people. Most houses have these things. The Toronto-Dominion Centre does not." DuBois's *propos* were emotional, polemical, but hardly logical or informed.

Assessment of the TDC by critics in the United States was quite different. Mildred Schmertz, writing in *Architectural Record* in 1971, recognized Mies's continued search to refine and develop an architectural language: "Mies's Toronto Dominion Centre — the last great work in which he [Mies] took an active part — is a structural and architectural development of ideas which have matured over four decades."[7] Similarly, John Winter in an *Architectural Review* of 1972 emphasized the importance of establishing standards: "with its generous urban spaces, its impeccable construction and the incorporation of many improvements worked out by Mies's office over the previous decade, it triumphantly reaffirms the virtues of consistent development. . . . In the TDC, Mies has left us a building which sets the standard for the architecture of our time. To his students he has bequeathed something greater — the Modern Movement's only on-going tradition."[8]

Winter compared the reception of the TDC to that of the Seagram Building: "While Seagram was world-famous before it was finished, the larger and more thoroughly worked out development at Toronto has caused barely a ripple on the architectural scene." He explained the reasons he saw for the reaction against Mies that had been gaining momentum since the middle 1960s: "Against the shifting background of willful form-making of American architects in the '60s, Mies stood alone, developing and refining what he knew. . . . The admirers grew bored because he would not produce a 'new architecture every Monday morning.'" In Canada, the nationalism of the Trudeau years was certainly another factor. Officially, in the 1960s Bregman + Hamann and the Parkin Partnership were the architects for the TDC, and Mies with his office in Chicago was credited only as consulting architect. The United States was seen as a greater threat to Canadian economic and cultural sovereignty than was Finland, where Revell lived and worked.

The tide of opinion is turning once again, this time in the direction of Mies. Regardless of fashion, the Toronto-Dominion Centre, as I have been intent on showing, occupies a major place in architecture and in Mies's work, as an exemplar of urban form and the evolved expression of the two building types that were his central preoccupation. Individually and together, the TDC buildings are outstanding contributions to the architecture of the twentieth century. Moreover, they show that at almost eighty years of age Mies was still doing what he thought to be essential: advancing solutions or, in his words, "punching through the clouds."

### Notes

1. A search for images of these designs has been carried out by the author: no record of the SOM scheme has been found to date in the Toronto-Dominion Bank archives, or by the archivist of SOM, New York, or by the office of Bregman + Hamann, Toronto. On the other hand, drawings for the 1963 Parkin scheme were identified by the office of Bregman + Hamann, who are listed as engineers for the scheme with SOM as consultants. See figures 4–6.

2. On my recommendation Mies became the architect of the Seagram Building in 1954. As Director of Planning, I was responsible for the coordination of the client, the builder, and all consultants and for assuring the quality of the building. As a silent part-owner of Fairview, I intervened in the TDC commission process once Bunshaft was removed. First, it was clear to me that hiring an architect to supervise the work of another architect would lead to conflict and irresolution — an architect must have the client's confidence. Second, the large site invited a new urban solution, not just a single tall building: Mies was the only architect who had consistently engaged the problematic of architecture and urban space.

3. The cantilevered skin was also an ideal solution for the centrally air-conditioned office building; space between the column line and the cantilevered skin allowed for the necessary continuous horizontal pipes and ducts to run around the perimeter.

4. The TDC complex was developed by Mies with Gene Summers of Mies's office. Peter Carter, also of Mies's office, worked on the construction phase of the complex, on the design of the shopping concourse, the details of landscaping of the plaza, and the interior design of the offices of the Fairview Corporation and the Toronto-Dominion Bank's superb entertainment suite on the top floor of the tower building.

5. I am grateful to Gene Summers for this information.

6. Macy DuBois, "Toronto Dominion Centre, a Critique." *Canadian Architect,* 12 (November 1967), pp. 31–45.

7. Mildred Schmertz, "Canadians build an office complex by Mies van der Rohe in Toronto," *Architectural Record,* 149 (March 1971), pp. 105–14.

8. John Winter, "Dominion Development," *Architectural Review,* vol. 151, no. 899 (January 1972), pp. 55–57.

1. Mies van der Rohe,
Toronto-Dominion Centre.
Night photograph of building under
construction, 1965.
Photo Metropolitan Photos.

Practice

## MIES'S SKYSCRAPER "PROJECT": TOWARDS THE REDEMPTION OF TECHNICAL STRUCTURE

*Detlef Mertins*

The skyscrapers of Mies van der Rohe imply a way of approaching the architectural "project" that may be helpful in working through the implica-tions, for architecture, of some poststructuralist critiques of humanist, and more specifically Enlightenment, projections of subjectivity. Although it may appear at first unlikely, I would suggest that there is an affinity between Mies's "project" and approaches put forward by Gianni Vattimo and Jean-François Lyotard, which go beyond simply problematizing the modern conception of the project to rewriting it. Vattimo has explicitly posed the task for architects and planners "to find legitimations for the project that no longer appeal to 'strong,' natural, or even historical structures,"[1] and Lyotard has pointed to the need to think again about a modality of presence, but one that would be an alternative to the modality of masterful intervention.[2]

While Mies certainly did appeal to "strong, natural, and historical struc-tures," and was complicit with precisely the kind of instrumental rationality that theorists of postmodernity have subjected to critique, his work should at the same time be situated within the history of anti-Enlightenment thought in Germany, including the pervasive and unresolved opposition between *Kultur* and *Zivilisation,* and a line of negative thought within critical theory from Immanuel Kant's sublime to Theodor Adorno's aesthetics, both of which have been taken up implicitly by Lyotard in his appreciation of twentieth-century Minimalist art.

In Mies's skyscrapers — both the early projects for the Friedrichstrasse competition of 1922 and the later North American work, of which the Toronto-Dominion Centre of 1963–67 will be taken as representative —

the architectural project may be understood as the artistic transformation of a form of construction ready-made by the circumstances of history and (human) nature. While Mies held that these projects were based in technology they were not to be understood as the projects of technology itself. Rather than the willful projection of a future, they suggest something of the modality of presence that Lyotard has called "passibility," which he likens to both Benjamin's "passage" and Freud's *Durcharbeitung,* or working through — a rewriting or reconstruction that entails a particular kind of listening and receptiveness. Neither passive nor active in the conventional sense, it may be possible to think of Mies's architecture in Lyotard's terms as "a working attached to a thought of what is constitutively hidden from us in the event, hidden not merely by past prejudices but also by those dimensions of the future marked by the pro-ject and the pro-gramme." For Lyotard, passibility is a state of mind in which the mind "gives itself as passage to the events which come to it from a 'something' (let us call it a something) that it does not know" — a state of mind that he characterizes in analogy to the "free-floating attention" of the psychoanalyst. Passibility, as the "possibility of experiencing" assumes a donation, "which is experienced before (or better, in) any conceptualization, gives matter for reflection, for the conception."

Where Lyotard may be understood as approaching the "project" from the perspective of the unprojectable event, Vattimo comes to it through the already-given mediations that constitute "reality," "community," and "rationality," which he points out have now become visible through their multiplicity. For Vattimo, "experience is mediated" and we have nothing by which to orient ourselves but indications that we have inherited from the past, from other cultures, and from the present. While acknowledging the structuring powers of the already-given systems of mediation, he aims beyond any simple historicism or repetition towards a kind of self-orienting activity engaged in what Martin Heidegger called *Überlieferung,* or handing down. The ability of listening to the handing down is necessary to achieve what Vattimo conceives of as a "new monumentality," the building of cities where one recognizes oneself and where one is, cities where there are distinguishing marks. For Vattimo, "once the architect is no longer the functionary of humanity, nor the deductive rationalist, nor the gifted interpreter of a world-view, but the functionary of a society made up of communities, then projection must become something both more complex and more indefinite," and, he adds, more rhetorical. In order to orient ourselves within the contemporary condition, after losing the innocence still contained in terms like "community" and "place," "one has to be able to work in an intermediary zone between an enrootedness in a place — in a community — and an explicit consciousness of multiplicity."

While Vattimo is clearly opening up a line of thought that remains anti-thetical to the modernism of a figure like Mies, there is, nevertheless, a similarity of approach between his listening to the *Überlieferung,* or handing down, and Mies's way of working from the givens, his simultaneous accep-tance and transfiguration of the mediations that history has already provided, and the capacity of his projects to orient people in relation to the larger world, be it the spatial world of the city or the temporal world of modern times. It may, then, be possible to explore the potential of such an affinity while acknowledging the differences between the imperatives of Mies's time and those of our own.

From his first ground-breaking proposal for a glass skyscraper for Berlin in 1922, Mies approached the skyscraper as a ready-made "technical form" in respect to which architecture needed to forge new artistic responses. Introducing his crystalline project to the readers of Bruno Taut's expression-ist magazine *Frühlicht* in 1922, Mies wrote the following well-known lines:

> Only skyscrapers under construction reveal the bold constructive thoughts, and
> then the impression of the highreaching steel skeletons is overpowering. With the
> raising of the walls, this impression is completely destroyed; the constructive
> thought, the necessary basis for artistic form-giving, is annihilated and frequently
> smothered by a meaningless and trivial jumble of forms ... and yet these buildings
> could have been more than just manifestations of our technical skill. This would
> mean, however, that one would have to give up the attempt to solve a new task
> with traditional forms; rather one should attempt to give form to the new task out
> of the nature of this task.[3]

While the idea of inserting high-rise towers into the urban fabric of Berlin was in the air after the Great War, none had been realized and the object of Mies's remarks was, rather, the American skyscraper. In this passage, Mies gave voice, like Walter Gropius and others before him, to the growing German admiration for American technical skills and technical forms, coupled with a radical critique of America's propensity to smother its modernity within the stoney cloak of outmoded European styles and "artistic" prejudices. This double movement of criticism and admiration became, in the following years, a *topos* of architectural modernism in Europe, from Le Corbusier to ABC.

In the text cited above, Mies emphasizes what he calls "constructive thoughts" that boldly break ossified conventions and, at the same time, open up the possibility for authentic expressions of the present. But in calling them merely the *basis* for artistic form-giving, he clearly reserves the category of "artistic form" for something other than construction. The task of architecture as art is, he suggests, not only to reveal the overpowering impression of the steel skeleton, and thereby to bring repressed natural forces into visibility, but also to be "more than just a manifestation of technical skill." In the virgin wilderness of American modernization, industry and capitalism had produced a seemingly authentic, objective and unmediated building form, an apparently natural outgrowth of the social, economic, and technological conditions of the modern metropolis. It remained, however, for Europe, more specifically for Germany, more specifically still for Mies, to transmute raw technique into the transcendentalized substance of new artistic expression.

But what is this "more" in the phrase "more than just technical", which resurfaces later in the dictum "less is more"? Or, to put that question another way, what kind of "projects" were Mies's skyscrapers in Berlin in 1922 and in North America in the 1950s and 1960s? Clearly Mies's conception of the architectural project was related to technology — it was as he said "based" in it — but it was hardly the project of technology itself. It accepted as given the legacy of Enlightenment rationality and the instrumental transformation of nature, but was not equated with them. It took the project of masterful intervention and the projection of subjective will as the "necessary" historical givens of the era — its destiny — yet sought to establish a domain of critical interpretation or "freedom" in relation to them, and to link "self-realization" to what Mies called "service." For Mies, we may say that the "project" resides precisely in the interconnectedness of service, the "more than just," the surplus or supplement to what is perceived to be the necessary, rational, and material base of modern civilization.

Having taken over the dictum that "building serves" from the Dutch architect H. P. Berlage, Mies distinguished himself within the avant-garde of German architecture after 1926, as Fritz Neumeyer has shown, by maintaining that the service of architecture could not be achieved simply by the functional, economic, and logical fulfillment of social needs or the constructive imperatives of modern industry.[4] Rather, it is clear from the passage cited, as well as later statements, that for Mies architecture served *artistically*. It aimed at the monumental, symbolic, and transcendental. At the same time, he distinguished his conception of art from the isolationism of the nineteenth-century discourse of the autonomy of art by relocating the aesthetic experience in the material world of industrial capitalism. In the case of Mies's skyscrapers, the architectural project operates to effect a passage from the objective, unconscious, spontaneous, and ultimately

uncontrollable productivity of modern industry and economy to the indeter-
minate realm of *Geist,* which combines the implications of "spirit" and
"intellect" and may even be open to "pleasure." Standing in critical dialogue
with the fateful unfolding of material history, Mies's high-rise buildings are
transformative projects springing from his simultaneous admiration and
criticism of the American skyscraper. While these statements apply to both
the 1922 and the 1963 projects, the "more" that distinguished architecture
from construction in 1922 was marked by naturalizing and aestheticizing
the technical structure of the skyscraper, while by 1963 Mies's strategy had
shifted to a reworking of the technical form, which served to re-present
that which is natural, elemental, and originary within technology. Where the
1922 project employed the forms and principles of nature metaphorically,
the later towers aimed at the artistic evocation of that which is natural
within technical forms themselves. But before turning to the later towers
and circumscribing my use of the term "representation," I want to pursue
the relationship between technical form, natural form, and artistic form
in the case of the 1922 skyscraper. I have three points.

First, although the visibility of the skeleton was one of his expressed
goals, Mies's drawings and descriptive text were much more concerned with
substituting glass for mass, and with the effect of glass on the observer.
Among Mies's drawings and montages of the building, there are more that
depict it as a solid, plastic, and visually affective form than there are
drawings that reveal the inner structure. While he ascribed a certain kind of
aesthetic value to the steel skeleton itself — he wrote of its "overpowering
impression" — he invested greater energy in pursuing the "rich interplay
of light reflection" made possible by the use of large surfaces of glass, in
contrast to the classical play of light and shadow characteristic of mass
architecture.

Second, Mies's engagement here with the perceptual and expressive
characteristics of surface and mass allows us to position this project in the
context of the nineteenth century's hesitancy about iron frame as a medium
for architectural expression. Karl Scheffler's remarks in his book *Moderne
Baukunst* of 1908 may be taken as typical of the widespread conviction that
frame construction — be it wood or iron — was unsuitable for architectural
expression because "there is no mystery . . . no mass, no surface." Mass and
surface were key because, for Scheffler, the artistic handling of construction
aims at "something soulful and fashions a body for this soulfulness with
the means of artistic forms that express this inner force."[5] Even the young
Walter Gropius, who extolled the virtues of North American grain silos
as early as 1911 — as the immediate, sensible, and plastic expression of
modern needs and spirit — could not ascribe artistic potential to frame

construction. He was interested in concrete grain silos precisely for the way in which they combined the expression of inner purpose with monumental effect.[6]

Primitive yet eminently modern, engineered yet seemingly free of intellectual prejudice, aesthetically self-sufficient and original, the grain silos and factories were mobilized by Gropius to stake out a position in relation to the desire for a new monumentality that had characterized the previous two decades. Informed by the sensibilities of art historians such as Heinrich Wölfflin, Alois Riegl, and Wilhelm Worringer, the quest for a modern monumentality had involved abstracting and psychologizing historical styles into simple, massive, and geometric forms capable of evoking powerful emotions. Projects representative of this would include Wilhelm Kreis's Bismarck Monument of 1899, Peter Behrens's exhibition buildings after 1904, and Heinrich Tessenow's crystalline School for Rhythmic Gymnastics of 1911. Within this context, Behrens's machine halls for the AEG became celebrated for precipitating the shift toward a monu-mentality of glass and steel, elevating technology to the level of art by means of geometry. Following from these projects, Gropius's appreciation of grain silos had the effect of dislodging the aesthetic value of simple masses from the domain of this new — yet still historicist — monumentality and resiting it in the ready-made monumentality of industrial constructions in the New World. He thereby displaced "history" as a source by what he took to be the "nature" of architecture itself.

Mies's Berlin skyscraper may be read in the context of this search for an alternative to the "false" monumentality of the architectural treatment given to skyscrapers in America in terms that parallel Gropius's admiration for the immediate expression and monumental value of grain silos. Sub-stituting glass for mass allowed Mies to employ one of the key tropes of nature — the crystal — and at the same time to produce a monumental form for the structural skeleton (figs. 2 & 3).

My third point, however, begins by recognizing that as paradigms for the presentation of objective, inner nature, or truth, grain silos and steel skeletons represent entirely different theories of knowledge, the silo being an indirect symbol of the interior in need of interpretation, the skeleton being a direct display of inner structure and in no need of interpretation. This distinction corresponds to the two modes of visual cognition repre-sented in the illustration to an article in the elementalist magazine G in which Mies was active (fig. 5). Entitled "The Pure Form is the Natural," the article appeared in the final issue of the magazine in 1926.[7] The image registers two notions of pure form — the elemental and the constructive — and two theories of expression — one based on the legacy of the eighteenth-

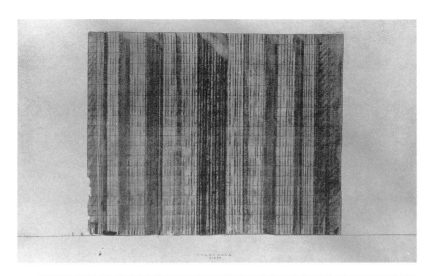

2. Mies van der Rohe,
Glass Skyscraper, 1922, Berlin. Elevation
(schematic).

3. Photograph of a grain silo in South
America from the photo collection of
Walter Gropius.

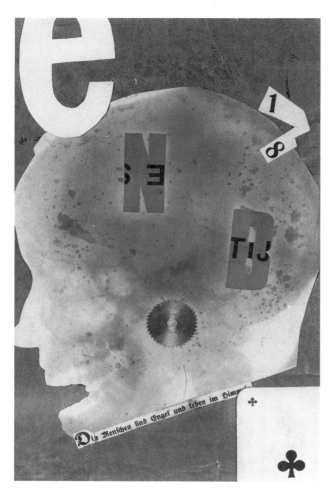

4. Raoul Hausmann,
People are Angels and Live in Heaven,
Collage of photographs and typography.
c. 1921.

5. Image of "two different perspectives
on the same object," which accompanied the
article "The Pure Form is the Natural" in G,
no. 5–6, April 1926 (Berlin).

6. Mies van der Rohe,
Glass Skyscraper, 1922, Berlin.
Photomontage of the second project.

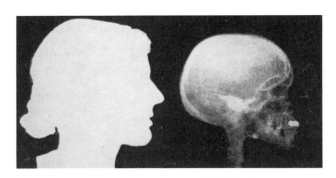

century science of physiognomy (and the later study of phrenology) and the other on the visual penetration of outward appearances by new optical devices such as X-ray photography. Physiognomic studies had taken the abstracted profile of the head to be an objective cipher of the character of the individual. And the practices of dissection in biology and medicine, as well as the invention of mechanical aids to natural vision, such as microscopes, had made it routine to see the inner biological construction of the body directly. These two paradigms of objectivity, of how inner nature was understood to present itself without mediation, interpenetrated in the discourse of *Gestaltung* — the German term for creation, formation, or creative force that El Lissitsky had suggested be abbreviated to "G" for the title of the magazine. Transposed into the realm of art, the physiognomic interest in the schematic outline is now marked by the "profile" of the pure form rectangle and its three-dimensional counterpart the elemental prism (as demonstrated in painting by Theo van Doesburg and in film by Hans Richter). In the realm of architecture it is active in the paradigm of grain silos and its extension into the schematic and elemental architecture of Ludwig Hilberseimer. The external visibility of the structural skeleton depended, as Mies demonstrated, on the new optics of mechanical reproduction, on the transparency, reflectivity, and color of large sheets of thermally-improved glass.

Mies's skyscraper of 1922 and his characterization of modern architecture as one of "skin and bones" — which prompted Theo van Doesburg to call him an "anatomical architect" — folded together these direct and indirect modes of exhibition (hypotyposis) — outline and skeleton — creating an architectural analogue to Raoul Hausmann's superposition of physiognomic outline and X-ray skeleton in a collage of c. 1920/21 entitled "People are Angels and Live in Heaven" (figs. 4 & 6).

But another reading of this folding leads into the distinguishing characteristic of Mies's high-rise projects in the United States and Canada. The desire for an architecture that would be both primitive and modern coincided with a theory of historical development that was based on Hegel's teleology of the spirit, from the originary solid and tactile masses of Egyptian pyramids to the optical interminglings of modern spatial sensibility. Put forward by the art historian Alois Riegl in the years around 1900, this notion was still active in the cultural imagination of the late 1920s, as evident in László Moholy-Nagy's book of 1929, *Von Material zu Architektur,* where he depicts an historical progression from the pyramidal "block" to a dematerialized "architecture" of light and space. After his experiments with the open spatiality of De Stijl and the free plan, Mies returned to an architecture of integral objects. Especially in the case of the skyscrapers, this reiteration of the elemental block was accompanied by intensive research into the possibilities of the dematerialized skin — research that would appear to follow studies in dynamic form such as the illuminated sculpture of Edmund Collein at the Bauhaus in 1928 (fig. 7). Instead of enclosing the structural skeleton with uninterrupted sheets of glass, the post-World War II skyscrapers develop the "curtain" wall into a diaphanous membrane that is both glass and steel. The same steel sections that make up the inner skeleton were now deployed to delineate an outer surface by means of a finely woven tracery of lines whose volumetric affect is most intense for a spectator in motion. In relation to the native American skyscraper, the mass of the building has first been rationalized into an elemental prism, which is consonant with the structural logic of the steel frame, but has then been transformed from "mass" into "spatial volume." While there is still a rich interplay of reflection in the bronze-tinted glass, this preoccupation in Mies's writings had been displaced after 1927 by a more direct approach to what he called "the spiritualization of technology." For, as he wrote, "only where the building art leans on the material forces of a period can it bring about the spatial execution of its spiritual decisions." Architecture should, he contended, "recognize the spiritual and material forces of our period, investigate them and draw, without prejudice, the consequences."[8]

Thoughts such as these, and the evidence of the projects themselves, demonstrate a shift in Mies's work from the metaphorical use of natural forms (crystals, skeletons) to signify the seemingly unmediated presentation of inner essence, toward a kind of critical mimesis, understood as a re-doubling, rewriting, reworking, or re-presentation of that which has already been produced spontaneously by natural history, that which has already happened — a critical "artistic" activity through which something "more" emerges that is capable of leading the mind from material phenomena to the contemplation of ideas. In the terms used by Mies around 1927, creation itself should be left to "the creative forces," the project of architecture being understood, instead, "to illuminate, make visible, and direct the currents of the spiritual and concrete situation in which we stand" rather than to evalu-ate it.[9] As Ludwig Hilberseimer astutely observed, Mies "is an artist — not a designer, not an inventor of everchanging forms, but a true master builder."[10] In his lecture notes of 1927–28, Mies suggests that in the modern era, the influence of the technical on the soul requires "complete renunciation of one's own aims in the work, of whimsies, or vanity." Instead he admonishes that what is needed is "not only self-revelation, but also service."[11] If we listen to his "not only" and "but also" we recognize that his thought draws together epochal unfolding and self-assertion in such a way that the

7. Edmund Collein,
Illuminated sculptural studies:
three-dimensional sculptural forms emerge
from the rotation of sticks in space,
1928, Bauhaus.

subject emerges as neither fully determined nor the agent of free will.

At the same time, Mies pointed to what he called the "misunderstanding" between materialism and idealism. While these notes remained fragmentary and the ideas undeveloped, the implications of thinking materialism and idealism together may be drawn out by turning to the theoretical writings of the critic Walter Benjamin, a fellow-traveller of the circle around Hans Richter and the magazine G. Benjamin's theory of contemplation, written in 1924–25 and published in 1928, may serve to clarify what I would like to draw from Mies's conception of the architectural project as a modality of presence within the conditions of the modern world.

In the theoretical text published as the prologue to his study of seventeenth-century German tragic drama, Benjamin begins by setting "contemplation" against "knowledge" as the genuine method for the philosophical presentation (*Darstellung*) of truth, which is his central concern. Extending the Platonic theory of ideas, Benjamin holds that because the object of knowledge is instrumental, knowledge cannot be identical with truth. "Truth," writes Benjamin, "bodied forth in the dance of represented ideas, resists being projected, by whatever means, into the realm of knowledge."[12] The proper approach to truth, then, is not that of intention or knowledge, but rather a "total immersion and absorption in it." Contemplation is the intentionless state of reflection called for by the intentionless state of being that is truth. "Tirelessly the process of thinking makes new beginnings, returning in a roundabout way to its original object (*auf die Sache selbst zurück*). This continual pausing for breath is the mode most proper to the process of contemplation (*die eigenste Daseinform der Kontemplation*)."

While Benjamin considers concepts to be spontaneous products of the intellect, ideas are already given, they pre-exist and are simply to be reflected upon. They belong to a fundamentally different world from that which they apprehend, and are the proper object of philosophical contemplation. Moreover, their being is not something that is accessible in the manner of a visible object, not even an object of "intellectual vision." In a thought that bears remarkably on Mies's North American towers, and through which he distances himself from Romantic theory, Benjamin contends that ideas are not like objects whose essence is standing naked behind a veil, waiting to be unmasked. Rather, Benjamin explains, ideas are related to phenomena in a dialectic as their representation (*Repräsentation*), "their objective virtual arrangement, their objective interpretation." While phenomena enter into the realm of ideas, they do not do so whole, in their crude empirical state, "adulterated by appearances," but only in their "basic elements, redeemed." They are divested of their false unity so that, "thus divided, they might partake of the genuine unity of truth." However, at

the same time that the realm of ideas redeems phenomena, the representation of ideas must necessarily occur through the medium of empirical reality. For ideas cannot be represented in themselves, but solely in "an arrangement of concrete elements in the concept: as the configuration of these elements." This dialectic of representation is encapsulated in an image that also registers the elusiveness of the object of contemplation: "Ideas are to objects as constellations are to stars."

In Benjamin's notes for his Arcades Project of the 1930s he reformulated the role of art in its dialectical movement toward nature and against it. The following passages demonstrate this movement in ways that are especially resonant for a consideration of Mies:

> It is the peculiar property of technical forms of creation (as opposed to artistic forms), that their progress and their success are proportionate to the transparency of their social content. (Whence glass architecture.) [V, N 4, 6]
>
> One can formulate the problem of form for the new art this way: When and how will the form-worlds of the mechanical, in film, in the building of machines, in the new physics, etc. rise up without our help and overwhelm us, make us aware of that which is natural about it? [V, K 3a, 2][13]

Standing as it did in a direct dialogue with the native skyscraper across the street — the Toronto Star Building of 1928 — the main tower of the Toronto-Dominion Centre seized hold of the inner logic of the skyscraper as a technical structure that is relatively transparent to its social and historical content. It does "more" however than just fulfill this inner logic, it "determines the nature of the technical."[14] It seeks to represent that nature as a luminous spatial volume, an image created entirely by means of the veil of the curtain wall that envelopes the internal structural skeleton and gives it the expressive presence of a body whose skin is at once pitch black, diaphanous, and glowing. Without the veil of elementalized matter, there would be no architectural body to stimulate aesthetic effect, no idea for the mind to contemplate, no evocation of an essential truth within the experience of modernization (fig. 8).

Mies's architectural project springs from, and leads to, the philosophical contemplation of life in modern times, the search for ideas informing and redeeming the specific historical experience of western civilization in the twentieth century. His curtain wall bespeaks neither a utopian projection, nor even the harmonious resolution of art and technology — both of which have often been ascribed to Mies's work. Rather, it leads the observer to a melancholic contemplation of the "idea" of "the modern" arising from the acceptance of a condition resolutely divided from nature, a contemplation

8. Mies van der Rohe, Toronto-Dominion Centre. Aerial photograph of project under construction, 1968. Photo Ron Vickers.

9. Mies van der Rohe,
Toronto-Dominion Centre: Curtain wall as
a mass ornament. Photo Steven Evans.

10. Women workers in one of the AEG
factories, 1906, Berlin.

Public, like waves in the sea.

Girls.
Legs.

11. Mass sport as mass ornament,
Germany, c. 1930.

12. A chorus line of legs depicted as a
mass ornament in László Moholy-Nagy's
film script for "Dynamic of the
Metropolis," 1927, Berlin.

of black furnaces producing intense heat and light along with new artificial materials, of the infinite horizon of steel rails and telephone lines, of the elemental units produced by machines and for machines, of the rhythmic repetition of the assembly line and the extension of its rationality into every aspect of metropolitan life, including, as Siegfried Kracauer already observed in 1927, the realm of mass entertainment and sport (figs. 9, 10, 11, 12). Kracauer argued for accepting the chorus line, whose entertaining legs correspond to the productive hands in the assembly line — as well as the endless rows of athletic bodies on sports fields and the mass ornament of the anonymous crowd configured into a symbolic image discernible only from an airplane — precisely for their ability to render visible the hitherto obscured reality of mass society.[15] Similarly, Mies rendered visible the material conditions of technology, industry, and labor by rewriting or reworking them and making of them an "ornamental" pattern that would redeem technical structure by transforming the calculus of means and ends into the evocation of an end in itself.

## Notes

1. Gianni Vattimo, "The End of Modernity, The End of the Project? On Architecture and Philosophy," *Journal of Philosophy and the Visual Arts* (1990), pp. 74–77.

2. Jean-François Lyotard, *The Inhuman. Reflections on Time,* trans. Geoffrey Bennington and Rachel Bowlby (Stanford, California: Stanford University Press, 1991). See especially Chapter 2: "Rewriting Modernity."

3. Ludwig Mies van der Rohe, "Skyscrapers," published without title in *Frühlicht,* vol. 1, no. 4 (1922), pp.122–24. In Fritz Neumeyer, *The Artless Word: Mies van der Rohe on the Building Art,* trans. Mark Jarzombek, (Cambridge, Massachusetts & London, England: MIT Press, 1991), p. 240.

4. Neumeyer, pp. 156–61.

5. Karl Scheffler, *Moderne Baukunst* (Leipzig: Julius Zeitler, 1908), p. 12.

6. Walter Gropius, "Monumentale Kunst und Industriebau," lecture of April 10, 1911 in Folkwang-Museum in Hagen, Germany. Published in Hartmut Probst and Christian Schädlich, *Walter Gropius. Band 3: Ausgewählte Schriften* (Berlin: Ernst & Sohn, 1988), pp. 28–51. See also Gropius's "Die Entwicklung moderner Industriebaukunst," *Jahrbuch des Deutschen Werkbundes 1913* (Jena: Eugen-Diederichs, 1913), pp. 17–22.

7. "Die reine Form ist die natürliche," G. *Zeitschrfit für elementare Gestaltung,* vol. 5–6 (April 1926), pp. 134–35.

8. Mies van der Rohe, "Lecture given at the 'Immermannbund' in Düsseldorf. Unpublished manuscript of March 14, 1927." In Neumeyer, p. 262.

9. Mies van der Rohe, "On Form in Architecture," in *Die Form,* vol. 2, no.2 (1927), p. 59. In Neumeyer, p. 257.

10. Ludwig Hilberseimer, *Mies van der Rohe* (Chicago: P. Theobold, 1956), p. 12.

11. Mies van der Rohe, "Notes for Lectures, 1927," unpublished notebook. In Neumeyer, pp. 278–79.

12. Walter Benjamin, *The Origin of German Tragic Drama,* trans. John Osborne (London & New York: Verso, 1977), pp. 27–56. All quotations are from the "Epistemo-Critical Prologue."

13. Walter Benjamin, *Gesammelte Schriften, V: Das Passagen-Werk* (Frankfurt am Main: Suhrkamp, 1982).

14. In his "Notes for Lectures, 1927," Mies wrote that "The nature of the technical is determined in its fulfillment." See Neumeyer, p. 275.

15. Siegfried Kracauer, "The Mass Ornament," (1927) *New German Critique,* no. 5, Spring 1975, pp. 67–76, translated by Barbara Cornell and Jack Zipes.

TECHNOLOGY

1. Mies van der Rohe,
National Gallery, 1962–68, Berlin.
Photo Fritz Neumeyer.

**A WORLD IN ITSELF:
ARCHITECTURE AND TECHNOLOGY**

*Fritz Neumeyer*

The convergence of technology and art may be considered to be the essential theme of the architecture of Mies van der Rohe, rather than the achievement of technical perfection, as many a critic has suggested. In his statement "Architecture and Technology" of 1950, Mies explained the fundamental issues of this fusion through a notion of technology as "far more than a method ... [albeit] superior in almost every respect;" rather, Mies held that technology was "a world in itself." Supported by a Hegelian conception of the spirit of the age, this world was taken to be a "real historical movement – one of the great movements which shape and repre-sent their epoch." To Mies, technology appeared to be so closely related to architecture that whenever technology reached "its real fulfillment" it would transcend into it. Architecture, which depends on facts but has its "real field of activity ... in the realm of significance," gave expression to what Mies called the "inner structure" of an age, "the slow unfolding of its form." Positioned on this Hegelian platform, architecture and technology were ready to be married by Mies, who concluded, "Our real hope is that they grow together, that someday one will be the expression of the other. Only then will we have an architecture worthy of its name: Architecture as a true symbol of its time."[1]

For Mies, the merging of technology and aesthetic modernism embodied the promise of a culture suited to the age, one in which form and con-struction, individual expression and the demands of the times, as well as subjective and objective values would converge into a new identity. However, the reciprocal interpretation of art and technology, and of modern and traditional concepts, which Mies used to pursue such a convergence of opposites, had its own dialectical problems. These problems required different conceptual maneuvers at different times. Mies's shifting positions during his long career as an architect can be explained by these moves, which proved in the end that the inherent ambiguity and conflict between art and technology could not be resolved.

The idea of convergence was built on the will to analogy: art was to be seen as an educator or mediator of technology, and, alternatively, technology was to be the educator and conveyer of art. The promise of a new synthesis between architecture and technology was expressed by Peter Behrens's Turbine Factory for the AEG in Berlin of 1909, which became one of the architectural landmarks of the century. Mies worked in Behrens's office at that time and recalled how he was involved in the window design of its courtyard façade. The merging of art and technology was successful in this project in a way that made it impossible to decide which one was the expression of the other. At first, the critics celebrated the Turbine Factory as liberating construction from the narrow confines of function, thereby allowing it to gain artistic expression. A decade later, however, Behrens was ridiculed for favoring formal properties over the "honest" use of construction.

Behrens's attempt to resolve the ambiguity between the image of form and the image of construction justified both ways of reading the building. The will to analogy, derived from Friedrich Nietzsche's concept of the revaluation of values, suggested a dynamic or Dionysian interpretation of classical form and, on the other hand, a classical or Apollonian interpretation of modern construction. Both intentions became apparent in the Turbine Factory, with the will to form domesticating modern technology by bending it backwards towards the classical form, and the will to modern expression evident in the injection of modern energy and dynamics into the static, classical form. Art had created a coherent, reciprocal syntax. It constructed an image of form and formed an image of construction, thereby recharging both entities with new functional and aesthetic credibility.

Perhaps this is what Mies had in mind when he characterized Behrens as the inventor of "die grosse Form," the grand form. A comparison could easily be drawn to Mies's own work, which also took the path of raising modern technology to a monumental form. In Mies's hands, the banal constructional element of the I-beam was elevated to the level of the classical, just as Behrens had done with the shape of the iron girder. Modern industry and the standards of technical perfection provided the means to create form out of necessity and architecture out of construction.

With the Turbine Factory, Behrens posed the question of the extent to which form should shape and limit technology or vice versa. By designing a

2. Mies van der Rohe,
Seagram Building, 1958, New York.
Photo Fritz Neumeyer.

3. Peter Behrens,
Hussitenstrasse front of AEG Assembly
Hall for Large Machines, 1912, Berlin.

building with two different faces, Behrens dealt with the two aspects of this ambiguity in an almost dialectical manner. While at the street corner, familiar from the much-reproduced photographs, the artistic will to form had the upper hand, the elevation on the courtyard side simply offered structure waiting to be discovered as architectural form. This is precisely what happened, of course, with the string of Mies's later projects, beginning with the buildings for the campus of the Illinois Institute for Technology in Chicago. In them, the process of excavating the skeleton and refining its structural members brought Mies to the gates of a new architectural syntax based on construction.

In his campaign for the discovery of a new artistic interpretation of architectonics, Mies benefited greatly from the archaeological investigations into the anatomy of architecture undertaken by his predecessors. Comparing the façade structures of a building by Behrens and one by Mies reveals his vital connection to a tradition that allowed Mies to abstract, meaning to do "almost nothing," as he characterized his personal approach to architecture. To complete the immanent logic of a concept, born of advanced techno-logical and artistic possibilities, was the fundamental transformative principle that informed Mies's architectural inventions. Where Behrens, at the AEG Assembly Hall for Large Machines (1912), needed all his energy to press a classical colonnade, with mighty brick pillars, onto the front of the factory, Mies's Seagram Building in New York (1958) arrived at a new architecture, seemingly without effort — an architecture discovered by turning ones eyes away from the classical pillars and deep into the struc-ture (figs. 2, 3, 4, 5). Here in the shadowy background, the I-beams that run down the façade lay ready, waiting simply to be recognized as a pri-mary element by being brought forward to replace the subtly classical brick pillars. Dipped into a bronze bath and then glued onto the façade of a high-rise building, the I-beam was turned into the abstract pilaster of the machine age.

For Mies, the discovery of the steel frame was linked not only to the technological progress of the age, but also to developing its metaphysical potential and refining the idealistic construction of modern architecture. Mies enacted the destruction of architecture, using the liberating forces of modern construction to free the wall from its obligation of carrying load and proudly presenting the skeleton as the constituent element of the new architectural project. The canonical designs of the 1920s — the Friedrich-strasse Glass Skyscraper, the Concrete Office Building, and the Concrete Country House — which were all accompanied by short manifestos that cleared the stage verbally — provided the prototypes for such a modern building art. And through the use of metaphors, such as the one of a "skin

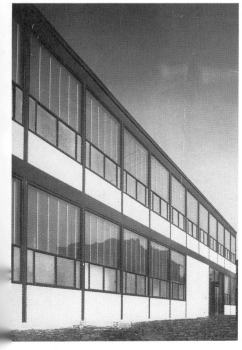

4. Peter Behrens,
AEG Assembly Hall for Small Machines,
1912, Berlin.
Photo Fritz Neumeyer.

5. Mies van der Rohe,
Alumni Memorial Hall, Illinois Institute of
Technology, 1945, Chicago.
Photo Hedrich-Blessing.

and bone" architecture, which served to draw nature and technology together, the architect tried to reach beyond the cultural limitations of "architecture." In order to ground the building of a new objectivity, to define the zero-point from which a building art suitable for the age could begin, it was first necessary for Mies to reject artistic will and subjectivity. This new objectivity was understood as architecture's primordial state of innocence in equilibrium with nature and as the point of departure for the modern architect to express the will of the epoch, one in which technology had become humanity's first nature.

The imperative of Mies's early manifestos thus proclaimed, "Create form out of the nature of the task with the means of the time. That is our work!" This meant that one should not think of art in order to create art, because, as Mies stated, "Form is not the goal but the result of our work."[2] The figure of the engineer served as the model for the architect, for he simply fulfilled the eternal laws of function, material, and purpose and did not think of art. This was seen to be the only possible way to achieve identity with the new age of objectivity, which forced the architect to find expression through the technology of construction.

Despite this imperative, one always finds discrete reverberations of humanism and traces of a secret classicism, even in Mies's radical designs of this period: for example, in the way in which the floors of the concrete office building step out a little one above the other, thereby adding some sort of entasis to the wall, which only reveals itself to the eye when comparing the windows at the corner of the different floor levels. With such refinements, Mies contradicted his own crude logic of positivistic form. Form was, after all, granted its right to exist, but only under the cover of avant-gardist radicalism, which the *Zeitgeist* demanded act with strict objectivity. This objective spirit was to be found in the skeleton of bare construction, in the support structure of posts and beams.

In the second phase of Mies's attempt to turn technology into art and to promote construction as architecture, the objective structure of the frame became an instrument of perception as well. Technology did not simply rule out art, but instead was treated as yet another instrument in the service of metaphysics. In his statement of 1932, "The New Time," Mies contended that whether one built high or low, in steel or glass, brick or stone, "would say nothing about the value of this way of building." Now Mies distinguished carefully between a "practical question" and "questions of value," giving the latter the privilege of being "decisive." "We must set new values," he wrote, "and point out ultimate goals in order to gain new criteria. For the meaning and justification of each epoch, even the new one, lie only in providing the conditions under which the spirit can exist."[3]

Figs. 6 & 7. Mies van der Rohe,
Barcelona Pavilion, 1929, Barcelona;
reconstruction 1986.
Photo Fritz Neumeyer.

Leaving behind his earlier, Darwinian, thoughts of architectural evolution, Mies transformed the frame into a reflexive architectural element and an instrument for perception and for exploring the realm between subjectivity and objectivity. No longer did the abstract ideal of a viewed construction provide the compositional model; rather its opposite, the perceptual frame or the construction of the view, served this role. As an essential architectural unit, the dialectical setting of podium and pavilion provided a thematic construct strong enough to reflect objectivity and subjectivity together, the self and the outer world.

As such a modern viewing machine, which constructs the viewer by arranging a set of frames and sequential spaces, the building now appears in a morphological transformation whose complexity is revealed only by passing through and strolling around. The sublimity of stepping aside engenders a new kind of awareness of the whole — a process of discerning the world and the self in one. The structure constructs a viewer who himself constructs a coherent space when moving through it. This moving through the building entails an ambiguous play of opposites, with the viewer participating in the process of setting and abolishing boundaries through the opening and closing of vistas.

In the Barcelona Pavilion, Mies demonstrated brilliantly the extent to which the observer had become an element of the spatial construction of the building itself. From one position, the viewer looking into the patio gains the impression of being in an enclosed space, sheltered by walls from all sides. In moving one step forward the side wall opens and reveals itself to be only a slab, thereby generating an ambiguous space; depending on the point of view this space can be closed as well as open (figs. 6 & 7).

By the end of the 1920s, Mies had arrived at a critical stance toward modern technology. His remarks at the opening of the *Weissenhofsiedlung* in 1927 mark the change of position that took place during those years. While the exhibition was meant to demonstrate the potentials of modern technology in the realm of housing, as its director, Mies warned against "the current slogans of rationalization and typification" in order "to raise tasks out of an atmosphere of the unilateral and the doctrinaire." Contrary to his statement of 1923, the problem of providing new housing still remained for Mies, in spite of its technical and economic aspects, "a problem of the building art."

The apartment building that Mies contributed to the Stuttgart exhibition underscored these thoughts. In depicting the building in the official publication, Mies paid less attention to representing the technical details of the steel frame than to demonstrating the elaborate multitude of spatial solutions in the organization of the ground plan, which modern construction made possible. Mies's buildings of the latter half of the 1920s were no longer dedicated to technology and construction. They behaved rather unspectacularly and unpretentiously in these terms and instead emphasized the creation of spectacular impressions of space. To this end, the achievements of technology in architecture offered new means that finally allowed the architect to develop a clear and simple construction and to clarify tectonics and architectural elements.

In one of his last statements in Germany, "What Would Concrete, What Would Steel Be Without Mirror Glass?" of 1933, which remained unpublished, Mies described the value of these technical means:

> [Steel and glass] are genuine building elements and the instruments of a new building art. They permit a measure of freedom in spatial composition that we will not relinquish any more. Only now can we articulate space freely, open it up and connect it to the landscape. Now it becomes clear again what a wall is, what an opening, what is floor and what ceiling. Simplicity of construction, clarity of tectonic means, and purity of material reflect the luminosity of original beauty.[5]

The structural liberation of the architectural body into "skin and bones" was turned into a reaffirmation of the classical language of architectural elements. The conceptual theme of Peter Behrens's work was repeated, only under more modern conditions. It is therefore not surprising to find a critic in 1927 calling Mies the "most promising of today's architects" for having penetrated "to the specific architectonic of Schinkel." Although his architecture no longer showed any traces of the so-called Schinkel style, he was to be looked upon as "one of the most original of Schinkel's followers."[6]

The Esters and Lange houses in Krefeld of 1927–29 make clear that the new spatial freedom in Mies's architecture owed as much to technology and modern construction as to the reinterpretation of the Schinkel villa, to which Behrens had introduced Mies around 1910. These houses are brick buildings, which, in spite of their abstract modern formal language, appear extremely heavy, even monumental. The spatial organization, however, in which the individual rooms project outwards from the core like the open drawers of a cabinet, offered a degree of openness and complexity that would be characteristic of subsequent projects, such as the Tugendhat House and the Barcelona Pavilion. Although built with brick, the Esters House allowed itself to be penetrated by the gaze, as if it consisted only of frames, like a pergola (fig. 8).

For Mies, the idea of the building as a frame could be linked easily to the villas of Karl Friedrich Schinkel with their pergolas and terraces, their complex spatial — almost philosophical — dialogue between connectedness

8. Mies van der Rohe,
Esters House, 1927, Krefeld.
Photo Fritz Neumeyer.

9. Mies van der Rohe,
Crown Hall, Illinois Institute of Technology,
1956, Chicago.
Photo Hedrich-Blessing.

and distance, and their morphological unity of architectural and land-scaping elements. In speaking of the "measure of freedom in spatial composition" as "the needs of modern man," Mies remained open as to whether he was referring to contemporary, modernistic concepts, such as those of De Stijl, or to the modernism of Schinkel, whose villas opened space freely and connected it to the landscape, marrying architecture and nature in an unsurpassed way.

New technology offered the opportunity of modernizing the frame as a linking and mediating element, which itself opened up a symbolic site for dwelling on the threshold between man and his environment. Modern technology could also help in building a bridge on which the spirit could enter into a world of otherwise meaningless facts and resolve the limited being of individual existence into a higher, metaphysical reality — one in which the opposing elements of mind and matter coincide as self-completing parts of a whole. This idealistic construction of a philosophy of opposites, motivated by the desire for continuity and participation in the absolute, was the essence of Mies's architecture.

In the Tugendhat House, the high-tech frame was mechanically equipped so that an entire wall of windows could slide down or be pulled up at the push of a button, just as we operate the windows in our cars today. This disappearance of the wall created a challenging ambiguity between inside and outside. The new measure of freedom, which the ground plan suggested, was enriched by an undisturbed communication with the absolute, the horizon and the sky.

In contrast to the rationalization of space, which other modern architects executed, Mies's buildings attached space to the modern subject — an ample space of concentration that allows the subject to step aside from the world while remaining *within* it, not retreating from it. As a threshold, the building offered distance from the mechanical bustle of modern life through the experience of something sublime and essential *within* it. The frame is the instrument of perception that creates isolation and connection at the same time. It frees objects and subjects from their context, puts them into a poetic dialogue that creates new relations and insights into the whole. The built frame gained its value and meaning by serving as such a place of encounter between opposite worlds, one that, in Mies's terms, provided the conditions under which the spirit can exist, whether one builds in steel or in brick, high or low. As an architect, one could as easily employ the logic of modern technology and its steel skeleton as the logic of the classical pergola.

With the help of both logics, Mies created a number of significant frame structures. Crown Hall was intended to be such a place of reflection and contemplation, operating, like an eye, as a viewing frame onto the city.

Especially at night, when the gaze can travel through the building undisturbed by reflections on the glass walls, it frames a view of the distant Chicago skyline like a picture (fig. 9). Lofty lobbies, such as those of the Seagram Building and the Toronto-Dominion Centre, provide another kind of such in-between space, a space for stepping aside. Just as the public life of the street seems to be pulled into the building, so the interior is connected to the public realm. In Mies's last building, the National Gallery in Berlin, this dualism works in the most convincing way: art can be viewed against the backdrop of the city, with the viewer being visually connected to it yet physically separated at the same time (fig. 1).

In Mies's search for what could be taken as constant in a changing world, the frame represented the promise of essential order. Architecture's duty to provide an element of cultural identity demanded the convergence of the opposite worlds of mind and matter, art and technology. Mies performed the laconic splendor of the Platonic frame, already manifest in simple beam constructions, on the highest technological level of advanced steel construction. Crafted and refined, architecturally and artistically and with the help of modern machine methods such as sandblasting that smooth the metal surfaces, the I-beam could become a cultural constituent of the new age.

How little was needed for the architect to turn modern construction into architecture and create art from technology is eloquently shown by Mies's project for a concert hall from the 1940s. A few space-dividing walls were sufficient to reveal the spatial potential of modern wide-span construction and to transform a bomber plant by Albert Kahn into a modern concert hall. This was a demonstration of what the cultural promise of modern technology could be: a transformation that worked as convincingly as Behrens's effort to make a temple emerge from the bottom of a factory, but with the same limitations.

How much, on the other hand, was needed to create art out of technology and to maintain the classical notion of a body under the conditions of the machine may be illuminated by a detail such as the famous "Miesian corner" of the IIT buildings. Brick and steel I-beam are joined together by an architectonic rationality not unlike that which the Renaissance architect Fillipo Brunelleschi had first applied in the pilaster system of the Church of San Lorenzo.

Mies refused to turn over the body of architecture, which was based on the principle of mimesis, to the machine and its abstract mechanical principles. With the help of the iron frame, the architect in the age of technology freed volume from mass and made the body disappear into a linear structure. This new structure had to be accepted as the basic condition for the making of modern architecture. The silent, minimalist buildings of Mies suggested an architectural body of a modern, lightweight monumentality in which, after more than a century's struggle, the opposite worlds of transparency and gravity, of technology and architecture finally were united.

Mies believed in the civilizing potential of modern technology while acknowledging its dehumanizing forces and the loss of spiritual values in the era of mechanization. Architecture served, for him, as a bulwark against the revolutionary forces of progress that were destabilizing the cultural conventions of architecture. Mies's continued belief in architecture kept him apart from the modernist euphoria, which turned building over to the paradigm of technological functionalism. As a world in itself, architecture had to come from within — a notion of the autonomy of the discipline that stands in provocative contrast to today's architectural discourse with its attempt to discover a world outside itself by pushing the center of architecture as far away as possible from architecture.

**Notes**

1. Ludwig Mies van der Rohe, "Architecture and Technology," *Arts and Architecture,* vol. 67, no. 10 (1950), p. 30.

2. Ludwig Mies van der Rohe, "Office Building," G, no. 1 (1923), p. 1; "Building," G, no. 2 (1923), p. 1. In Fritz Neumeyer, *The Artless Word: Mies van der Rohe and the Building Art,* trans. Mark Jarzombek (Cambridge, Massachusetts & London: MIT Press, 1991), p. 324.

3. Ludwig Mies van der Rohe, "The New Time," *Die Form,* vol. 7, no. 10, p. 306. In Neumeyer, p. 309.

4. Ludwig Mies van der Rohe, "Foreword," *Bau und Wohnung* (Stuttgart: Deutsche Werkbund, 1927). In Neumeyer, p. 259.

5. Ludwig Mies van der Rohe, "What Would Concrete, What Would Steel Be Without Mirror Glass?," 1933. In Neumeyer, p. 314.

6. Paul Westheim, "Mies van der Rohe: Entwicklung eines Architekten," *Das Kunstblatt,* vol. 11, no. 2 (1927), pp. 55–62. In Neumeyer, p. 76.

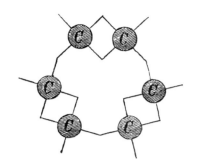

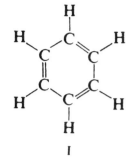

Kekulé formula

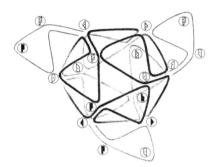

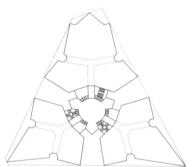

1. Model of Benzene ring (after August Kekulé).

2. Modern symbolic notation for the Benzene ring.

3. Rudolf von Laban,
Choreutic shapes performed by the body.

4. Mies van der Rohe,
Glass Skyscraper (project), 1922, Berlin, Plan.

## MIES AND MOVEMENT:
## MILITARY LOGISTICS AND MOLECULAR REGIMES

*Sanford Kwinter*

The title of this paper, as originally conceived, was "Mies van der Rohe and the Autobahns." It seemed worthwhile at the time I was first invited to participate in this conference — when one could already feel the advancing tremors of a neo-minimalist, Mies-revivalist mannerism about to shake the avant-garde architectural world — to play the part of the wary historian — to problematize Miesian space by rooting it as firmly as possible within the specific totalitarian system of scientific and economic rationalization that characterized the unprecedentedly huge public works initiatives introduced by the Nazi Party virtually from the moment that they came to power in the early 1930s, and of which the celebrated Autobahn project was but a single facet. At the time however, I was relatively innocent of the vast literature on Mies, of the mounting political controversies, and especially of the specific denunciations that had already been launched by scholars such as Richard Pommer, José Quetglas, Elaine Hochman, Lewis Mumford, and others. I confess that I retreated from this initial impulse, first, because to indict Mies in this way could appear now only an ordinary thing to do, and second, because after reading these arguments — and they were often compelling, occasionally breathtaking — I was simply no longer convinced. What I mean is that I no longer even felt susceptible to being convinced, at least not within the given configuration of the moral arena in which the questions had been formulated and the answers sought. Many scholars, Quetglas foremost among them, can be credited with the largesse of having used Mies's works — rather than his social and business relations — as the basis for a sometimes savage, sometimes mainly rhetorical condemnation. This approach, of course, is the one far more likely to interest a theorist. These arguments largely break down to the problem of Mies's own peculiar space, whether it is judged to be static or mobile, fixed or fluid, physically and psychologically inhabitable, or merely irritatingly and perpetually routing and repellent. But these arguments are not so simple as they seem: rather, they are distillable to a simpler, but far more critical opposition — indeed an opposition historically nowhere more critical than in Mies's work — that between the technical concepts of "wall" and "space."

Those critics who have fixed their attention on Mies's slabs, plateaus, and closure-refusing but barrier-creating quasi-walls — with their obsessive, multiple curtain and screen effects — have seen the works as Trojan horses, offering shimmering chimeras of flight and freedom but delivering only frustration, obstruction, monotony, and intractability. Those who have focused on trajectories — the winding intervals and synaptic spaces — have found something else, a type of flow that is certainly slow, but steady and redolent with the democratic values and the capacious imagination and explicit materiality of the preceding generation's architecture, that which arose out of the American Midwest.

Can these problems, however, be posed together, I began to wonder? Can space and wall, fixity and flow be thought together, part of the same *Gestalt* as it were, in a way that would serve to reconfigure the Mies problem and break the impasse — not necessarily the political one, for this will likely remain forever fugitive, but the epistemological-historical one at least?

What I will do is suggest three new pathways — all of which will certainly seem very spurious at first — three historical developments of significant morphological consequence, whose sphere of effects are inseparable from the technical milieu out of which Mies's own astonishing and deceptively elementary spatial lexicon arose.

I will deal schematically with three areas of modernist scientific and technological development: one, Adolf Hitler's Autobahn program and other, secondary forms of rationalization of movement such as are found in Rudolf von Laban's system of dance notation; two, the question of organic *synthesis* in the German pre-war chemical and pharmaceutical industries; and three, the discovery of certain new structures — mesoforms and other intermediate states of matter — in the theoretical biology of the 1920s and 1930s.

## The Autobahns

"All strategic roads," claimed Hitler, "were built by tyrants. They go straight across the country [while] other roads wind like processions and waste everybody's time." Just after his rise to power in 1933, Hitler appointed

Julius Dorpmüller to head the *Reichsautobahn* Agency, and Fritz Todt, the engineer who would mastermind most of the pre-war public works programs (including dams, fortifications, bunkers, strategic defense lines, communications systems, logistic coordination, encryption programs, etc.), to begin construction of the Nazi regime's greatest, and perhaps only surviving, technological monument, a *Gesamtkunstwerk* of Roman Imperial proportions: a network of brilliantly and uncompromisingly engineered highways spreading from border to border across the entire country. The program was initially justified as a benign, job-creating project (workers however, were in fact cataloged and conscripted under pain of forfeiting rights to unemployment support, then paid slave wages and interned in quasi-military barracks — this until concentration camp prisoners could later take over these duties at even less expense) but no time was lost developing the Autobahn's military potential. "Once we have secured our grip on the Eastern territories by means of the construction of the Autobahnen," Hitler later declared in 1942, "the problems of distance, which worry us little today, will cease to exist." The *Motor Hitler-Jugend* (Motorized Hitler Youth) and the *Nationalsozialistisches Kraftfahrkorps* (National Socialist Motor Corps), as well as the motorized units of the German *Wehrmacht* all profited from the use of the straight new highways whose efficiency for short-term troop movements far exceeded that of the railway. The Autobahns, he proclaimed "swept away the internal frontiers of the Reich," and what's more, the vast network of highways, "where uniformity in all aspects has been the guiding principle, allows anyone to travel anywhere he likes and still feel at home. It is only after passing the frontier of the Reich ... that he may expect to meet the first pothole."

But the Autobahns were not simply new forms of *tabula-rasa*-rationality deployed at a new, evermore gigantic, monumental scale; indeed they were meant to blend harmoniously into the grand and undulating German landscape. According to Fritz Todt, writing in 1934, "Fulfillment of the simple transportation function is not the ultimate meaning of German road construction. The German road must be an expression of its landscape, and an expression of the German essence." Punctuated with free-standing columns to support images of swastika-bearing eagles and other Nazi regalia, the highly engineered space of the Autobahns literally may be said to have set the course for the more subjective forms of national conformity, without which state Fascism would not have been possible.

"Our Nazi character," wrote Eduard Schönleben in 1943, "corresponds to the new roads of Adolf Hitler. We want to see our goal far ahead of us, we want to strive directly and steadily toward that goal; intersections we cross, unnecessary delays we do not suffer. We will not yield."

I trust it is not necessary further to belabor the obvious correspondences in language, concept, and tone between Nazi civil and aesthetic engineers and the work of Mies and the "modernist" theorists he is claimed to have read. Taylorist and Fordist modernization theory had already clearly emerged in the design philosophies of Mies's predecessors, Hermann Muthesius and Peter Behrens. Yet this type of argumentation is alone too facile and the situation far more complex and ambiguous than it might seem. The Autobahns were almost unprecedented examples of integrated engineering, mathematics, and logistics. The roads are so constant and homogeneous, so gently inflected and perfectly banked that even with today's automobiles they can be continuously travelled at speeds close to 180 miles per hour. But let us especially not forget that they are first and foremost assemblages of circulation; they are concerned with the problem of movement in a smooth and unobstructed linear space without asperities.

These were also the same years that saw the rise of the sciences of ergonomics, time and motion studies in places of increasingly rationalized manufacturing, and the effort-shape analysis in dance and eurythmy in general. Effort-shape analysis and the rational notational form that emerged from it, known as Labanotation after its inventor Rudolf von Laban, had the double effect of providing the first rigorous metalanguage for documenting movements of the body in space and for allowing such movement-events for the first time to be abstractly notated, studied, recorded, and then reproduced simultaneously in, say, fifteen cities at once, while the inventor-choreographer is absent from all but one (figs. 1 & 2).

In summary, my point is the following: the problem of political space cannot be stated so simply as one of fixity-homogeneity versus mobility-singularity. Indeed both of these qualities actually came historically to depend on the other at this historical moment. The change here, in other words, is not simply a quantitative one, a sliding from one pole or term to the other; what is at question is the appearance of an entirely new type of historical mixture, one whose properties and affects remain — at least within architectural theory — fundamentally unformulated and therefore incompletely defined.

## Aromatic Polymerization

The next "pathway" has to do with the history of German chemistry both during and between the two wars, specifically with the assembly of the huge industrial-chemical-pharmaceutical combine known as *Interessen Gemeinschaft Farbenindustrie, Aktiengesellschaft* — IG Farben for short — and primarily its significant roots in nineteenth-century science. This question forms a labyrinth of colossal political intricacy, a significant portion of which was uncovered and documented during IG Farben's war crimes trial after the Second World War. I will resist the temptation to fall into the endlessly fascinating quagmire and hold fast to the single development in which I am interested here.

IG Farben's primary fortune was amassed in the nineteenth century by means of discoveries — instantly patented, of course — of a plethora of new dyes and colors (whence *Farben*) extracted in molecular form from the sticky black sludge known as coal-tar, a by-product of coal-burning and a substance considered by most other national chemical industries as so much repulsive waste but that, in fact, held within it such a rich store of new molecules that it is now commonly said to have laid the foundation for virtually all of twentieth-century organic chemistry, an industry whose profits and strategic knowledge were funneled, if not directly into the Nazi campaign, then into the broader war effort in general. The story goes back to the German chemist, Friedrich August Kekulé, and to his discovery one afternoon in 1865, while riding on a London bus, of the specific spatial arrangement of atoms in the benzene molecule. Not only did Kekulé, an ex-architect turned chemist, conceive of the benzene molecule as a perfectly symmetrical ring of carbon atoms, he actually introduced the very idea, and demonstrated the inestimably important concept of spatial or architectonic structure or plan in formulaic chemical description (figs. 3 & 4). With Kekulé, chemistry *became* architecture (or at the very least, applied geometry) and a whole new branch of science — stereochemistry — opened up.

Now this precise piece of work, besides supplying the key to the treasures hidden in coal-tar, also laid down the theory of the "aromatic" group of molecules, a class of compounds structurally related to, or based on, the six-carbon benzene ring. When looped and attached together these simple compounds, known as monomers, are able to form linked chains or polymers, very large and complex molecules, based on simple, but infinitely repeatable units. In such cases the carbon hexagon ring keeps returning cyclically in what is known as an aromatic heterocyclic polymer.

Polymerization — combining elements in cyclic repeating patterns in space — is recognized by most historians of science as belonging to the most important technical inventions of the century, and this technique lies at the basis of all synthetic fibers, as well as plastics, many drugs, etc.. Nylon, synthetic rubber (neoprene), and polyester are but a few of the polymers synthesized in the 1920s and 1930s, which played crucial roles in logistics and deployment in the Second World War. (The synthesis of nitric acid made possible new explosives such as the liquid rocket fuel that is said to have provided the sinews for both of the World Wars. The complex geo-politics of natural rubber, its importance and denial in the Pacific Theater and subsequent synthesis in laboratories and factories in the Second World War is also a well-known story.)

Of course, I want to point out that this work in stereochemistry was crucial to the developments of all technical culture in the West in the 1920s and 1930s and that Mies's work — his specifically modernist "pattern-matrix" — might be seen in relation to these advances in geometric modeling and their relation to second-order, emergent material properties (fig. 5). His architecture is, after all, nothing if not a *tour de force* in an aesthetic of units and series and of seemingly infinite repeatability. This fact alone certainly does not condemn him *a priori* as a stooge of Nazi science fetishizing the techniques of artificiality, synthetic chemistry, and the evil uses to which they were put. But one more thing is worth noting before moving on. Mies's work is aggressively and almost unrelievedly horizontal in its orientation, seemingly uninterested in any complexity, interaction, or development that can occur between horizontal strata (except for infinitesimal and nearly unregistrable deviations in which the vestigial influence of Behrens may still be felt). It turns out that one of the great breakthroughs that stood between the work of Kekulé and the flourishing of spatial chemistry in the modern period here under consideration was the — at least, then – shocking discovery, that the carbon valencies in his molecule in fact could not lie in the plane at all, but rather must stick out into space. It was this introduction of the variable of the third dimension (by Jacobus Henricus Van't Hoff and Joseph Achille Le Bel) that made it possible to analyze and then to synthesize very complicated compounds. It was this discovery more than any other that gave birth to chemical engineering.

Now *plastic* is the crucial word here, and this concept cannot be underscored powerfully enough. The invention of polymerization introduced real, not only metaphoric, plasticity into the everyday material world. Chemists (and other practical geometers at other scales) could now decide what properties they wanted a molecule (or structure) to possess and could then build them in. But in those days, for obvious political and military reasons, the target property was most often strength. Advertisements throughout German cities, publicizing the new aromatic polyamides, announced the triad of Plasticity's virtues: *Kraft, Standfestigkeit, Weisse* (strength, stability, and whiteness; the early aromatic compounds were usually white). These words — in this conjuncture — were ominous to say the least, and could easily have passed for Nazi graffiti.

**Liquid Crystals**

The final set of developments that I would like to present concerns the discovery in microbiology and physics of states of matter known as paracrystals or aperiodic solids. In 1944, in his book, *What is Life?* — a work that we know from Fritz Neumeyer actually existed in Mies's library alongside hundreds of other volumes of mostly crackpot para-science and pseudophilosophy so popular in the Weimar era — Erwin Schrödinger hypothesized that there was a fundamental difference between the structure and arrangement of atoms in living organisms and those found in virtually every other type of matter studied by physicists. The phenomenon of life seemed to embody mysteriously active, labile structures known as *aperiodic* crystals, whereas among the most complex objects that physicists had ever studied were periodic crystals. He characterized their differences in structure as comparable to the difference between an ordinary wallpaper on which a pattern is repeated with a regular and monotonous periodicity and that of an embroidered Raphael tapestry "which shows no dull repetition, but an elaborate, coherent, meaningful design." These irregular, or aperiodic — that is, repeating, but not quite perfectly repeating — crystals, he surmised, were somehow the material carrier of life. Yet by the time Schrödinger was writing, these chemical "mosaics" had already been studied for well over a decade with great excitement by theoretical biologists who had begun to intuit the central role that the science of morphology would again come to play in biology, even now at the biochemical level. In the finale to his Terry Lectures of 1935, Joseph Needham, drawing on the previous work of J. D. Bernal and Friedrich Rinne, presented in a speculative yet prescient mode the idea that liquid crystals — or paracrystalline solids — were possibly responsible for most of the active, spontaneous, self-sustaining *pattern-based* processes that are generally associated with life. Liquid crystals are essentially solids in which the rigid symmetries of pattern are not entirely fixed, but in which a certain amount of liquid-like flow remains possible. Many substances, when heated, for example, do not pass immediately from a regularly ordered solid to a randomly ordered liquid at a specific threshold point. On the contrary, many substances pass through a succession of states known as "mesoforms," in which there is a mixture of both flow and fixity through a definite and regular arrangement of molecules. I will show and explain a few of the standard types already identified, though these are still, to this day, rather poorly understood.

We will begin with standard crystalline solids, that is, plain solids, like nearly all of the materials of the objects around us (fig. 6). What we are looking at are two different configurations, on the left what is known as a *smectogenic* crystal — the word smectic alludes to its tendency to separate itself into horizontal layers or strata — and on the right, a *nematogenic* one — "nematic" referring to its elongated strandlike qualities and its tendency, when melted, to become nematic and fluid. Above we see the crystal in section or elevation, and below in plan. Note, in both cases, the *regular periodicity in all three dimensions.* The individual molecules or "integers" do not budge — neither in position nor direction, but remain in fixed lockstep in an only slightly varied pattern. Such a system is entirely immobile — unless one decreases the pressure, or increases the heat. If indeed such a formation corresponded to the deep structure of Miesian space, one could, without fear of being accused of lacking nuance, declare the work to be rigid and static.

At the very opposite end of the spectrum I now show you a formation (fig. 7) that is properly no longer a crystal at all, because it has, presumably through heating, lost all of its order or structure, indeed it has lost these entirely and in all directions (both plan and section diagrams would here be identical). We are now looking at a pure fluid, a molecular system in its liquid state: there is no pattern or orientation, no position, direction, or periodicity. The molecules touch and move in unconstrained fashion, and the material flows freely.

As I have implied from the beginning of this paper, it is precisely the *intermediate states* of material organization that are interesting, the so-called mesoforms, the partly-fixed-partly-fluid liquid crystals, or aperiodic solids. I will show three examples of these states, though there are certainly many more (and I have discussed some of these elsewhere[1]).

The first is a liquid crystal in the nematic phase (fig. 8). Here the elongated molecules show directional orientation — they all face the same direction — but no periodicity, which means they can move at will — let us say flow — along each of the x, y, and z axes. They are quite fluid, but not entirely so, because they manifest a minimum amount of structure or order through their adherence to a directional orientation.

The second is a liquid crystal in what is known as the normal smectic phase (fig. 9). The orientation or direction of the molecules is very clearly established, as are the smectic strata or planes that further restrict and structure the material into equispaced rows. Notice, however, that there exists no periodicity *within* each of the rows; the molecules are free to flow about in two dimensions, and this freedom is legible in the plan or section diagram despite the apparent rigidity expressed in the elevation. Note that this substance is solid globally and externally, but internally sensitive and fluid.

The third and final paracrystal is in what is called the low-temperature smectic phase (fig. 10). Remember that I said decreasing pressure or

5. Crystalline Solids.

6. Liquid State.

7. Liquid Crystal in the Nematic Phase.

8. Liquid Crystal in the Normal Smectic Phase.

9. Liquid Crystal in the Low-temperature Smectic Phase.

increasing heat will bring a substance closer to its liquid phase and take it further from its solid, fixed crystal phase. Here then, low temperature smectic must mean "more highly structured smectic" and less fluid, yet, because it is still partially aperiodic, it still has *some* flow. Let us find it.

Again we see the characteristic smectic layers, but something has changed, something that is more comprehensible in the plan/section than in the elevation. This liquid crystal is clearly periodic in the y, z plane like its smectogenic relative, which is no surprise: lowering the heat increases the order, but its *periodicity varies from strata to strata.* Quite simply, whereas the normal smectic was free and fluid in two "dimensions," the low-temperature smectic has lost one dimension of freedom (gained one more dimension of order), and flows in one dimension only.

Note that what we are now calling "dimensions" are in fact dimensions in modeled, or *phase space,* not Euclidean space; these dimensions are what are today often referred to in the literature on dynamics as "degrees of freedom," and a given material system may possess anywhere from one, to thousands of degrees of variability or freedom, all of which must be inventoried and taken into account in any responsible analysis.

Perhaps we can free our imaginations now from the too-obvious, literal correspondences and resonances of the diagrams I have shown to the basic and apparent morphologies developed in Mies's work, and think the problem through rather in its conceptual aspect, remembering the Autobahns and Labanotation and the rationalizing *espousal* — rather than the fixing — of movement, remembering the dynamics and structure of heterocyclic polymerization and the way its products and effects came to saturate our lifeworld in nothing less than a total, economic-industrial-scientific *Blitzkrieg* in the 1920s, 1930s, and 1940s. Then, perhaps, we can allow ourselves the indulgence of reconsidering hasty and reductionistic political judgments on the difficult subject of historical space, especially when the technical and epistemological factors that shape this space so clearly belong to a field so saturated, contradictory, and hybridized, and so superficially studied, that the standard aesthetic/analytic models are practically no longer of use.

"To whom," some of you are already undoubtedly asking, "does Mies belong?" To the architects? To the art historians? To the warlords? Or to the twentieth century itself? Depending on what answer one gives, a predictable political judgment will easily follow. But I cannot hide my own bias, and I will affirm it here in ending today: Mies is a problem for the twentieth century, and to this infinite *Prozess* (to use Franz Kafka's German) that is our century no witnesses may justifiably be excluded.

**Notes**

1. Sanford Kwinter, "Emergence: or the Artificial Life of Space," *ANYwhere*, 1992.

**Bibliography**

Aftalion, Fred, *Histoire de la chimie,* (Paris: Masson, 1988).

Bernal, J. D, *Science in History, Volume 2: The Scientific and Industrial Revolutions* (Cambridge, Massachusetts: MIT Press, 1971).

Kekulé, Friedrich August, *Lehrbuch der organischen Chemie, oder, der Chemie der Kohlenstoffverbindungen* (Erlangen: Ferdinand Enke, 1861–87).

Needham, Joseph, "The Hierarchical Continuity of Biological Order," *Order and Life* (Cambridge, Massachusetts: MIT Press, 1968).

Pynchon, Thomas, *Gravity's Rainbow* (New York: Viking, 1974).

Sasuly, Richard, *IG Farben* (New York: Boni and Gaer, 1947).

Schreiber, Peter Wolfram, *IG Farben: die unschuldigen Kriegsplaner: Profit aus Krisen, Kriegen und KZs: Geschichte eines deutschen Monopols* (Stuttgart: Verlag Neuer Weg, 1978).

Schrödinger, Erwin, *What is Life?: The Physical Aspect of the Living Cell.* (Cambridge: Cambridge University Press, 1951).

Schrödinger, Erwin, *Mind and Matter.* ( Cambridge: Cambridge University Press, 1967)

Zentner, Christian, and Friedemann Bedürftig, eds., *Encyclopedia of the Third Reich* (New York: Macmillan, 1991).

Bitomsky, Hartmut (director), *Reichsautobahn,* 1987 (Film).

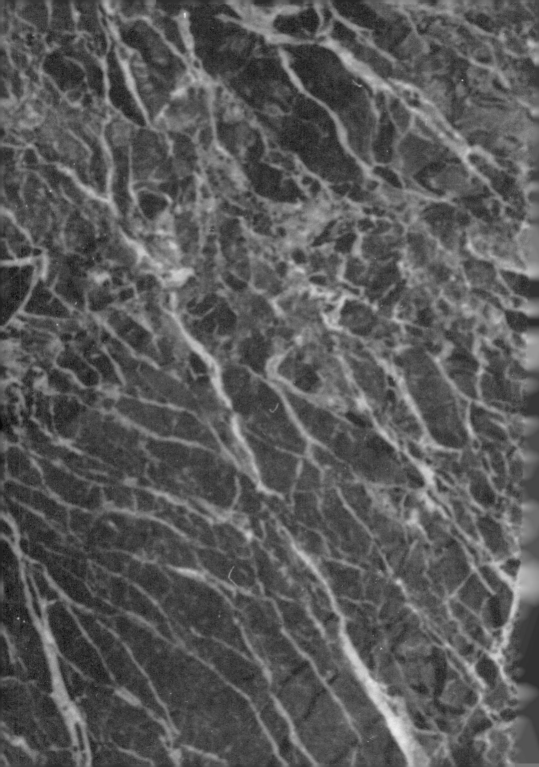

REWORKINGS

1 & 2. Dan Hoffman,
Recording Wall, August 1991.

# THE RECEDING HORIZON OF MIES – WORK OF THE CRANBROOK ARCHITECTURE STUDIO

*Dan Hoffman*

## Introduction

Reflecting upon the Toronto-Dominion Centre and the "presence of Mies,"
I am struck by the feeling of a passing age that the center evokes. I am not
speaking here of the twenty-five years that have elapsed since its completion
but of a broader, historical era against which its dark towers are inscribed.
The age to which I am referring is that of perspectival culture, a culture
characterized by a manner of thinking that measures itself according to the
idealizing abstractions of an ever-receding horizon.

In building monuments of this age, Mies van der Rohe worked from
within its logic. He had little choice since the complex nature of a building
endeavor demands a form of organization that addresses the comprehensive activities that constitute a culture. As an inheritor of perspectival logic,
with its inherent desire to refer thought to the idealized abstractions of
a distant horizon, Mies practiced a thinking that reduces architecture to
an abstract system of notation through which the diverse conditions of a
building activity are organized and focused. This abstract system has strong
parallels to the forms of Euclidean geometry; points, lines, planes, etc.,
and istherefore subject to a questioning that focuses upon the ideality of
a given form in relation to its circumstantial execution. As a result, the
realm of human activity and the nature of the surroundings within which
they occur are constantly referred to the constructs of geometry and
their inherent perfectibility.

The horizon is symbolic of this manner of thinking. The horizon defines
the limit of the territory that exists before it. It functions both as the visual
and abstract symbol of this limit, appearing before us in its dual aspect of a

physical and conceptual line. Mies reduced architecture to the "transparent bones" of its geometry, employing both technical and aesthetic means with which to organize and promote the building process. The eminently visual aspect of the horizon line also permits Mies to symbolize its presence through the spatial and formal dispositions of his compositions. Seeing, and the thinking that it represents, becomes both the program and the structure of his work.

The age of perspectival culture is characterized by a focusing of concerns within the context of a limit-horizon. The horizon is understood as the repository of all possible perspectives of an object, the place from which the object is comprehensively viewed. A single perspective must therefore be understood as much by what it excludes from view as by that which it includes. Understood in this way, a perspective is permeated by the condition of the not-seen, a condition that destabilizes the authority of a singular view. We get a sense of this in the perspective drawings of Mies where the figures in the architecture are reduced to shades that pass across an ever present yet distant horizon extending laterally beyond our view.

This manner of thinking and feeling is also found in the Sartrean condition of the *négatité* that he defines as ". . . realities which are not only objects of judgment, but which are experienced, opposed, feared etc. . . . by the human being and which in their inner structure are inhabited by negation."[1] The not-seen, or the area outside the limits of a perspective, forms the background of our understanding of the scene within which it is located. Like the *négatité,* it permeates the scene as a potential negation of that which is seen. Understood in this more comprehensive manner, the négatité of the picture functions as "a type of synthesis of negative and positive in which the condition of negation is the condition of positivity."[2] In other words, the *négatité* describes a circumstance in which the object of one's attention is informed as much by the presence of the object in its positive aspect as by all that is *not present* to view or immediate understanding. The tension between its negative and positive aspects is understood as the "regulative concept" that informs our understanding of a situation, a concept that extends beyond the situation, forming a horizon against which the situation is understood.

We are not so far here from the phrase "less is more" often attributed to Mies, a phrase that transforms a negative (less) into a positive (more) as well as serving as a regulative concept in the consideration of an architectural context. In this way Mies was able to structure the many and diverse claims that surround a building proposition, focusing their aspects while maintaining a sense of the broader context from which they emerge.

For Mies, the condition of the horizon and its perspectives is symbolized in the notations of an architectural syntax. The operations of this syntax with its geometric referent enabled him to fulfill one of the primary aspects of perspectival culture: that the measure of rational thought exists in the form of an idealized abstraction, which can be approached but never fully materialized. The modernism of Mies exists in this pursuit for the materialization of abstraction, a pursuit whose ends are always receding from view while acting simultaneously as the regulative concept for the pursuit itself.

The work of the Architecture Studio at Cranbrook has developed in the aftermath of this modernist pursuit of Mies. We are impressed by the singularity of its vision, but find ourselves questioning a number of its assumptions. For example: does the reductivism often associated with negation (in terms of the mechanism of neither-nor) still operate effectively to inform the complexities of building and architecture? Is the singular pursuit of a regulative concept still an appropriate philosophical program for architecture? And a related question, can geometry and the perspectives that it offers still be employed with the authority that it exercised for Mies? The studies that follow begin to address these questions. For the most part they involve material studies done in the context of an architectural studio. As architects we are driven to work in this manner partly in reaction to the strong emphasis that Mies placed upon the abstract representations of drawing despite his counter-claims regarding the primacy of the building. Our own studies have shown that building activity resists the order and control described by Mies and cannot always be organized according to the abstractions that he emphasized in his drawing. We have also found that the building act is filled with possibilities that cannot be anticipated in the reasoned disciplines of drawing and reflection alone. Our questioning of Mies, then, has grown out of an intuition that building is also conditioned by bodily acts and conditions that remain outside the reach of a focused logic. A more realistic understanding of architecture would consider the trans-parency offered by reasoned thought as well as the opacities buried in the body that both builds and inhabits its constructions.

For the remainder of this paper I plan to review a number of studies undertaken by myself and members of the Architecture Studio. For the most part these studies were not conceived with a specific reference to Mies, though after reflecting upon the influence of his work it became evident that we are still tied to many of the same issues, albeit from another perspective. I welcome the opportunity to consider how much we have actually left behind.

As an introduction to one of my own studies entitled "Recording Wall," I would like to refer to a detail of a brick wall designed by Mies for the Wolf House (1925–27) (fig. 3). Although brick was not considered to be a "modern" building material at the time, Mies was able to employ it in a manner that recognized the traditional craft embodied in brick construction while at the same time signifying a decidedly modern attitude in its detailing. The story goes that he took great care in the selection of the individual bricks since at the time they were not produced with the "technological precision" that we find in contemporary brick production, checking for uniformity of edge as well as demanding great care in the alignment of the coursing during construction. The story comes into focus when one examines the completed wall and recognizes that the combined precision of the brick units and mortar coursing produces a grid of mortar of such exactitude that it visually dominates the materiality of the individual brick units. Here we find that craft is brought to the point of invisibility and thereby negated relative to the abstracted, geometric pattern of the grid. Mies develops and refines the idiosyncratic craft of the hand so that the brick detailing represents a *technological* perfection in which any trace of the hand is erased. In so doing he submits the technique of bricklaying to what Edward Husserl refers to as an "idealizing praxis,"[3] wherein a limit-horizon such as "the straightness of a line" or "the smoothness of a plane" is approached through the perfection of an instrumental technique.

Husserl considered this *striving towards perfectibility* through mathematically based and instrumentally driven techniques as a defining characteristic of the modern age, a striving that becomes, if considered uncritically, a fate whose end is determined by the apparent autonomy of instrumental logic. Mies also saw this striving as a defining aspect of the age but took a surprisingly uncritical approach to the issue as evidenced in his statement, "Fulfill the law to gain freedom."[4] For Mies the issues of universal *mathesis* and technologically driven praxis are considered as *a priori* factors rather than problematic questions that threaten to undo the very accomplishments upon which they are based. For Mies these questions are laws to be fulfilled rather than questions to be posed.

For the study entitled "Recording Wall," a masonry wall of concrete blocks is stacked up without mortar to nominal dimensions of 8 feet by 16 feet (figs. 1 & 2). During the stacking or construction process each block is photographed as it is being put into place. (Cameras are located on both sides of the wall and are activated by an extended shutter release located by the foot of the builder.) The resulting photographs are then printed onto the surface of each block using a liquid photo emulsion. All information recorded by the photograph that is not part of the wall is then painted over

3. Mies van der Rohe,
Wolf House, 1925–27, Guben. Terrace.

4. Mies van der Rohe,
Project for the Alexanderplatz
Competition, 1928, Berlin.
Photomontage (no longer extant).

on one side in black and on the other in white. The resulting wall becomes a literal recording of its own construction or de-construction.

As opposed to the Miesian wall, where a latent, gridded geometry is emphasized through a perfection of building craft, the geometry of the concrete block wall is assumed to be present and without need of emphasis, because it is already a product of technologically controlled means of production. What is of interest, then, is the supplementary reading of the wall made possible by the layer of recorded information placed upon it through the photographic process. Here we see evidence of a crafting activity as the blocks are put into place and we become aware of the construction process itself as an issue in the perception of the wall. The index of the photograph is now used to supplement the found technology of the block wall, thereby returning it to a presence lost in the production of the masonry units.

To bring this short discussion of technology and praxis to a close, I would add Gianni Vattimo's observation that rather than providing us with new freedoms, advances in technology appear to produce as many problems as they claim to solve — producing the paradoxical situation and feeling of moving forward while remaining in the same place.[5] The desire to move towards the horizon of ideality now finds us simply trying to keep up with its ever-receding ends.

The use of an indexical recording device (or camera) is actually anticipated by Mies in the documentation of a number of his early projects. In his proposal for the Alexanderplatz in Berlin (1928), for example, a drawing of the project was inserted within an edited photograph of the site (fig. 4). The stark simplicity of his proposal as drawn into the site is in marked contrast to the variegated confusion of the surrounding urban scene, its repetitive and minimally articulated walls maintaining the absence of the initial erasure or clearing while simultaneously positing a new construction in its place. The deliberate choice of the two means of signification, the representationally constructed drawing and the indexically recorded photograph, underscores the operation of the *négatité* that Mies employed for this urban project. By literally erasing a photograph of the city, Mies negates or absents the site and replaces it with a construction that sustains the negation of the original act. The result is a double negative that gives forth the positive residue of a building proposal.

One might add here that the Toronto-Dominion Centre establishes a similar relationship with its context. The dark stillness of the simple, geometric volumes that characterize the composition contrasts with the active, urban life that surrounds it. Surely it is this stillness that Mies had in mind when representing his Alexanderplatz proposal.

In later projects such as the Resor House (1937–40), Mies inserts a photograph within perspective drawing to depict views of the site from the interior (fig. 5). The difference between the photograph and the drawing is emphasized both by the minimal articulation of the drawing itself and by the dramatic choice of a mountain range as the subject for the photograph. It should be noted that in this case it is the *representation* of architecture that is framing the view. The reduction of architectural notation to the simple outline of a column represents the floor and ceiling while flattening the space of the foregrounded interior. Through its framing, the view is also drawn close to the surface of the architectural frame, although the cubist inversion of near and far is never attempted. This is understandable since by definition a perspective is constructed as a subjectively determined distance between an object and the horizon. Mies pressures this relationship by reducing the foreground elements of architecture while emphasizing the horizon itself as an object, maintaining the spatial hierarchy of perspective by bringing it up to but not over its limit.

The importance of Mies's drawing-photographs lies in the manner in which differing means of signification are used to challenge the symbolic and spatial meanings of a project relative to its context. It is this aspect that we have attempted to push further in our investigations at Cranbrook.

In a study by Kamol Jangkamolkulchai, a camera is used to orthographically survey a room, recording the floor, walls, and ceiling (fig. 6). By positioning the camera in such a manner, the perspectival depth between the camera and the surface is compressed to a flatness approaching that of a geometric plane, drawing the perspective to the verge of collapse onto the flatness of the plan. The "ground" in these images is no longer generated from an objective, geometric reference but is produced from the compression of a subjective point of view onto a surface. Any protrusion on the surface is thereby infected by the perspective mechanism of the lens and further destabilizes the abstract, geometric reference of the surface plane. The compressed photographs are then used as drawings on which to make minimal interventions of linear elements that are then built or inscribed into the space itself setting up another round of photographic recordings. The cycle between photography, drawing, and construction is repeated again and again to the point where it is impossible to determine the means of signification within the documentation. Lines are now suspended in the space between media and material. It is impossible to determine whether they are located upon the surfaces of the drawing, photograph or wall, whether the lines are to be understood as being material, notational, indexical or representational.

Here the architectural object and context are brought into a spatial and representational ambiguity, a charged field that denies the distance critical to perspectival thinking. The equivalence demonstrated between index and representation, as well as the spatial ambiguity between near and far are both steps that Mies resisted in his work. For Mies, architecture assumes a dialectical stance in relationship to its context. It is critical that the two remain distinct so that a distance can exist between them, no matter how small it may be. His construction of vision brings us up to the surrounding horizon but does not venture beyond it. It is important to consider this tendency in Mies's work since a number of his contemporaries were already venturing to cross this line in their work. Speculations on this subject are far beyond the scope of this paper, but I would suggest that his hesitation can be understood in the context of a mourning attitude that he assumed with regard to the historical disruptions of modernism, remembering the basic assumptions that constitute its intellectual structure while also attempting to bring them to an end. In this light, it is appropriate to describe his work as "monumentalizing" his age, an act of remembrance that sets the stage for our own investigations.

The Barcelona Pavilion (1929) remains the paradigmatic example of the reductivism of Mies (fig. 7). The significance of the pavilion, however, is not only due to the minimal use of architectural elements but their reduction into the symbolic forms of geometry. It is here that we must look to observe how the limit-horizon is approached and possibly inhabited. In the familiar front view of the pavilion, for example, it is evident that the space of the pavilion is limited by the inside surfaces of the section between the roof and plinth, a space that is filled in elevation by the vertical thickness of the marble-faced walls. When projected towards the horizon, however, the surfaces of the roof and plinth begin to converge into a single line that is conceptually without thickness. This line surrounds the pavilion and though it is never visible serves as its conceptual horizon, organizing the multi-directional views that are offered in the free plan of the ground plane. The compression of architecture into this conceptual thickness of the space within a line demonstrates how far Mies goes in thinking towards the formal limits of architecture. It is these very limits that contextualize and organize his work.

The formal function of the horizon is examined further in a study by Adam Womelsdorf (fig. 8). In this case, the horizon line is actually a rectangular section of mirror suspended horizontally by four wires. A light source is located above the mirror, producing a reflection and shadow upon the wall surface beyond. Because the light comes from a point source, reflections and shadows upon the wall appear in the triangulation of a perspective, the horizontal mirror appearing to bisect the view of the two

5. Mies van der Rohe,
Resor House, 1937–38, Wyoming.
Interior perspective of living room
(view through north glass wall).

6. Kamol Jangkamolkulchai,
Drawing in the Spaces of Construction,
April 1992.

receding planes. One is reminded here of the horizontal symmetry implicit in the formal structuring of the horizon line used by Mies, where the floor of the plinth and the roof plane are understood as reflections of a horizontal section. Another look at the frontal view of the pavilion confirms this with the dark reflecting pool acting as the shadow and the underside of the roof acting as the reflection for the virtual horizon line.

What Womelsdorf's study demonstrates is that the virtual horizon line of Mies has a direct correlate in physical phenomena, that the horizon reflects itself upon the material structure of the world as well as upon thought. The reflective surfaces of the pavilion compound the horizontal reflection in other dimensions, filling the primary, horizontal section of space with a multiplicity of views. But it is important to keep in mind that the horizontal section remains as the encompassing orientation, the horizon from which all views emerge and within which all experience is bounded.

As already mentioned, perspectival culture sees the horizon as an ideal limit-form from which constructions are viewed and measured. This understanding maintains that the horizon can never be surpassed, which makes a view from the position of the horizon an impossibility. But what if the horizon itself is considered as a human construct, something particular to our way of seeing and understanding, something particular to our embodied consciousness in the world? These questions are provoked in a study by Francis Resendes in which a horizon line of water is constructed in a series of thin, rectangular, glass tanks installed over a row of windows of the same size (figs. 9 & 10). The tanks are all connected by rubber tubing attached to the bottom of a cylindrical reservoir set at the height of Resendes's eyes. When the reservoir is filled, its level is reproduced in the rectangular, glass tanks due to the phenomenon of water always seeking its own level.

Looking through the water level of the glass tanks to the horizon beyond, we are reminded of the coincidence of the material aspects of water as a self-leveling substance and the idealized, geometric aspects of the horizontal line. This coincidence is threatened, however, when the physical conditions of the horizontal line are drawn over the horizon, as it were, beyond the "Newtonian oasis" of the middle ground of centralized vision where the rules of Euclidean geometry hold sway over our perceptions.[6] Questioning the perceptual nature of the line at the periphery of our vision asks us to consider its limit not as an idealized limit-form that orders our understanding, but as a circumstantial relationship between our body and its environment. Rather than focusing upon the *idea* of the horizon we may ask how a correspondence is made between the *acts* of the body and the world within which they occur. In other words, we are in search of a verb rather than a noun to describe how the phenomenon of the horizon works.

7. Mies van der Rohe,
German Pavilion, Barcelona, 1928–29.
View from the edge of the large pool.

8. Adam Womelsdorf,
Reflection Shadow, October 1991.

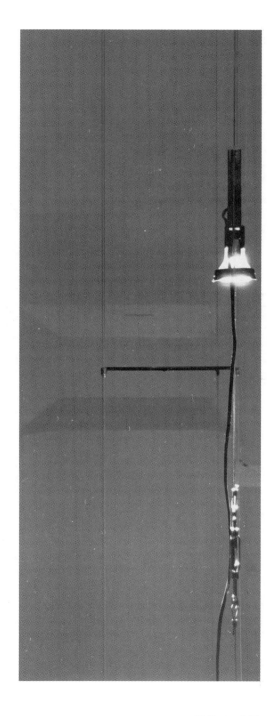

9 & 10. Francis Resendes,
Horizon Level, May 1991.

Resendes's study indicates that the fluid action of leveling is critical to the formation of the horizon and the horizon-idea. The significance of this intuition is that this phenomenon operates on both a local and global scale. By using a fluid level we can always locate ourselves perpendicular to the surface of the earth at a particular point, therefore releasing the necessity to refer our posture to the abstraction of a horizontal plane. This emphasis upon localized leveling also permits us to consider the limits of the earth in terms of the continuity of a fluid limit rather than as the brittle abstraction of a geometric plane.

The phenomenal circuit is completed when we realize that leveling also occurs *within* the body in the liquid balance in the cochlear chamber of the ear. Given this *sense* of the horizon, the globes of our eyes act as ocular joints between internal and external realms. We externalize this relationship to the world with the aid of the instruments that are used to construct our buildings. M. Merleau-Ponty has observed, "our organs are no longer our instruments, rather our instruments have become our detachable organs."[7] The float level is the instrument that brings the measure of the horizon to construction and, along with the plumb line, permits its development in the world. Equipped with this physical understanding we can determine a tangent to the surface of any point on the globe. The geometry of this condition is determined by the ever-changing topology of the surface rather than the fixed idealization of parallel lines that one finds in Euclidean geometry. It is important to remind ourselves of this when we see through the gridded and parallel frames of a Mies building. The world is not flat and the horizon is not straight, rather they are part of a continuous surface that comes back around upon itself. With its liquid level and motility, the body makes itself at home upon this surface. In this context, the perspectival extension to the horizon appears as an act of will born from the desire to fix the limits of the world, making it objectifiable within the abstract frame of a perfected and perfecting representational system.

Referring back to the fluid level study of Resendes, it is interesting to note how we look *through* the level of the water in the glass frames out to the view beyond. The fluid beyond us is also that which is within us, a liquid environment that dampens the dry physics of Mies, making it more pliable and responsive to the physical aspects of embodied consciousness. As I hope I have demonstrated, Mies's interest in the physical aspects of building is always inflected by a corresponding concern with the abstract limits that organize a construction. A building detail is understood to be the intersection of a geometrically driven syntax and the material concerns of production. Details therefore have a historical dimension in Mies, carrying forth discussions within the context of an established discourse in Western

11. Mies van der Rohe,
Aerial·view photomontage of the campus
of the Illinois Institute of Technology,
1939–41, Chicago, Illinois.
Photo Hedrich·Blessing.

12. Dan Hoffman,
Altered aerial photograph of downtown
Detroit, 1992. Areas that have been
blackened are vacant parcels of land.

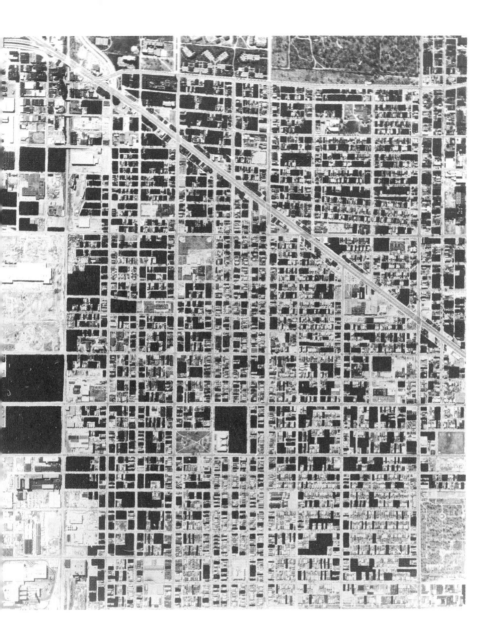

culture. In the case of Resendes, the detail works its way back into consciousness through the intuition of the body and its sympathetic understanding of the horizon as a level. It presumes an a-historical context of understanding, one that relies upon the assumption that the body is the primary reference for an orientation upon the surface.

In closing I would like to offer two images: a photograph of a model for the campus at IIT designed by Mies (fig. 11) and a recently altered aerial photograph of Detroit (fig. 12). The black areas in this photograph are painted-out parcels of empty land. The information for the altered photograph comes from the city administration's "vacant land program" which is an attempt to identify and assemble parcels of land to be purchased for future development. Unfortunately, no development has taken place and the parcels are growing larger and larger. Though the comparison with IIT might appear superficial, the formal similarities between the two are too close to be dismissed. In seeing the two together, I have come to understand that Mies and the thinking that he represents have left an inheritance that still exerts a profound influence upon our culture although it is manifested here in the activity of unbuilding rather than building.

Mies's contribution, like that of any great architect, was to synthesize the contradictions of an age. How else can one mobilize a culture towards the great investment of effort and displacement of material that is required to build? With respect to this view, it is our feeling at the Architecture Studio that the contradictions inherent in the perspectival paradigm have become too great and that it is now too crude an instrument with which to deal with the inherent complexities found in building. The darkened, aerial photograph shows us that negation has taken to the streets and has exceeded any possibility of a positive turn. This transformation of building into unbuilding is occurring at a rate that makes the dialectical relationship of a building to its context impossible to consider. Nevertheless, we are inspired by the challenges that such environments offer, depleted as they are of the structures inherent in perspectival ordering. What remains is the activity of wild negation, a type of vernacular that does not order itself in such determined and opposing ways. The complexities and richness of such conditions will be an exciting challenge for the studio to pursue once Mies finally disappears from view.

**Notes**

1. Jean-Paul Sartre, *Being and Nothingness*, trans. Hazel E. Barnes (New York: Washington Square Press, 1966), p. 5.

2. Sartre, p. 5.

3. Edmund Husserl, *The Crises of European Sciences* (Evanston, Illinois: Northwestern University Press, 1970), p. 41.

4. Fritz Neumeyer, *The Artless Word: Mies van der Rohe and the Building Art,* trans. Mark Jarzowbek (Cambridge, Massachusetts & London: MIT Press, 1991), p. 195.

5. Gianni Vattimo, *The End of Modernity,* trans. Jon R. Snyder (Baltimore: Johns Hopkins University Press, 1988), p. 7.

6. Patrick Heelan, *Space Perception and the Philosophy of Science* (Berkeley: University of California Press), p. 28.

7. Maurice Merleau-Ponty, *The Primacy of Perception* (Evanston, Illinois: Northwestern University Press, 1964), p. 178.

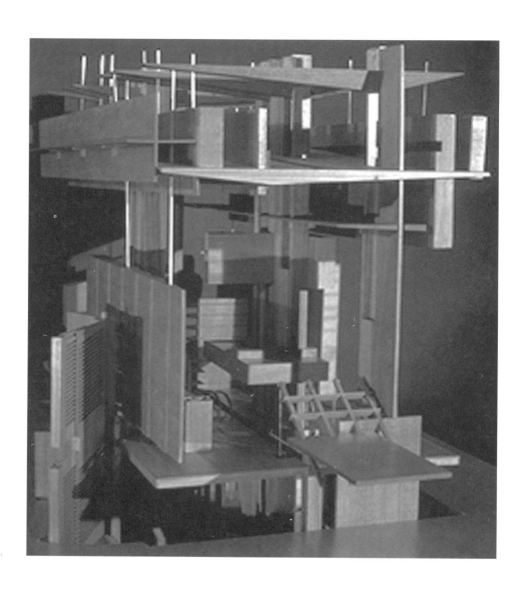

1. Loaf House,
Model, constructed by Amy Berka,
Tim Burke, Fritz Head, Jason Kerwin, and
Veronica Pazaran.

## RENOUNCING AUTISTIC WORD

*Ben Nicholson*

### An Audit of the Pedagogy

In 1989 the Illinois Institute of Technology (IIT) decided to take on the task of replacing the pedagogy of the College of Architecture. The strategy of the then-new dean, Gene Summers, was to establish a number of semi-autonomous studios in which all courses in design, visual training, and city planning are taught. As a studio leader, my participation in the reworking of the curriculum began with the commencement of these studios in 1990. I add that I am an implant to the College, not having passed through the official rites of initiation of Mies van der Rohe's curriculum, which has remained intact until now.

On reading Mies's texts and seeing the work of students at the College, the existing curriculum can easily be aligned with the tradition of architectural education. The form of both his words and works differs little from the traditional model in which the artifact is understood to be based on a "philosophy," imbued with "fine craft," and a manifestation of the processes of its constitution.

Makers and architects have frequently taken on the task of describing how they think about architecture and art: Leo Battista Alberti, Albrecht Dürer, Sebastiano Serlio, and Andrea Palladio all left documents that would lead the architect or painter reading the text right up to the brink of creation. A similarly reflective process exists in our century, and Mies's strategy for thinking about architecture is part of that lineage. The IIT curriculum, formed in 1938, was a gritty total work forged by Mies and then hammered and polished by Walter Peterhans and Ludwig Hilberseimer to run smoothly for ten years, yet it slipped into blind perpetuity. Once the vim and vigor of creating this system had reached a plateau, only the slightest trimming was needed for its maintenance.

The instigators of the pedagogy left in their wake little more than cryptic aphorisms and a legacy of impeccable drawings. The evidence that remains of the original working pedagogy comes to us in four forms: 1) the text of the "Inaugural Address" and "The Program for Architectural Education"; 2) student drawings and models, for the most part now dispersed; 3) the legacy of word of mouth; and 4) the buildings of Mies.

Practically speaking, the pedagogy became an artifact of sworn silence, unavailable to the uninitiated, for there is only one way to it — to do it. A legacy of word of mouth accompanied participation in the curriculum, yet this is a paradox; for it is nonsensical to articulate the contemplative silence surrounding the studied gaze of Mies's critique, punctuated by his famous remark, "Try it again!"

A legacy of silence has its difficulties, for once the artifacts are gone and the story-tellers leave, there is nothing to grasp, no written word to set the imagination afire. The physique of Mies's buildings is too large to put into one's lap and mull over. Without a key, the buildings are going into a slow feint, and residents are now more frequently leaving articles propped up against the glass walls. They are admonished for doing this by those who know — yet without understanding exactly why.

**Reworking the Inaugural Address**
The text of the 1938 inaugural address is a compaction of succinct aphorisms around four topics: the binding of practicality and values; order emerging from chaos; working in the Spirit of the Age; and formal and organic order. The remarks are qualified by the activity of building.

*Chaos and Order*
The second wave of remarks in the Address settle on chaos and order. Mies states:

> – Education must lead us from irresponsible opinion to true responsible judgement.
> – It must lead us from chance and arbitrariness to rational clarity and intellectual order.
> – Therefore let us guide our students over the road of discipline from materials, through function, to creative work.[1]

The value of Mies's thoughts on chaos and order is in the promotion of a journey from one state of being to another. The specific examples used in his remarks are, however, not so useful to us: being led from chance and arbitrariness to rationality and intellectual order is a proposition that sticks in the craw, for it deposes the potential value of chance before it has had an opportunity to establish its self-worth.

The texts that Mies refers to, and which guide his pedagogy, are by St. Augustine and St. Thomas Aquinas. We can see how the logic of their thought fits the logic of his thought. However, his chosen books are not our chosen books. Since his writing, architects have imbued chance and the arbitrary with a furious logic, and even mathematicians have formed a Theory of Chaos. It is curious that Mies preferred not to speak of the rationality and order present in the work of people such as Kurt Schwitters, whose collages he owned.

Today's cultural interests and accompanying models gleaned from the past are radically different from those stated in the Address. Since 1938, interests have focused on other texts. The careful logic of Marcel Duchamp has become a contender for an appropriate model for logic in our age. Duchamp's *Large Glass* and accompanying manual, *The Green Box,* is as well-reasoned and well-crafted as anything offered by the party line of order. We are also reminded of the crisis in thinking in the sixteenth century in which paradox and incommensurability were viewed as more fitting models of life than the rational systems that preceded them. For example, the introduction of irrational dimensions and irregular geometry, present in the 1540s pavement in Michelangelo's Laurentian Library, might be a more apt model of intellectual order today than anything based upon the Hesiodian flight of Chaos making a beeline for Order. Mies's Address gives us the *structure* to think about philosophical models, even though ours are different from his.

In the opening sequence of his Address, Mies sets practicality and virtue apart and then reinvites them back into each other's company, as mutual counterparts. It is our task to complete this structure of thinking and to bring together those ideas in the address that he identified but was unable to commingle. Having located our own philosophical models, we have found a way to invite issues, such as chance and the arbitrary, to consider clarity and intellectual order. A wistful retention of the modernist interpretation of St. Augustine and St. Aquinas as contemporary models is nothing more than a sheepish longing for the good old days. Mies asks us to engage in philosophy, not sentimentality.

*The Shake-out of Ordered Chaos*
We are no longer willing to engage the pedagogical sequence leading from materials, through function, to creative work. That sequence echoed Mies's personal journey from the stone yard, to the making of programmed

houses to the symphonic works. Between his time and our time, a generation of architects — such as James Stirling, John Hejduk, Peter Eisenman, and then Daniel Libeskind — had to unlearn modernist dogma and rediscover architecture through a long and silent search, characterized by the abstract discipline of drawing, to arrive at a point from which they could consider themselves ready for big building. In practical terms, the avant-garde of architecture have forged a course of action diametrically opposed to that suggested by Mies. Their first activity was to pose questions that lead to creation; their second action was to look for function; and finally they grappled with materials in the building site. It must be added that Hejduk and Libeskind have paid enormous and visible tribute to Mies by rediscovering his spirit, strategy, and method.

*The Spirit of the Age*
The third sequence in the Address centers on the necessity to remain in step with the Spirit of the Age. Mies suggests:

> – Just as we acquaint ourselves with materials and just as we must understand functions, we must become familiar with the psychological and spiritual factors of our day.
> – No cultural activity is possible otherwise; for we are dependent on the spirit of our time.
> – Therefore we must understand the motives and forces of our time and analyze their structure from three points of view: the material, the functional, and the spiritual.
> – We must make clear in what respects our epoch differs from others and in what respects it is similar.[2]

Our times are not his time. His epoch was begun by endgame belligerence, followed by the fresh face of being on a winning team that went on to pursue a vision of life characterized by optimism and prosperity. Furthermore, IIT — his laboratory of architectural thought — was set down in a city eager to practice the ideas of urbanism formulated by Mies and his collaborators. But, in 1992, it is no longer appropriate to found a curriculum based upon that kind of cultural optimism, particularly when the age is uncertain whether it is coming or going. Yet architecture is not a fairweather activity: its responsibility is to decode whatever conditions we find ourselves in and we are charged to find the appropriate manner of practicing — building or otherwise.

## Ways of Thinking in the Spirit of the Age

The intellectual activities that we practice in the Studio are guided by considering incidents and past structures of thinking that are pertinent to our age. For example, Robert Graves notes that the Bible was translated by Hebrew scribes who thought that the clay tablets, upon which the original texts were cut, were inscribed repeatedly from right to left, in the Hebrew manner of writing. The tablets were in fact cut in boustrophedon — written from left to right and then from right to left, etc.. The consequences of this, he suggested, is that every other line in the Bible has been interpreted backwards and that two religions have emerged from a dramatic misinterpretation of a text.

The creativity of text-making is in the struggle to interpret words even if they do not make sense. There is a passage from Mies's address that has also fallen foul of the translating process. This passage — "Durch nichts wird Ziel und Sinn unserer Arbeit mehr erschlossen als durch das tiefe Wort von St. Augustin, 'Das Schöne ist der Glanz des Wahren!'" — is translated in Werner Blaser's book as "Nothing can express the aim and meaning of our work better than the profound work of St. Augustine, 'Beauty is the splendor of Truth.'" The same passage is translated by Rolf Achilless as "Through nothing the sense and goal of our work is made more manifest than the profound words of St. Augustine, 'Beauty is the splendor of Truth.'"[3] Obviously there is a glitch in the translation of the second version that makes it read as if nothingness is more valuable to the process of work than St. Augustine's aphorism, "Beauty is the splendor of Truth" — an interesting concept and perhaps more provocative than the right reading.

Potential can fall out of stock attitudes should one wish to look for it. Contemporary readings of texts (and architecture) have fulfilled the work of the Dadaist and surrealist thinkers, ways of thinking with which the German Mies had an intimate liaison — more so than Mies's North American circle cares to admit. These right readings make it easier to comprehend his enigmatic activity of setting incongruities into the bowels of North American cities.

The form of Mies's Address still stands. The form of the remarks still allow his intentions to be readily available. The actuality of thinking and doing today is quite changed: clearly the spirit of our time is not the one practiced in the middle of this century. However, once it has been identified and unscrambled, it conforms — to the letter — to Mies's statement.

## One Design Practice at IIT

At IIT, each of the autonomous studios is responsible for designing and building a house with the students. Our task is to see if it is possible to make a house according to the reverse of the order that Mies recommended, that is via the route of creativity, through function, to materials. Our house is two years into its four-year cycle, and we have produced a set of drawings from which the function will follow.[4]

Our studio's house, the Loaf House, is sited in an area off-campus that is referred to as the Gap, so named because it is an urban void. Now full of cavity lots and the quietness of weed patches, the site (or the Gap) is synonymous with the aftermath of an urban storm that has blown itself out.

With the Loaf House we wish to make a place that continuously reveals itself, in which the inhabitants could touch a place of shifting divisions. To catalyze this intention, the student team was presented with a drawing of a multiple elevation of a wall-sized window. Two plans of the window were drawn at different levels (fig. 2). Despite the fact that the students conversed carefully, the new dimensions would not align. Rather than crow at the lack of alignment, the drawing was left in an unknowing potent state.

These drawings were reworked, this time allowing the pieces in the plans to drift on orthogonal tracks across the page until they crossed other paths (fig. 3). At these points of conjunction the pieces of paper spliced into each other, in the monkey grip of collage. Within this net of impossibilities, foreign bodies in the form of aircraft parts or Spanish onions were set in, giving perspective to the inbreeding that collaging of collaging can spawn. The finished collage drawings were recalibrated to note the points of origin from which the instigative pieces had been set adrift.

The unstable, volatile drawings now had to be pegged to the Gap site. A half-lot was selected for a small house. The lot perimeter, hemmed in by the surrounding buildings, was drawn onto paper and into it the collaged fragments of the previous campaign were reined in, along new cut rails — the component pieces moving across the paper in a disciplined, yet unbridled state (fig. 4). Once again, the moments of commingling were arbitrated with the precision of cut collage and three more plan sections were tamed for the house.

The dissipated state of the house was then freeze-dried into eight pieces located in the three axes. There is now a desiccated rectangular space defined by five sets of drawings, each of which somersaulted out from its former state. At each turn the zone of the former spin is crafted with a watertight exactitude, yet something unutterable happens between maneuvers and it is deliberately noted and drawn (fig. 5). Duchamp's word for this zone was *inframince,* meaning the warmth of a seat that has just been vacated. The desire of the Loaf House is to become a constructed state of the in-between, in homage to Mies's Brick House, but diagnosed as such via our own strategy.

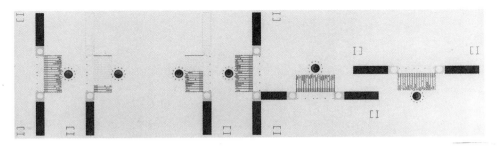

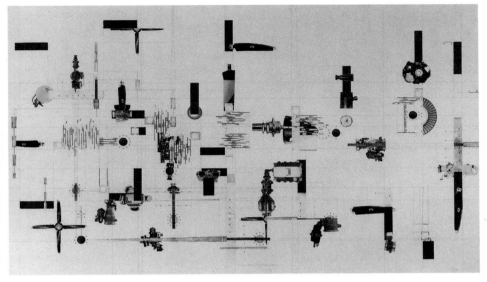

2. Loaf House,
Static Plan, drawn by Boris Cubas.

3. Loaf House,
Commingle Plan, drawn by Kristina Yu.

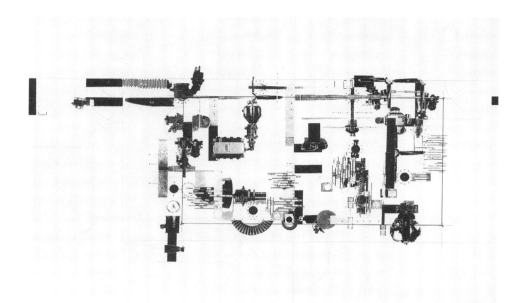

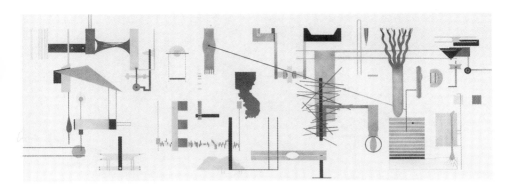

4. Loaf House,
Contract Plan, collage by Nathaniel
Lindsey.

5. Loaf House,
Non-specific Section, drawn by Kristina Yu.

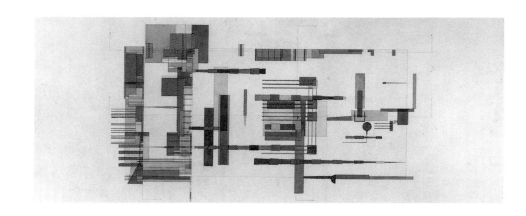

6. Loaf House,
Cartographic Plan, drawn by Kristina Yu.

The Loaf House drawings are constructed to have their own past; the genes of each drawing are traceable through five generations to their hereditary great great grandfather. When the drawings move to a new state,where a mismatch of plan and function may arise, the impasse can be arbitrated within the history of the drawings. The five generations pass along what they can to the construct: different maturities of form tumble out of their respective logics to coalesce into a single set of measured drawings: plans, sections, and elevations (fig. 6). The set is latent with a strategy for structure, for a structural system that permits an interdependence of parts where each is suspended, balanced, supported, or wedged against its neighbor's nature. The Loaf House is now in a drawn and modeled state, as yet unset with function and materiality (fig. 1). This will be the next task.

## Paying our Respects

To be an uninitiate within IIT's guild of pedagogical knowledge is daily unnerving, but I am — as many architects and thinkers outside it are — respectful of, and grateful to, Mies. Yet there cannot be a monopoly held over what Mies has left. We all have a right to his work irrespective of our scholastic aptitude — to learn from it what we are able and what is appropriate to our lifework, whatever that may be. What is readily available from his work is his intention, his conviction and his method. His product — his architecture — remains his alone. It is appropriate to heed his polemic carefully and to translate the materiality of his work to ours. The resulting architecture will not look the same as his, but will have been faithful to its tenets. At IIT we are reworking the pedagogy by reinventing and realigning the materiality of his legacy while being careful not to undermine or contradict his principles.

**Notes**

1. Ludwig Mies van der Rohe, "Inaugural Address as Director of the Department of Architecture at Armour Institute of Technology, Chicago, November 20, 1938," in Werner Blaser, *Mies van der Rohe, Principles and School* (Basel and Stuttgart: Birkhäuser, 1977), p. 28.

2. Blaser, p. 29.

3. See Fritz Neumeyer, "Mies as Self Educator," in *Mies van der Rohe: Architect as Educator*, eds. Rolf Achilles, Kevin Harrington, and Charlotte Myhrum (Chicago: University of Chicago Press, 1986), p. 35.

4. The Loaf House has been worked on by seventeen students at the Illinois Institute of Technology during the 1991–92 and 1992–93 academic years under the co-direction of B. Nicholson and C. Wetzel.

# MINIMALISM

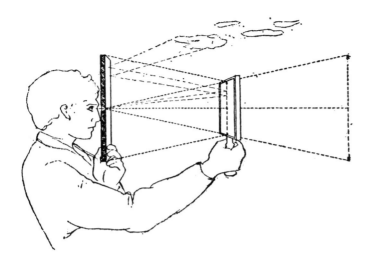

1. Reconstruction of Brunelleschi's
first experience of perspectival
representation.

## THE GRID, THE /CLOUD/, AND THE DETAIL

*Rosalind Krauss*

As I was reading some of the recent literature on Mies van der Rohe, I encountered a phenomenon I had not known of until then: I came across the politically correct Mies, the poststructuralist Mies, almost, we could say, the postmodernist Mies. Which also means that I began to understand what I had not before, namely, why I had been invited to a conference on the "presence of Mies."

For it seems that a certain reading of Minimalism — let us call it phenomenological — had been imported into the field of architectural criticism to attack received opinion about Mies's purported classicism, his formalism, his aloofness. If Minimalist sculpture was initially understood — indeed in certain circles continues to be understood — through a set of classicist and idealist terms, understood, that is, as projecting timeless, unchanging geometries, what we might refer to in shorthand as Platonic solids, this reading was challenged (by myself and others) as entirely inappropriate to work that immersed itself in the actual, contingent particularities of its moment of being experienced, insisting that its very point was to focus its viewer's attention on how it changed from moment to moment of its perception in real time.[1]

What this second reading underscored was the way geometric shape was shown to be entirely context dependent — as in Robert Morris's three identical but perceptually very different L-beams — and thus open to the cat's cradle of the interface between viewer and viewed — as in much of Donald Judd's work; the way it exploits a geometry that exists in and through the flux of tension and gravitational force (Judd, Richard Serra), so that, far from having what we could call the fixed and enduring centers of a kind of formulaic geometry, Minimalism produces the paradox of a centerless because shifting geometry, in objects with no fixed armature, objects that can be rearranged at will (Morris). Because of this demonstrable attack on the idea that works achieve their meaning by becoming manifestations or expressions of a hidden center, Minimalism was read as lodging meaning in the surface of the object, hence its interest in reflective materials, in exploiting the play of natural light. And hence the analogy that could be formed between conditions of meaning suggested by this work and those being developed in both structuralism and its post-structuralist radicalization.

In the revisionary readings of Mies that I encountered this summer, all of these notions were being put to work to create an anti-formalist, anti-classical Mies, one who — and here I am quoting K. Michael Hays — "insists that an order is immanent [only] in the surface itself and that the order is continuous with and dependent upon the world in which the viewer actually moves. This sense of surface and volume," he continues, "severed from the knowledge of an internal order or a unifying logic, is enough to wrench the building from the atemporal, idealized realm of autonomous form and install it in a specific situation in the real world of experienced time, open to the chance and uncertainty of life in the metropolis."[2]

Indeed, in one description after another of the Barcelona Pavilion (by Robin Evans and José Quetglas, for example) the emphasis had shifted entirely away from the kind of contrapuntal but nevertheless classical logic of plan and elevation to which I had been introduced back when Mies was seen as the very epitome of the International Style, and instead what I was now being shown was a structure committed to illusionism, with every material assuming, camelion-like, the attributes of something not itself — columns dissolving into bars of light, or glass walls becoming opaque and marble ones appearing transparent due to their reflectivity — but even more importantly, with a mysteriousness built into the plan such that the building is constructed without an approachable or knowable center and is in fact experienced as (to use these authors' word) a labyrinth.[3]

This resistance to the spectator's grasp, to what we might call the building's making the terms of its production or its function transparent and thus reproducing the technical or economic means of production that structure its social field, is finally seen as having political overtones, as when K. Michael Hays says that although Mies's work is immersed in the space/time of its viewer, its resistance to meaning constitutes a "critical interpretation of its worldly situation," critical in so far as it confronts us with a refusal to construct an "efficient representation of pre-existing cultural values."[4]

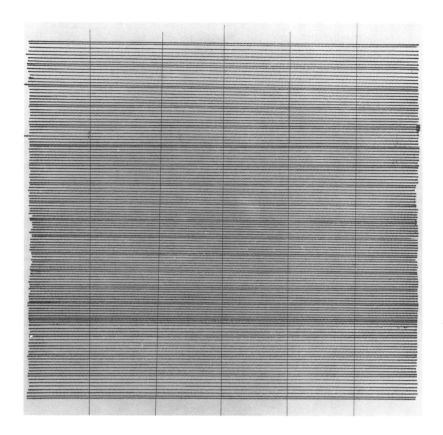

2. Agnes Martin,
Untitled, 1961.
Black ink on paper.
8¾″ x 8⅛″.

Thus, from the poststructuralist, labyrinthine Mies, the one involved in the play of the signifier, we end up with the politically correct Mies, whose resistance to the existing terms of the social field at large includes a resistance as well to the idea of aesthetic autonomy, the notion that art and architecture should be self-enclosed cultural projects unconcerned with and unable to address and thus to offer a critique of the context — political, social, economic — in which they arise. The very title of a recent essay by Ignasi de Solá-Morales Rubió spells this out by demanding that architecture now move "From Autonomy to Untimeliness."[5]

Now, while I was very interested in the arguments laid out on behalf of this anti-classical Mies, I must say that I was far more riveted by another Mies, to whom I was re-introduced by Franz Schulze's critical biography, the Mies who, in perfect International Style manner continued to insist on architecture and the production of truth as generated by a set of *a priori* and universalizing laws, and who was caught up in the entirely modernist obsession of repeating a very small repertory of structural ideas — namely the prismatic tower and the universal space of the clear-span pavilion — and was, throughout his career, committed to the use of the grid.[6] It was this Mies who, one chilly day in April 1967, presided over the nine-hour procedure of slowly jacking up the 1000-ton plate of the gridded roof of the Berlin National Gallery so that it could be lowered onto the pin-joint connections of the eight columns that were to support it — making it seem therefore to float slightly above the columns and the glass of the pavilion's walls like a strangely weightless and buoyant cloud.

It appeared to me that there was a connection here between this Mies and another figure from the recent history of Minimalism, one who also spent an artistic lifetime committed to the problem of the grid but who nonetheless opened that problem to some surprising developments. The figure I have in mind is Agnes Martin; and if I spend the rest of my time here speaking about her work, it is because the literature on the poststructuralist Mies has shown me that architectural criticism is interested in sophisticated readings of contemporary painting and sculpture, which I am far more capable of producing than such readings of any work of architecture we might wish to name, and because I feel that the door has perhaps been closed a bit too quickly not only on how to think about grids but also on the whole question of autonomy.[7]

The very quintessence of a Minimalist artist, Agnes Martin has spent her entire mature career, from 1960 until the present, painting works that always measure six feet square and are always constructed of penciled lines applied over lightly gessoed canvas grounds, the lines themselves arranged to form grids, in the first half of her career, and bands, in the

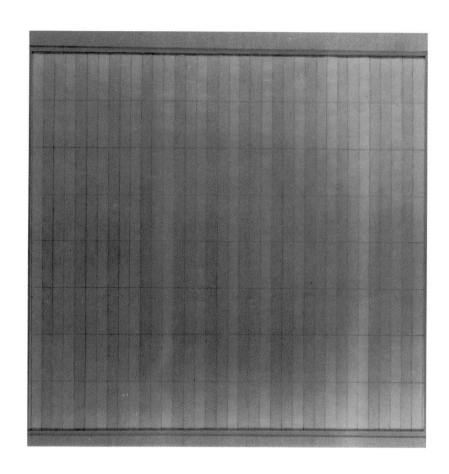

3. Agnes Martin,
Untitled, 1977.
Watercolor and graphite on paper.
9″ x 9″.

second. Nevertheless, no matter how unflinchingly abstract these creations are, there has developed a persistent reading of Martin's work, in all of its luminous silence, as opening onto what came to be known as the "abstract sublime." This reading, initiated by Lawrence Alloway in a 1973 essay, comprehends the canvases as analogues of nature, "both," as Alloway wrote, "by inference from her imagery and from judging her titles."[8] And indeed, Martin's titles have always held out an invitation to experience her work as an allusion to nature, with names such as *The Beach, Desert, Leaf in the Wind, Milk River, Night Sea, Orange Grove, White Stone, Falling Blue.*

Nonetheless Alloway was careful, in his text, to acknowledge all those admonitions Martin herself had always pronounced against understanding her work as an abstracted nature: "My paintings have neither objects, nor space, nor time, not anything — no forms," he quotes her saying. Or again, he cautions, "Referring to one of her poems she notes: 'This poem, like the paintings, is not really about nature. It is not what is seen. It is what is known forever in the mind.'"

It is one thing, however, to listen to Martin insisting, "My work is anti-nature," and it is another to hold this claim steady as one approaches her paintings. Alloway's reading became the standard for interpreting Martin, as the rubric "abstract sublime" slid into the space between her work and its succession of interpreters/viewers. Characteristically, Carter Ratcliff referred Martin's work to Edmund Burke's *Philosophical Enquiry into the Origin of our Ideas of the Sublime and Beautiful,* which, in the mid-eighteenth century, laid down a recipe for satisfying the growing taste for "sublime effects." Burke's description of a "perfect simplicity, an absolute uniformity in disposition, shape and coloring," his call for a succession "of uniform parts" that can permit "a comparatively small quantity of matter to produce a grander effect than a much larger quantity disposed in another manner" seemed made for Martin's work, just as that work — as pared down and simplified as it might appear — could be thought nonetheless to smuggle within it diffused references to the repertory of natural "subjects" that followed from Burke's analysis: "the sea (Turner), the sky (Constable), foliage (Church) and, simply, light."[9]

It is this covert allusion to nature that the category "abstract sublime" has come to imply, with the abstract work always able to be decoded by its romantic double: Mark Rothko read out through Caspar David Friedrich; Jackson Pollock by J.M.W. Turner's storms; Martin by Turner's skies.[10]

But again it has consistently been Martin herself who has cautioned against a romantic context for her work. Repeating that she sees herself joined to an ancient tradition of classicists — "Coptic, Egyptian, Greek, Chinese" — she defines this tradition as something that turns its back on

4. Agnes Martin,
Untitled #4, 1977.
India ink, graphite & gesso on canvas.
6´ x 6.́

nature. "Classicism forsakes the nature pattern," she writes. "Classicists are people that look out with their back to the world. It represents some-thing that isn't possible in the world. It's as unsubjective as possible. . . . The point — it doesn't exist in the world."[11]

In the exceedingly superficial and repetitive literature on Agnes Martin there is one arresting exception. It is a careful phenomenological reading by a critic named Kasha Linville, in which, for the first and only time, there is a description of what it is actually like to see the paintings, which, she explains, "are sequences of illusions of textures that change as viewing distance changes."[12]

First there is the close-to reading, in which one is engaged in the work's facture and drawing, in the details of its materiality in all their sparse precision: the irregular weave of the linen, the thickness and uniformity of the gesso, the touch in the application of the pencilled lines. "Sometimes," Linville explains,

> her line is sharp, as in an early painting, *Flowers in the Wind,* 1963. Sometimes its own shadow softens it — that is, it is drawn once beneath the pigment or gesso and then redrawn on top, as in *The Beach.* Most often, her line respects the canvas grain, skimming its surface without filling the low places in the fabric so it becomes almost a dotted or broken line at close range. Sometimes she uses pairs of lines that dematerialize as rapidly as the lighter-drawn single ones. As you move back from a canvas like *Mountain II,* 1966, the pairs become single, gray horizon-tals and then begin to disappear.

But this "moving back" from the matrix of the grids is a crucial second "moment" in the viewing of the work. For here is where the ambiguities of illusion take over from the earlier materiality of a surface redoubled by the weave of Martin's grids or bands; and it is at this place that the paintings go atmospheric. Again, Linville's description of this effect is elegant and precise. "I don't mean 'atmosphere' in the spatially illusionistic sense I associate with color field painting," she writes. "Rather it is a non-radiating, impermeable . . . mist. It feels like, rather than looks like atmosphere. Somehow, the red lines [she is writing here of a work called *Red Bird*] dematerialize the canvas, making it hazy, velvety. Then, as you step back even further, the painting closes down entirely, becoming completely opaque."

That opaqueness of the third "moment," produced by a fully distant, more objective vantage on the work, brackets the atmospheric interval of the middle-distance view, closing it from behind, so to speak. Wall-like and impenetrable, this view now disperses the earlier "atmosphere." And this final result, as Linville again writes on Martin, is "to make her paintings impermeable, immovable as stone."

The "abstract sublime" consideration of Martin's art, never so careful or accurate as this one, implies that atmosphere or light are a given of the paintings, which, like a certain kind of landscape subject — clouds, sea, fields — can simply be observed from any vantage one might take on them. The landscape subject, no matter how reduced or abstracted, simply defines the work as an objective attribute of it, like the color blue, or red. But Linville's three distances make it clear that /atmosphere/ is an effect set within a system in which an opposite effect is also at work, and that it both defines and is defined by that opposite.[13] Linville's three distances, that is, transform the experience from an intuition into a system, and convert *atmosphere* from a signified (the content of an image) into a signifier — /atmosphere/ — the open members of a differential series: wall/mist; weave/cloud; closed/open; form/formless.

By a curious coincidence, it was just when Linville was noticing Martin's production of the three distances that Hubert Damisch was completing his study *Théorie du /nuage/,* a book that rewrites the history of Renaissance and Baroque painting according to a system in which the signifier /cloud/ plays a major, foundational role.[14] This role, which is that of a "remainder" — the thing that cannot be fitted into a system but which, nevertheless, the system needs in order to constitute itself as a system — finds its most perfect illustration in the famous demonstration performed by Filippo Brunelleschi at the opening of the fifteenth century, the demonstration that both invented and supplied the complete theory of perspective.

Having painted the image of the baptistery in Florence on a wooden panel into which a tiny peephole had been drilled at the exact vanishing point of the perspective construction, Brunelleschi devised an apparatus for viewing this image. Its reverse side would be placed against the brow of the observer, whose eye, right at the peephole, would gaze through the panel, while in front of the panel, the observer would hold up a mirror at arm's length. The depicted baptistery, reflected in this mirror, would thus be guaranteed a "correct" viewing according to the theory of perspective's legitimate construction, in which the vanishing point and viewing point must be geometrically synonymous. In this sense, the representation is the function not of one but of two constructed planes: that of the "viewer" (stationary, mono-ocular) and that of the display (constructed in terms of measurable bodies deployed in space, thus capable of being submitted to the determination of geometry).

But between those two planes of the perspective apparatus something was necessarily added, slipped into the construction as though it were a measurable, definable body, but which gave the lie, nonetheless, to this very possibility of definition. This something was the /cloud/. For the sky above the baptistry on Brunelleschi's panel was not depicted in paint; rather the area given over to it was executed in silver leaf so that, acting as a mirror, it would capture the reflections of the real sky passing over the head of the viewer staring into the optical box of the perspective construction.

Perspective was thus understood from the first to be a matter of architectonics, of a structure built from delimited bodies standing in a specific space and possessing a contour defined by lines. The immeasurability and ubiquity of the sky, however, and the unanalyzable surfacelessness of the clouds render these things fundamentally unknowable by the perspective order. "The process to which Brunelleschi had recourse for 'showing' the sky," Damisch writes,

> this way of mirroring that he inserted into the pictorial field like a piece of marquetry and onto which the sky and its clouds were captured, this mirror is thus much more than a subterfuge. It has the value of an epistemological emblem . . . to the extent that it reveals the limitations of the perspective code, for which the demonstration furnishes the complete theory. It makes perspective appear as a structure of exclusions, whose coherence is founded on a series of refusals that nonetheless must make a place, as the background onto which it is printed, for the very thing it excludes from its order.[15]

It is in this sense that painting understands its scientific aspirations — toward measurement, toward the probing of bodies, toward exact knowledge — as always being limited or conditioned by the unformed, which is unknowable and unrepresentable. And if the /architectural/ came to symbolize the reach of the artist's "knowledge," the /cloud/ operated as the lack in the center of that knowledge, the outside that joins the inside in order to constitute it as an inside.

Thus, before being a thematic element — functioning in the moral and allegorical sphere as a registration of miraculous vision, or of ascension, or as the opening onto divine space; or in the psychological sphere as an index of desire, fantasy, hallucination; or, for that matter, before being a visual integer, the image of vaporousness, instability, movement — the /cloud/ is a differential marker in a semiological system. This can be seen, for example, in the extent to which cloud elements are interchangeable within the repertory of religious imagery. "The fact that an object can thus be substituted for another in the economy of the sacred visual text," Damish writes, "this fact is instructive: the /cloud/ has no meaning that can be properly assigned to it; it has no other value than that which comes to it from those serial relations of opposition and substitution that it entertains with the other elements of the system."[16]

Meaning, according to this argument, is then a function of a system that underpins and produces it, a system — /cloud/ versus /built, definable space/ — with its own autonomy, that of painting, which precedes the specifics of either theme or image.

Autonomy, of course, has come by now to have indescribably bad associations; like formalism, it is thought to be the blinkered product of ideological construction. Yet much art has been produced within this ideology and in relation to a conception of autonomy; and the rush to move beyond the circumscribed aesthetic sphere to the *hors-texte,* the context, the legitimating "real" text, often produces superficial readings, as in the case of leaching out Agnes Martin's painting into the concealed landscapes of the "abstract sublime."

But if we allow ourselves for a moment to entertain this transgressive thought of autonomy, we come upon a position, itself the founding moment of art history as a discipline, that sets up, along with Damisch's, a model for Agnes Martin's three distances. This is the work Alois Riegl developed over the course of his *Stilfragen* (1893) and *Spätrömische Kunstindustrie* (1901), studies that fend off all hypotheses about the putative effect of external factors on art's development — whether in the material field, as in Gottfried Semper's theories of art's genesis out of building practices; or in the field of the "real," as theories of mimesis would have it; or due to the contingencies of history, as the "barbaric invasions" explanation of the supposed decline in late Roman art would imply. Instead, Riegl posits an entirely internal or autonomous evolution, one that continues without gap or deflection from the most ancient civilizations of the Near East up through Byzantium.

This evolution, "dialectic" in nature, arises from the desire, externalized via art, to grasp things in the most objective way possible, untainted, that is, by the merely happenstance and contingent vantage point of the viewing subject. But in acknowledging the object in terms of almost any level of sculptural relief (that is, in promoting an experience of its tactility), shadow is necessarily admitted into the confines of the object — shadow which, marking the position of the spectator relative to the object, is the very index of subjectivity. "The art of antiquity," Riegl wrote, "which sought as much as possible to enclose the figures in objective, tactile borders, accordingly was bound from the very beginning to include a subjective, optical element; this, however, gave rise to a contradiction, the resolution of which was to pose a problem. Every attempt to solve this problem led in turn to a new problem, which was handed down to the next period, and one might well say that the entire art history of the ancient world consists of a developmental chain made up of such problems and their solutions."[17]

The development Riegl charts goes from what he calls the haptic objectivism of the Greeks — the delineation of the clarity of the object through an appeal to, and a stimulation of, the tactile associations of the viewer — to the optical objectivism of Roman art, in which the need to set the figure up in space as radically free-standing led to the projection of the rear side of the body and hence the use of the drill to excavate the relief plane. It arrives finally at the most extreme moment of this opticalism carried out in the service of the object. When the relief plane itself becomes the "object" whose unity must be preserved, this leads, in examples Riegl drew on from late Roman decorative arts, to the construction of the object itself in terms of a kind of moiré effect, with a constant oscillation between figure and ground depending — and here is where this begins to get interesting for Agnes Martin — on where the viewer happens to be standing. Writing that now "the ground is the interface," Riegl describes the fully optical play of this phenomenon once what had formerly been background emerges as *object:* "The relationship of the bronze buckle alters with each movement of its wearer; what was just now the light-side can become at the next moment shadow-side."[18]

Since this figure/ground fluctuation varies with the stance of the viewer, one might argue that the object, now fully dependent upon its perceiver, has become entirely subjectivized. And indeed, although Riegl argues that this development ultimately gave rise to the subjective as a newly autonomous problem for the history of art, one that would fulfill itself in the efforts, for example, of seventeenth-century Dutch portraitists to portray something as non-objective as states of attention, he does not read this late Roman moment as itself subjective. Rather, he wants to argue, with this optical glitter organized into the very weft of the object, that it is the subject-viewer who has been fractured, having now been deprived of the security of a unitary vantage. This is still the *Kunstwollen* of objectivism at work, but in the highest throes of its dialectical development. The filigrees of late Roman relief, far from being a regression to a more ancient or barbaric linearism, are the sublation of this aesthetic problem. "The screw of time has seemingly turned all the way back to its old position," Riegl writes, "yet in reality it has ended up one full turn higher."[19]

Agnes Martin's claim to be a classical artist — along with the full complement of Egyptians, Greeks, and Copts who make up Riegl's objectivist *Kunstwollen* — has been in the main disbelieved by her interpreters. How can her interest in formlessness, it is argued, be reconciled with such a claim, given classicism's complete commitment to form? When Martin observes, approvingly, "You wouldn't think of form by the ocean," or when she says that her work is about "merging, about formlessness, breaking down form," this is thought to underwrite the idea that she has transcended classicism for a newly ardent and romantic attitude toward the sublime.

Yet let us take Martin at her word and allow her her affiliations to a classicism that, in Riegl's terms, would commit her to an objectivist vision, no matter how optically fractured, and to a place within a development internal to the system of art, a system within which the marker /cloud/ has a foundational role to play.

This objectivism, unfolding within the twentieth century, would itself have to be seamed into the fully subjectivist project that was put in place following the Renaissance, a Cartesian project that has only intensified steadily into the present. Except that at the beginning of the century, modernist painting opened up, within an ever growing dependence of the work on the phenomenology of seeing (and thus on the subject), what we could call an "objectivist opticality," namely, an attempt to discover — at the level of pure abstraction — the objective conditions, or the logical grounds of possibility, for the purely subjective phenomenon of vision itself.

It is in this context that the grid achieves its historical importance: as the transformer that moved painting from the subjective experience of the empirical field to the internal grounds of what could be called subjectivity as such, subjectivity now construed as a logic. Because the grid not only displays perfectly the conditions of what could be called the *visual* — the simultaneity of vision's grasp of its field dissolving the spatial (tactile) separation of figure against ground into the continuous immediacy of a purely optical spread — but also repeats the original, antique terms of a desire for objectivity and extreme clarity. Like the Egyptian relief, the grid both enforces a shadowless linearity and is projected as though seen from no vantage at all. At least this is so in what could be called the classical period of the modernist grid, for which Piet Mondrian would stand as the prime figure.

Let us say further that this attempt to grasp the logical conditions of vision was, like the dialectic of the ancient drive toward the utterly independent object, continually forced to include its opposite. For as the grid came to coincide more and more closely with its material support and to begin to actually depict the warp and weft of textiles (Anni Albers's work is a case in point), this supposed "logic of vision" became infected by the tactile. Two of the possible outcomes of this tactilization of what I've been calling an "objectivist opticality" are: first, to materialize the grid itself, as when Ellsworth Kelly constructs the network of *Colors for a Large Wall* out of sixty-four separate canvases (nonetheless retaining the optical or the indefinite in the form of chance); or, second, to make the optical a function of the tactile (kinesthetic) field of its viewer, that is to say, the succession of those viewing distances the observer might assume. This latter is the case with Agnes Martin. And in her work it also remains clear that the optical, here marked as /cloud/ emerges within a system defined by being bracketed by its two materialist and tactile counterterms: the fabric of the grid in the near position and the wall-like stele of the impassive, perfectly square panel in the distant view. It is this closed system, taken as a whole, which pre-serves — like the moiré belt buckle — the drive toward the "objective," which is to say the fundamental classicism of its *Kunstwollen*.

To say all of this is, of course, impossibly outmoded, formalist, deter-minist, empty. But the /cloud/ remains bracketed within its peculiar system; and it is what Agnes Martin painted for these last thirty years. She destroyed all the rest.

Whether it is accurate or relevant to read the Barcelona Pavilion in terms of the /cloud/, I leave to far more astute analysts of architecture than myself. But should it be, I would say that this interpretation would not necessarily write an end to a conception of the work within the terms of aesthetic autonomy; rather, I would argue, it reinforces it. Untimeliness is not achieved quite so easily.

### Notes

1. See my analyses of Minimalism in *Passages in Modern Sculpture* (New York: Viking, 1977) and *The Originality of the Avant-Garde and Other Modernist Myths* (Cambridge, Massachusetts: MIT Press, 1985). Also see Hal Foster, "The Crux of Minimalism," in *Individuals: A Selected History of Contemporary Art* (Los Angeles: The Museum of Contemporary Art, 1986).

2. K. Michael Hays, "Critical Architecture: Between Culture and Form," *Perspecta* 21 (1984), p. 20.

3. José Quetglas, "Fear of Glass: The Barcelona Pavilion," ed. Beatriz Colomina, *Architectureproduction* (Princeton: Princeton Architectural Press, 1988), pp. 130, 135; Quetglas and Hays ("Critical Architecture," p. 24) use the word "labyrinth." See also Robin Evans, "Mies van der Rohe's Paradoxical Symmetries," *AA Files*, vol. 19 (Spring 1990).

4. Hays, p. 15.

5. Ignasi de Solá-Morales Rubió, "From Autonomy to Untimeliness," *ANYone*, ed. Cynthia Davidson (New York: Rizzoli, 1991).

6. Franz Schulze, *Mies van der Rohe* (Chicago: University of Chicago Press, 1985), p. 309.

7. This reading was initially developed for the catalog of the Agnes Martin retrospective at the Whitney Museum of American Art, November 1992. What follows is adapted from my essay there.

8. Lawrence Alloway, in *Agnes Martin*, exhibition catalog (Philadelphia: Institute of Contemporary Art, University of Pennsylvania, 1973), reprinted as "'Formlessness Breaking Down Form': The Paintings of Agnes Martin," *Studio International* 85 (February 1973), p. 62.

9. Carter Ratcliff, "Agnes Martin and the 'Artificial Infinite,'" *Art News* 72 (May 1973), pp. 26–27. For other discussions of Martin's work in relation to the abstract sublime, see Thomas McEvilley, "Grey Geese Descending: The Art of Agnes Martin," *Artforum* 25 (Summer 1987), pp. 94–99; and for her general placement within the category see Jean-François Lyotard, "Presenting the Unpresentable: The Sublime," *Artforum* 20 (April 1982), and "The Sublime and the Avant-Garde," *Artforum* 22 (April 1984).

10. Robert Rosenblum's "The Abstract Sublime," *Art News* 59 (February 1961), in which such comparisons are made for Pollock and Rothko, laid the foundation for later discussions in this vein.

11. Dieter Schwarz, ed., *Agnes Martin: Writings/Schriften* (Winterthur: Kunstmuseum Winterthur, 1992), pp. 15, 37.

12. Kasha Linville, "Agnes Martin: An Appreciation," *Artforum* 9 (June 1971), p. 72.

13. In the formal notation of semiological analysis, the placement of a word between slashes indicates that it is being considered in its function as signifier — in terms, that is, of its condition within a differential, oppositional system — and thus bracketed off from its "content" or signified.

14. Hubert Damisch, *Théorie du /nuage/* (Paris: Editions du Seuil, 1972).

15. Damisch, pp. 170–71.

16. Damisch, p. 69.

17. Alois Riegl, "Late Roman or Oriental?" ed. Gert Schiff, *Readings in German Art History,* (New York: Continuum, 1988), pp. 181–82.

18. Quoted in Barbara Harlow, "Riegl's Image of Late Roman Art Industry," *Glyph,* no. 3 (1978), p. 127.

19. Riegl, p. 187.

Mies van der Rohe,
Toronto-Dominion Centre.
Interior of Banking Pavilion, 1987.
Photo Steven Evans.

## MIES VAN DER ROHE AND MINIMALISM

*Ignasi de Solá-Morales Rubió*

During the course of the identity crisis that beset the Modern Movement in architecture in the 1960s, one of the theoretical tasks approached with the greatest commitment was the reappraisal of the work of the masters of modern architecture. This cultural operation was begun at a moment of crisis, not only in architecture, but in the visual arts in general. The post-painterly situation saw the emergence of various, diverse, alternative, and radical lines of working. Amongst these, minimalism and pop art constituted two opposing lines of exploration, both having their origins in the same dissatisfaction with the subjectivism of the expressionist tradition and the formalism of painting on conventional supports. The question of signification was of central concern for the artists working in either one of these directions. For the minimalists, the object was to return to a zero point, a *writing degree zero,* to adopt the title of Roland Barthes's famous text of 1953, on the basis of which to construct, painstakingly, a number of minimal aesthetic significations. For pop art, in its symmetrical and opposing way, the signification could be found in the imitation of the models established by the tradition or in the new repertoires — evident and popular — diffused by the new mass communications media.

In architecture, there was a clearly parallel phenomenon. Faced with the no longer tenable clichés of the modern tradition, there were those who sought, through a return to origins, to the pure wellsprings of enlightened architecture or the purism of the Modern Movement, the essential words, the founding gestures of the language of architecture. Others, in marked contrast, believed that they saw in the diffusion of the popular or in the prestige of classical architecture a fountain with the power to renew signification. Curiously, the return to Mies van der Rohe was undertaken from both of these standpoints — two points of view that were not always well defined and often held simultaneously.

What is now clearly apparent is that the problem of signification prompted a powerful need to see in Mies's architecture, above all, a reminiscence of the classical architectural tradition, thus giving rise to a false and mistaken reading of his work. Claiming a basis in his apprenticeship to Peter Behrens and in his Berlin-nurtured sympathy for the work of Karl Friedrich Schinkel, a classicist Mies van der Rohe has been put forward in recent years, an atypical master of the Modern Movement drenched in classical tradition for all the apparent modernity of the glass and steel of his buildings. This is an enterprise that it is now time to publicly denounce. It resembles too closely what has also been attempted with Frank Lloyd Wright and Le Corbusier; behind all of these endeavors, we can detect the desire of architects and critics to find a consistent signification in the work of an architect whose solutions, duly standardized and manipulated, had become the most rhetorically representative commonplace of commercial architecture.

Yet the classicism to be found in certain of Mies's buildings is far from constituting an argument capable of explaining all of the aesthetic intensity of his work. The references to Doric temples and to the Erectheum, the parallels with Schinkel's *Altes Museum* and the *Neue Wache,* the surprising views of the Barcelona Pavilion through Ionic columns or the carving up of the columns of the *Neuenationalgalerie* in Berlin as a redesigning of the classical orders: these correspond to an anxious search for meaning by the path of imitation, of classical mimesis, in an ideological operation that is difficult to justify on the basis of Mies's attitude, his writings, and the body of his work as a whole.

Mies's work was not born of the desire to recreate a permanent, trans-historical nature based on the classical orders and their grammar. Nor is it licit to think of Mies, after the manner of Marcel Duchamp, as the author of a series of architectonic *ready-mades* where the signification would be the product of some kind of modern nominalism, thanks to which the redundancy of the classical icons employed would serve to guarantee the meaning of the work of architecture. Thierry de Duve, in an intelligent recent book on Duchamp, coined the expression *pictorial nominalism.* This refers to the conventional procedure by which aesthetically non-significant objects — the *fontaine,* for example — are transformed into works of art. This nominal-ism, based on the *de facto* acceptance of the artistic status for any object whatsoever, takes the place of the Platonic essentialism in terms of which it is the order obtaining between nature and art, in the harmony of a unique cosmos, that guarantees the profound signification of the work of art. The semantic procedure is based on the imitative condition — *ars simiae naturae,* art imitates nature — intrinsic to the classical *modus operandi.* Architectonic nominalism, conventionally, makes use of the classical as a sign, as a surface display denoting the artistic, in the same way that so-called postmodern architecture, in Charles Jencks's version of it, has contrived to do *ad nauseam.*

In Mies there is no reference to the totality of the cosmos within which classical art constructed meaning, orders, types, proportions, perspective. It makes no sense, then, to turn to Mies as the last classicist. Yet neither is there a pop Mies, capable of freely appropriating the significations of the classical tradition with the cool daring of a bankrobber, a kidnapper. On the contrary, in the construction of a degree zero of the architectonic text the procedure is entirely different.

Mies's work is developed, not out of images, but out of materials — materials in the strongest sense of the word, that is naturally, the matter from which objects are constructed. This matter is abstract, general, geometrically cut, smooth and polished, but it is also material that is substantial, tangible, and solid. And at the same time, it implies a wider materiality that takes in the gravity and weight of the elements of construction, the tensions in their static behavior, their hardness or fragility, and the material artifice of the technology that prepares and handles the elements from which the building is raised. This is a materialism, finally, that sets out from the origin of the material problems of lighting, air conditioning, sealing of the outer skin, and the satisfactory functioning of the building in relation to the use for which it was designed. The whole tremendous body of innovation in Mies derives neither from imitation nor from the abstract discourse of concepts of space, light, or territory. In Mies, the realities are, from the very outset, material for the work of architecture, and his calls to understand architecture solely as building, as *bauen,* are no mere paying of lip-service to a fashionable functionalism, but rather are proof that for the creator of the Tugendhat house, the perceptual conditions established by the materiality of the building are at the very origins of its spiritual signification. It is only by way of the material conditions that we can arrive at "the forces which act in their interior" and the "authentic field of action which is, without a doubt, that of signification."

Of course, the relationship that is established between the materiality of the architectonic object and its reception as spiritual signification does not, for Mies, take place in some previously elaborated tissue of abstract elements such as rhythm, balance, proportion, and measure. These values are, in any event, an outcome. To put it another way, the architect does not adapt the forms of his materials to laws or conventions that have to be imitated or reproduced.

Our relationship with the architecture is im-mediate. The work of modern art, as Deleuze and Guattari observe in their most recent book, *Qu'est-ce que c'est la philosophie?* — is a block of sensations, that is to say a compound of perceptions and affections (*percepts et affects*). Such sensations do not pass us on to other objects or images serving as points of reference. The material and its durability are what support and produce both the perceptions that we receive by means of our senses and the affections that are neither merely subjective nor to be considered pure reactions on the part of the individual confronted with the work of art. The radical architecture of Mies is a consolidated, permanent block for the production of sensations, through which the materials pass and the concepts are reached.

The abstract condition of the Miesian sensibility reinforces the transition from sensation to perception and from perception to concept. A concept that has nothing to do with science or philosophy, which steers well clear of the dangers associated with so-called conceptual art. Through the extreme dematerialization of its messages, this tended, in effect, towards pure information, towards taxonomy, towards the formulation of general aims and projects. Mies's art, like the work of Donald Judd or Dan Flavin, has a material component that delimits it. The concrete materiality, which these have in common, makes them not general but particular. Their works are not the expression of a general idea, but tangible physical objects, the producers of perceptions and affections.

It is wrong to think of the architecture of Mies as a stage, even an empty one. The metaphor, as it has been used by Manfred Tafuri and certain of his disciples in reference to the Barcelona Pavilion, betrays once again the modernity of Mies's work by reducing it to a framework — the stage — that is by definition a previously determined visual convention. To speak of the empty stage is to see the perceptive discharges constituted by Mies's buildings as the last redoubt of the work of art as representation. Yet the modern sensibility has abandoned this procedure. Since the empiricism of the eighteenth century, since David Hume and Edmund Burke, since Uvedale Price and Richard Payne Knight, the aesthetic experience has been the unexpected commotion provoked by a course pursued at random, by an accumulation of images, by an excess of stimulations.

In his essay of 1931, "A Small History of Photography," Walter Benjamin said, "The cinema provides material for collective, simultaneous perception, just as architecture has always done." In Mies's work, the perception that we are offered presupposes neither point of view nor order of reading nor hierarchy. Modern vision, which photography developed, has resulted, as Paul Virilio suggests, in the disappearance not only of spatial distance but also of distance in time. There is nothing fortuitous about Mies's interest in photomontage and in having control of the photographs reproduced in his books; photographs, it should be noted, for which all notions of stage-setting or theatricality prove entirely inadequate.

In the same way, to speak of context in the work of Mies is to introduce another inadequate, inappropriate conceptual paradigm. His works of architecture were not produced in relation to the context, nor did they constitute a commentary on, or mimesis of, the place in which they were situated. Once again, looking at things in this way is a trick whose purpose is to carry Mies's work beyond the architect's own intentions. In the words of Harold Rosenberg, with reference to works of minimalist art, these "affirm the independent existence of the artistic object as significative in itself," rather than in relation to works from the past or to social ideas or to individual emotions.

This isolated, autonomous condition of the aesthetic experience has some bearing on the self-referential character of Mies's architecture. With Mies, the architecture is never a monument. It is not a monument in the strict etymological sense of that word: a work that refers to, recalls, something outside itself, such as an event, a moment in history, the community, its origins, or certain civic or moral values. In his writings, Mies appeals time and again to the spiritual signification that the work of architecture ought to attain. In his excellent exegesis of the sources of Mies's thinking, Fritz Neumeyer has underlined the importance to Mies of the phenomenological tradition of the followers of Max Scheller. Romano Guardini and Paul Landsberg are two contemporary thinkers whose influence on Mies seems beyond doubt. Perhaps, however, Neumeyer might have laid greater emphasis on the fact that there was a religious problem occupying a central place in the concerns of each of these thinkers. In the case of Guardini, a Catholic priest, this was an endless search for meaningful relations between human beings, things, and technology. He was trying to reconstruct meaning in a post-Nietzschean world in which not only was God dead, but the Hegelian proclamation of the death of art was at the roots of the activities of the avant-garde. Guardini, whose most developed thought on aesthetics is found in his texts on liturgy and sacred symbols, meditated throughout his life on transcendent significance as something stemming from, but going beyond, the concrete materiality of the objects, the gestures and words of human life. Landsberg, who was a Jew by birth and died in a concentration camp in 1944, was a friend of Mounier and the French personalists and devoted his working life to elaborating a philosophical anthropology, a body of thought that was to reconstruct a place for humanity, human production, and interpersonal relations.

This is the context in which Mies developed his self-referential conception of the work of art. Perhaps the difference between Mies's use of the notion and that of the minimalists derives precisely from the degree to which this self-reference is held as being open or closed in relation to other values. For the minimalists of the 1960s and later, the work neither appeals to nor evokes anything other than itself. It partakes of the pure randomness inherited from Stéphane Mallarmé and the final silence of Kasimir Malevich. The work of art is self-referential because it begins and ends in itself and explains only its own materiality, factuality, obviousness. In Mies there is much of this same spirit, which preserves the work of architecture from any temptation to make it the vehicle for some other signification or the expression of some other content. In Mies, too, the architecture refers to itself. It explains how it is and makes of its own presence, the primordial act of its signification. But in Mies there is an ethical project that is carried out precisely in the work. The entire debate regarding technology in the period between the wars is an ethical debate. Whether it be Oswald Spengler or Martin Heidegger, Thomas Mann or Ernst Jünger, the reflections on technology and its products are framed from an ethical viewpoint within the perspective of reconstruction following in the wake of Nietzschean nihilism. Analyses of the differences between *techne* and *poesis* in Greek thought, such as were being undertaken by Werner Jaeger, were born of a prevalent preoccupation of the time, from which Mies was by no means immune. The reconsideration of Medieval aesthetics, in which production and meaning were perceived as indivisible, provided the thinkers mentioned above, and Mies amongst them, with an indisputable point of reference. The autonomy of the work of architecture, the project of making of it once again a "solid and enduring compound," as Paul Cézanne said of his project for painting, is the very heart of Mies's work. Architecture should not be solipsistic, closed in on itself, complacently satisfied with its own interests, nor purely empirical, the "I don't search, I find" of Pablo Picasso. The Miesian project in architecture is inscribed within a wider ethical project in which the architect's contribution to society is made precisely by means of the transparency, economy, and obviousness of his architectonic proposals. This is the contribution of truth, of honesty. That is his message.

The year 1968 marked, symbolically, the end of the Modern Movement and the explosion of postmodern culture. At that time, minimalism, as a current, had already been given not only its name, but also its definition through the writings of Clement Greenberg, Barbara Rose, Harold Rosenberg, Irving Sandler, and Richard Wollheim, amongst others. It was the year in which the *Neuenationalgalerie* opened in Berlin, the last of Mies's buildings to be completed in the architect's lifetime. And it was at this moment that Gilles Deleuze published his most important book of philosophy, *Différence et répétition.* "I think we will have this work going round our heads for a long time to come. Perhaps one day the century will be Deleuzian," Michel Foucault prophesied.

To cite Deleuze's text here is relevant because it contains a figurative thought capable of formulating the evident nexus between the aesthetic experience of minimalism and the work of Mies. Conceived as a way of breaking away from the rigidity of structuralist thinking and at the same time escaping the pure decomposition of the post-Nietzschean carnival, Deleuze's text establishes the bases for a process of signification and the construction of meaning grounded in the imbalance that results from the introduction of repetition into the monist idea of the same and the uniform. Repetition as innovation, as a mechanism of liberation, of life and death; repetition as will, as the opposite of the laws of nature; repetition as a new morality beyond habit and memory; repetition that only attains tension and creativity with the fissures of difference, with disequilibrium, innovation, opening, and risk.

**Bibliography**

Roland Barthes, *Le degré zero de l'écriture* (Paris: Éditions du Seuil, 1959).

Thierry de Duve, *Pictorial Nominalism: On Marcel Duchamp's Passage from Painting to the Readymade* (Minneapolis & Oxford: University of Minnesota Press, 1991). Translated by Dana Polan with the author. This work originally appeared as *Nominalisme pictural* (Paris: Éditions de Minuit, 1984).

Gilles Deleuze, *Différence et répétition.* (Paris: P.U.F., 1968).

Gilles Deleuze and Félix Guattari, *Qu'est-ce que c'est la philosophie?* (Paris: Éditions de Minuit, 1991).

Ludwig Mies van der Rohe, "Aphorisms," in *Perspecta* 3 (1953).

Neumeyer, Fritz. *The Artless Word: Mies van der Rohe on the Building Art*, trans. Mark Jarzombek (Cambridge, Massachusetts & London: MIT Press, 1991). This work originally appeared as *Mies van der Rohe. Das kunstlose Wort. Gedanken zur Baukunst* (Berlin: Wolf Jobst Siedler, 1986).

OPENINGS

1. Mies van der Rohe,
Toronto-Dominion Centre,
Construction photograph showing the first tower
facing the Toronto Star Building across the plaza
and King Street. (c. 1965)
Photo Ron Vickers.

## LOOKING FOR "THE PUBLIC" IN MIES VAN DER ROHE'S CONCEPT FOR THE TORONTO-DOMINION CENTRE

*George Baird*

### Introduction

Detlef Mertins invited Rebecca Comay and me to speak together at this symposium, since he knew Comay to have an interest in the possible relationship of the ideas of Martin Heidegger to architecture, and he knew I had been interested for some time in the relationship of those of Hannah Arendt to it. Since Arendt had herself been a student of Heidegger, and since both she and Mies van der Rohe had come under the influence of the Berlin scholar Romano Guardini during the 1920s, it looked on the face of it as though this set of overlapping circumstances might well yield interesting new theoretical perspectives on Mies's architecture.

Well, yes and no. To start with, it turned out to be rather difficult for the three of us even to agree on a name for the common theme it was thought our presentations might explore. Given Arendt's and Heidegger's shared concern with the phenomenology of "the world," Mertins initially suggested the term "worldliness" to head both our presentations. But this caused concern to Comay who, while she recognized the clear relationship of "world" to "worldliness," nevertheless felt that the psychological and moral ambiguity often associated with "worldliness" would sit quite awkwardly in a Heideggerian philosophical context. She pointed out that the German term *Öffentlichkeit* (characteristically translated in contexts associated with Hannah Arendt or with Jürgen Habermas as "publicness" or as "public sphere")[1] had for Heidegger always been an unequivocal pejorative. Thus, between Comay's Heideggerian perspective and my own Arendtian one, the term "worldliness" soon came to seem problematic.

It is worth noting that since the symposium, I have realized again how aware Arendt was of the important ambiguity in question. In her introduction to the collection of essays published in 1968 under the title *Men in Dark Times*, Arendt commented on the conditions, which

> Heidegger described with uncanny precision in those paragraphs of *Being and Time* that deal with "the they," their "mere talk," and generally everything that, unhidden and unprotected by the privacy of the self, appears in public. In his description of human existence, everything that is real or authentic is assaulted by the overwhelming power of "mere talk" that irresistibly arises out of the public realm, determining every aspect of everyday existence, anticipating and annihilating the sense or the nonsense of everything the future may bring. There is no escape, according to Heidegger, from the "incomprehensible triviality" of this common everyday world except by withdrawal from it into that solitude which philosophers since Parmenides and Plato have opposed to the political realm ... the sarcastic, perverse-sounding statement "*Das Licht der Öffentlichkeit verdunkelt alles*" ("The light of the public obscures everything") went to the heart of the matter ...[2]

Given this clear acknowledgement on Arendt's part of Heidegger's position, it was evident that I was obliged to relinquish the too-volatile term *Öffentlichkeit*. As an alternative, the related term *Offenheit*, or "openness," was proposed. While less contentious, it seemed to me not only to be less pithy, but also so vaguely related to the concept of "the public" as to be rather questionable. Still, its appropriateness to a possible Heideggerian perspective on Mies van der Rohe was evident enough.

Then too, it is worth noting that, even at this early stage of my thinking about the topic, I was skeptical as to whether it would prove possible to discern any tangible evidence of a Miesian preoccupation with "the public" in any event, even after the close re-examination of his *oeuvre* in this respect, which it was thought my paper might constitute. Instead, I had a rather opposite impression. Mies's well-known preoccupation with the so-called "spirit of the age" would, in all likelihood, have precluded any profound or considered engagement on his part with matters of "publicness" or of "plurality." I had, of course, been influenced in my thinking in this regard by Fritz Neumeyer's compelling recent reinterpretation of Mies's thinking, *The Artless Word*.[3] Neumeyer has made it newly clear how Mies had sustained an intense commitment throughout his career to manifest in his works what he saw as the deep and inexorable forces of the age, be they congenial or uncongenial. A statement from Mies's "Baukunst und Zeitwille" of 1924 seems apt: "The individual becomes less and less important; his fate no longer interests us."[4]

Viewed in the light of such a comment, the familiar photomontage from 1953–54 (fig. 2) for the interior of a project for the Chicago Convention Hall can be seen to manifest a concept of "the public" that has more to do with Jean-Jacques Rousseau's fateful concept of the "general will," or Elias Canetti's more recent idea of "the crowd," than with the much more pluralistic notion of "voluntary association" that Arendt and others have taken over from Jeffersonian political theory.[5]

To sum up, given Comay's reservations (given, as well, my own doubt as to where my assignment would lead), I agreed to the title "Openings" for the session she and I would share.

### The Historical Context for a Possible Connection between Mies, Arendt, Guardini, and Heidegger

Prior to her fateful first encounter with Martin Heidegger in 1924, Hannah Arendt had attended classes given by Romano Guardini at the University of Berlin. For a short period early in her academic career, Arendt was interested in the "Christian existentialism" that Guardini represented — particularly in so far as it was derived from Sören Kierkegaard, whom she admired. But it would appear from the material published concerning this period of her life that this interest was very short-lived.[6] By the time she came under the sway of Heidegger — and subsequently Karl Jaspers — Arendt's thinking had moved rapidly onward. Interestingly enough, in 1952, during one of her return visits to Europe, she saw fit to attend a lecture — which turned out to be highly charismatic and very well-attended — given in Munich by her former teacher, Guardini. But she described her reaction afterward in a letter to her husband: "It was moral philosophy on the highest level but entirely inadequate."[7]

In *The Artless Word* Neumeyer speculates that Mies may have met Guardini for the first time in November 1925. He shows how Guardini's influence on the evolving thinking of the architect grew rapidly over the next two or three years. Indeed, Neumeyer sees Guardini as having had the decisive, final influence on the formation of thought that had been in process since the beginning of the decade. Having begun in a sort of tectonic medievalism deriving from the work of H.P. Berlage, Mies moved through a phase of keen interest in *Naturphilosophie,* and then into the spare and reductivist materialism that he saw as both required and guided by the "spirit of the epoch." It was, according to Neumeyer, Mies's encounter with Guardini's thought that moved him from this well-known phase into that of his full theoretical maturity as an architect, first manifest in the key text of 1928, "The Preconditions of Architectural Work." In that text, Mies demonstrated his realization that the rigorously reductive materialism of

2. Mies van der Rohe,
Chicago Convention Hall (project), 1952, Chicago.
Photomontage of the interior.
Preliminary version (1953).

his immediately preceding position was, in fact, insufficient. As Neumeyer puts it,

> Guardini called for something with which Mies was in profound agreement: another new, but not unilateral modernism in which subjective forces were restrained by objective limits, but in which, conversely, the potentially threatening powers inherent in technology were subordinated to the subject, to man and his life.[8]

By 1928, of course, Arendt had become the student of Heidegger, and had also begun and ended the personal relationship with him that only came to light after her death in 1975.[9] In a text prepared in honor of his eightieth birthday in 1969, Arendt reflected on the "student rumor about the young professor at Marburg" that had attracted her — like so many of her generation — to him:

> The rumor about Heidegger put it quite simply: Thinking has come to life again; the cultural treasures of the past, believed to be dead, are being made to speak, in the course of which it turns out that they propose things altogether different from the familiar, worn-out trivialities they had been presumed to say.[10]

But of course, while books of Arendt's other key mentor, Karl Jaspers, were found in Mies's library, there appears never to have occurred any connection between him and Heidegger. In sum, then, it would seem that the evident historical connections linking Arendt to Guardini and Heidegger, and Mies to Guardini, do not lead any further than the brief account above suggests. There does not appear to be any real historical justification for positing an explicitly Heideggerian Mies.

This having been said, however, another interesting analytical possibility does seem to exist — one that I rehearsed before the symposium, and that seemed to gain credibility during the event, in an interesting convergence of comments by various speakers. Might it be possible, I asked myself, to detect implicit, perhaps only intuitive, intimations of some sort of edified public life in the Miesian *oeuvre* itself; some evidence, one might say, of a deliberate intention to heighten the consciousness of the passer-by in the historical particulars of his or her situation; to bring to the front of the mind some broader possible significances of the physical artifacts amongst which he or she is located at that moment?

Having raised that conceptual possibility in advance, I was struck by the real palpability of its coming into being at the symposium. In this regard, let me speak first of a matter that has been of profound importance to Arendt, Heidegger, and Mies; that is, the "thingliness" of things.

## The Sheer "Thingliness" of the Characteristic Miesian Construct

Having lived with Mies's Toronto-Dominion Centre (TDC) in my home city for some quarter century, I have been struck by the very subtle shifts in its public image during that period. Upon its completion — and it was the first of the major downtown redevelopments of the 1960s in Toronto — it was, of course, largely seen by the public simply as "the modern new high-rise office tower" in the downtown core. As it came to be surrounded by a series of other office towers of a similar scale in the following decade — most of which were of far less architectural distinction — the TDC became a victim of the public's growing overall disillusionment with modern architecture. The late 1970s and early 1980s probably constituted the low point of its public reputation. Yet even at this stage, independent architectural observers in Toronto were beginning to look at Mies's project differently. In 1983, I myself published a commentary on it as part of a tour of downtown Toronto, already noting that the building had "a complex public reputation — disliked by perhaps even more Torontonians than admire it."[11]

I concluded my 1983 comments with a reference to the Toronto-Dominion Centre's

sheer architectural authority. In its elementarist simplicity, it creates an even-subconsciously perceptible symbolic unity; in its subtle modulations of scale, it creates a system of proportions which relies on astonishingly few motifs; in its use of materials, it paradoxically attains what we might call a sumptuous austerity.[12]

In recent years, the complex's reputation has risen rapidly, this time in a mysterious, symbolic interrelationship with a number of the putatively more "post-modern" buildings that now surround it. I discussed this fascinating interrelationship in a conversation with Fritz Neumeyer in 1989, on the occasion of his first visit to the complex:

I ask why it is that the productions of [Mies's] disciples — which after all spring from absolute faithfulness to his principles — through an imperceptible evolution, shift toward a perfunctory banality. In its turn, this banality typified the modernism which enabled the possibility of a post-modern critique to be mounted. Yet in the case of Mies himself, the works actually appear to have the ability to gather significance from their surroundings, and to project that significance back at you in a shockingly powerful way. I think this probably has to do — at least in part — with his uncanny choice of materials and with his relatively restricted palette. I am thinking of the Banking Pavilion: the green marble duct shafts which loom so powerfully in the space are, after the glass enclosure itself, the primary referent other than the ceiling. There is a complex relationship between the very discreet character of the enclosure and the very aggressive character of these two "dolmens." The ceiling, in its turn, is a datum which brackets the overall image. Finally, the wood panelling provides a material texture with a certain voluptuous quality.

As far as I can tell, this set of elements constitutes the vehicle which gives Mies's image in Toronto its power to keep picking up oppositional references over time. They permit the Toronto-Dominion Centre to continue to transform its own evolving readings in opposition to its surroundings.[13]

Given the trajectory of my thinking about the complex the parallels in the presentations of other speakers at the symposium were striking. For example, Fritz Neumeyer cited the overwhelming *gravitas* of the complex, and its utterly compelling address to the question, "What will remain?" For his part, Ignasi de Solá-Morales Rubió insisted that "Mies's work is developed, not out of images, but out of materials — materials in the strongest sense of the word, that is naturally, the matter from which objects are constructed. This matter is abstract, general, geometrically cut, smooth and polished, but it is also material that is substantial, tangible, and solid."[14] Dan Hoffman noted Mies's "obvious concern with the material processes of building," and showed in his presentation of work from his Cranbrook Architecture Studio how a new reading of this concern, focusing on the question of the "horizon," could demonstrate how "mourning his work both activates a memory of its historical context as well as offers the possibility of its overcoming."

It would seem to me that these provocatively parallel trains of thought all point to a decisive characteristic of Mies's buildings that I would, following the parlance of Heidegger, call "thingliness," a condition of authentic presence "in the world." An understanding of this condition was, of course, one of Arendt's key lessons from her mentor, and she made it a central element of the entire account of "the things of the world" in her 1958 text *The Human Condition.*[15] Like Heidegger, Arendt saw the authentic presence of such "things" as having been gravely threatened by the instrumentalism typical of Enlightenment rationality, and argued strenuously that the preservation of a world for human affairs would require radical reconsideration of the ascendancy of instrumentalist criteria and a renewed acknowledgement of the "intrinsic natural worth"[16] of things themselves.

Should it be the case that such an acknowledgement is indeed an essential condition of "worldliness" in our time, then I think it can be said that Mies's deep concern for the "substantial, the tangible, the solid" constitutes a quite thought-provoking — and perhaps even fundamental — contribution to the possibility of an edified public life in our time, notwithstanding his declared lack of interest in the fate of the individual. And perhaps this is not even the end of a possible revisionist, phenomenological reading of Mies. Perhaps it will be possible for me to speculate further still on the question of whether one may even be able to detect, implicitly and by intuition, evidence of a certain "space of appearance," in Arendt's terms, within Mies's characteristic urbanism — particularly as manifested in the Toronto-Dominion Centre.

## The Space of Contemplation and the Viewing Frame;
## Part One: The Figures

In order to launch my speculation with respect to this possibility, I will make use of, and attempt to extend the potential significance of, two concepts for understanding Mies which have been put forward by Neumeyer: the "space of contemplation," and the "viewing frame." For Neumeyer, the "space of con-templation" typifies the psychological realm of Miesian space. Such a space must, in the first instance, "not dissolve into function, for in it, 'something remains aloof, beyond time.'"[17] Beyond that again, according to Neumeyer,

> Secluded from the noisy turbulence of the city and yet visually connected to it, man is here thrown back upon himself and encounters his second nature, culture. Culture steps forward to meet him in double configuration, in the work of art and in the spirit of a built order, and even as the urban environment, in order to become — as Mies outlined as the aim of his art — "part of a larger whole."[18]

It would appear to be possible to take Neumeyer's concept of the space of contemplation and to read it back onto a series of key representations by Mies of his projects, representations that encompass not just the "built order" and the "urban environment," but even human figures. His employ-ment of photomontage as a technique of representation was referred to by a number of speakers at the symposium, and it is surely true that in such images, culture does indeed step forward to meet contemplative man. But such images — even as early as those of the project for a Bank Building in Stuttgart from 1928 (fig. 3) — also depict persons in the quotidian terri-tory of urban space. What is more, such figures even appear in images that are not based on photographs, examples being drawings of later projects, such as an early study for the Commons Building at IIT from 1946 (fig. 4). Neumeyer has gone so far as to speculate that it is possible to read photo-graphic images of completed projects as depicting figures within the space of contemplation. And Peter Carter's *Mies van der Rohe at Work*[19] includes an image of "an inter-media theatrical event" on the plaza in front of the Seagram Building in New York in 1972, suggesting that the space in question is sufficiently provocative in human terms to actually *evoke* such praxis (fig. 5).

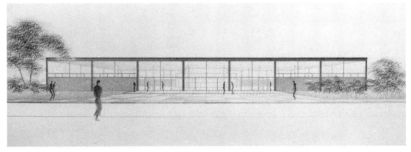

3. Mies van der Rohe,
Bank Building (project), 1928, Stuttgart.
Photomontage (no longer extant).

4. Mies van der Rohe,
Commons Building, IIT, 1946, Chicago.
Perspective of an early version of the project.

5. Photograph of an inter-media theatrical
event presented by Marilyn Wood on
September 29 and 30, 1972 on the plaza of
the Seagram Building in New York.

## The Space of Contemplation and the Viewing Frame;
## Part Two: The "World"

In positing his concept of the space of contemplation, Neumeyer of course suggested that a more precise version of it depended on the presence of what he named a "viewing frame." He saw this characteristic device as a basic architectonic apparatus that had the specific human effect of both facilitating and encouraging a view of a world beyond the immediately inhabited one. For Neumeyer, Mies's utterly characteristic urban "loggias" — following on from those of Karl Friedrich Schinkel — conceptually constitute such frames (fig. 6). This idea of Neumeyer's has provoked me and has prompted a meditation on a whole series of analogous images, both Miesian and non-Miesian.

A photograph (fig. 8) taken shortly after the building's opening shows that the Banking Pavilion at the TDC embodies formal characteristics very similar to the loggias that have been cited by Neumeyer. Note the complex axiality of the image, the compelling presence of the ceiling as spatial boundary, and the highly "contemplative" stance of the photographic eye; all these characteristics are as typical of this image as they have been of the entire series just discussed.

Interestingly enough, in its orientation towards the street, this image may be juxtaposed to an image by Leon Krier from his 1978 competition submission for La Villette in Paris (fig. 7). It is, of course, uncustomary to compare Mies with Krier. Still, in so far as Schinkel constitutes such a decisive precedent for both of them, it does not seem unreasonable to look at these two images together — particularly when considering the possible relationship of Neumeyer's concept of the viewing frame to my own speculations on the possibility of discovering any images of an edified public life in the *oeuvre* of Mies. For if Mies found an image for that characteristic space of his work that Neumeyer has called the space of contemplation, Krier has surely looked to the same source for a possible frame for public life in his own work. What is more, the comparison does not seem unlikely, for the very condition of contemplation constitutes the beginning of edification, such as a world for public praxis (as Arendt would define it) would undoubtedly require in order to come into being.

This possibility strikes me as a very exciting one, for it would enable me to return to an old preoccupation of mine with one of the original site plan characteristics of the Toronto-Dominion Centre. As with the relationship of the Seagram Building to the Racquet Club in New York, so Mies positioned the original Toronto-Dominion tower on the axis of the then-extant Toronto Star Building across the street. As figures 1 and 10 both show, this gesture of his made the Toronto Star Building the "fourth side" of the plaza in front

Karl Friedrich Schinkel, Roman baths in Potsdam, 1826.

Gallery of the Twentieth Century (New National Gallery), Berlin, 1962–1967.

234

6. Fritz Neumeyer's juxtaposed images of
"loggias" by Schinkel and Mies, as depicted in
*The Artless Word*.

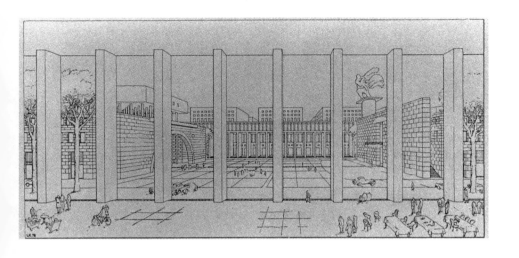

7. Leon Krier,
Project for the district of La Villette, Paris, 1976.
Perspective drawing of a public square.

8. Mies van der Rohe,
Toronto-Dominion Centre.
Photograph from inside the
Banking Pavilion looking
north to King Street, 1968.
Photo Panda.

9. Aerial view of the block that was to become
the site of the Toronto-Dominion Centre, 1964.

of the tower. Given that the "third side" was created by the single-storey Banking Pavilion, this spatial conception was a fragile one, but one nonetheless tangible and readily discernible, in my view, as the aerial view shows (fig. 8 in Mertins). Sadly, when the site of the Toronto Star Building was redeveloped a few years later, Mies's subtle urbanistic gesture was lost and the main tower of the new First Canadian Place now sits in no particular relationship to Mies's tower.

This episode in Toronto's recent urban history has caused me to ponder again the question of what influence Mies thought his Toronto-Dominion Centre (the first major downtown project of the 1960s) would have on its successors. For his gesture to the Toronto Star Building leads me to think that he imagined that the set of buildings extant at the time on all four sides of his site (as seen in the historical aerial view of the block before the construction of the TDC, fig. 9) would probably remain (or, failing that, at least be replaced by similar, if taller, "street-wall" buildings). What happened instead was that a whole series of further "towers in plazas" was erected around the TDC, so that now — not only is the delicate original relationship to the Toronto Star Building gone — so also are any other such relationships, even those of a secondary kind. I find myself supposing that Mies must have imagined, however naïvely, that some form of "other" realm beyond, onto which the evocative viewing frame of his breathtaking Banking Pavilion looked, would have stood there indefinitely, in a complex urban dialectic with his own proffered space of contemplation.

In light of this commentary, examine again the view depicted in figure 8. This time concentrate on the view from the Banking Pavilion out into the space of King Street. For here is presented, within the quintessential Miesian viewing frame, quotidian, heterogeneous Toronto in 1968, represented by a series of characteristic building facades, most of them derived from the nineteenth century.

If this hunch of mine can be thought to be credible, it would then also logically follow that Neumeyer's ideas of the space of contemplation and of the viewing frame are capable of extension to encompass some implicit and — admittedly only tentative — inclination on Mies's part, not just to erect a material world that is "substantial, tangible, and solid," but even to begin to go beyond that. Is it possible this inclination went so far as to proffer a grave and reflective public realm, one which was intended consciously by him to give onto some ineffable "beyond"? Is it even possible to suppose, following the association I have seen fit to make between "thingliness" and "world," that this "beyond" might even, following Arendt's divergence from Heidegger, constitute an "authentic" redemption of worldliness, after all?

10. Opening ceremonies for the Toronto-
Dominion Centre, May 14, 1968, Toronto.
Photo Metropolitan Photos.

## Notes

1. The most familiar usage in English is probably that associated with the translation of the title of Habermas's *Strukturwandel der Öffentlichkeit,* originally published in German in 1962 and translated into English as *The Structural Transformations of the Public Sphere* (Cambridge, Massachusetts & London: MIT Press, 1989).

2. Hannah Arendt, *Men in Dark Times* (New York: Harcourt Brace & World, 1968), p. ix.

3. Fritz Neumeyer, *The Artless Word: Mies van der Rohe on the Building Art,* trans. Mark Jarzombek (Cambridge, Massachusetts & London: MIT Press, 1991).

4. Ludwig Mies van der Rohe, "Building Art and the Will of the Epoch," published originally as "Baukunst und Zeitwille," in *Der Querschnitt,* vol. 4, no. 1 (1924), in Neumeyer, p. 246.

5. For a detailed account of Arendt's view of the general will as hostile to plurality and of voluntary association as essential to it, see her *On Revolution* (New York: Viking Press, 1965), especially Chapter 2 for Rousseau and the general will and Chapter 6 for the concept of voluntary association. For a more recent account, see Jean L. Cohen and Andrew Arato, *Civil Society and Political Theory* (Cambridge, Massachusetts & London: MIT Press, 1992).

6. My historical account is derived from Elisabeth Young-Bruehl, *Hannah Arendt: For Love of the World* (New Haven: Yale University Press, 1982).

7. Hannah Arendt, quoted in Young-Bruehl, p. 283.

8. Neumeyer, p. 201.

9. See Young-Bruehl, "Chapter 2: The Shadows," pp. 42–76.

10. Hannah Arendt, "Martin Heidegger at Eighty," *New York Review of Books* (October 21, 1971), p. 51.

11. George Baird, "Ten Buildings to See on Bay Street," *Section a,* vol. 1, no. 5 (October–November 1983), p. 27.

12. Baird, p. 28.

13. George Baird in conversation with Fritz Neumeyer in "The Toronto-Dominion Centre," *Section b,* forthcoming.

14. Ignasi de Solá-Morales Rubió, "Mies van der Rohe and Minimalism" (in this volume).

15. Hannah Arendt, *The Human Condition* (Chicago: University of Chicago Press, 1968). See especially Part III, Chapter 12, "The Thing-Character of the World," pp. 93–95.

16. Arendt took this striking phrase from John Locke. See Arendt, *The Human Condition,* p. 64.

17. Neumeyer, p. 235.

18. Interestingly enough, juxtaposed here to an image of Schinkel.

19. Peter Carter, *Mies van der Rohe at Work* (Washington: Praeger, 1972), p. 129.

Note: Many thanks to Detlef Mertins for finding figures 1, 2, 3, and 10.

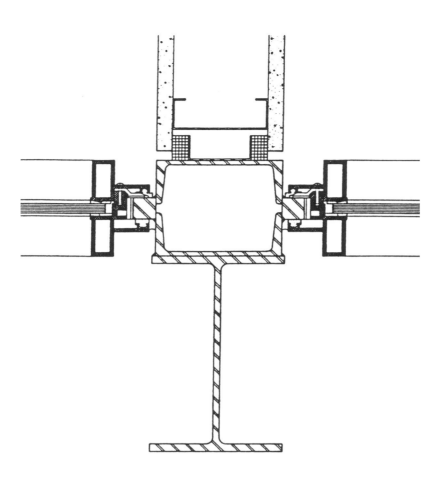

Mies van der Rohe,
Toronto-Dominion Centre,
Detail plan of curtain wall.

## ALMOST NOTHING: HEIDEGGER AND MIES

*Rebecca Comay*

"Almost Nothing": the Miesian title not only more or less captures what I know about architecture in general, Mies van der Rohe in particular, but seems to sum up as well just what there is to be said about Mies-and-Heidegger (the conjunction), my topic today. I am referring not only to the difficulties inherent in any effort to formulate linkages, bridges, common grounds (or, conversely, clearly marked barriers, walls, or fences) connecting or dividing philosophical and architectural discourse. The immediate proliferation of architectural metaphors ("bridges," "walls," "barriers," and so on) will have already by now signaled all the essential risks. For it will at the outset have problematized (indeed, will have problematized precisely as *unphilosophical*) any pretension on the part of philosophy to establish its priority to (but, equally, immunity from) architecture, whether as its "ground" or "foundation" or, alternatively, as a clearly demarcated "field" or "domain."

More specifically: any attempt to connect Martin Heidegger (the thinker) and Mies (the builder) would be subject to the following additional constraints. Heidegger will have unambiguously branded as "metaphysical" every temptation to establish philosophy as the ground or foundation of local or "regional" disciplines — whether as the enunciation of a universal truth to be instantiated in "examples" or as a "theory" to be applied in "practice" — a naïvely instrumentalist (strictly speaking, technological) temptation resting, ultimately, on a confusion between the ontic and the ontological registers, that is to say, for Heidegger, "the confusion *par excellence.*"[1] Such a confusion would assume particular significance where it is a question of establishing linkages between art and philosophy — what Heidegger will call, broadly, *Dichten* and *Denken* — simultaneously as close and as distant, he insists somewhere, as two mountaintops.[2] It should not be a question, then, of "applying" Heideggerian principles to Miesian practice.

So the difficulties are from the outset rather more than the obvious (perhaps trivially obvious) embarrassments: even if, thanks to Fritz Neumeyer[3], we revise the once-standard picture of Mies as the know-nothing ("Create, artist, do not talk!"[4]) builder, the linkage between Mies and Heidegger still remains difficult. I am referring to more than the obvious: among his scattered pronouncements and proverbs, Mies says nothing of Heidegger, seems to read all the "wrong" authors, is prone to citing St. Thomas Aquinas on *adaequatio*[5] and to invoking a neo-Hegelian *Zeitwille*[6]; Heidegger has "almost nothing," and in any case nothing very nice, to say about any modern art or architecture, that is to say, art arising in the age of (and thus conditioned by the imperatives of) advanced industrial technology or what Heidegger calls *Gestell*: our age. Tempting as it may be to recycle through the Heideggerian idiom the by now somewhat wearisome attacks on architectural modernism — metaphysics of the subject elaborating itself in the advent and ideology of global technology; "international style" as the simultaneous triumph of the "planetary" and of "style" (internationalism itself as "style," that is, as the global articulation of the Will to Power in its stiletto hammerings); "optical" desire for transparency, visibility, or self-evidence (glass skins, exposed bones); *Entortung,* or the reduction of finite, situated place to abstract, universal space[7] (the "same" box, allegedly, indifferently housing museum, chapel, theater, bank, classroom, office, apartment, etc.); "gigantism" as the escalation of sheer quantity[8] (skyscrapers, bank towers, everything conjured by Rilke's notion of "Americanism"); in short, for it essentially comes down to this, the elimination of the last vestige of "dwelling" [*Wohnen*] from the domain of "building" [*Bauen*], and thus the oblivion of the latter's "real meaning"[9] — tempting as it may be, therefore, to dismiss the very proposal or demand to think or celebrate here today the "presence of Mies" as already summing up the whole problem (in a word: metaphysics of presence), something more, I think, needs to be said.

Something more needs to be said. Even if it were simple to pit Heidegger against Mies — country versus city, house of Being versus bank tower, low-tech versus high-tech, and all the rest — something more would still need to be said. As it happens, of course, it isn't so simple: Mies'srelationship to rationality, technology, enlightenment modernity, both in theory and on the ground, was at the very least nuanced, if not deeply ambivalent; while, despite appearances, Heidegger wasn't really, after all, not really and truly, proposing a return to Greece. I'll assume that these points are by now generally conceded and will simply point to the most obvious lines of argument.

Thus, briefly: Mies's notorious injunctions ("We do not need less, but more technology . . ."[10]) no more constitute a "gospel of technology"[11] or naïve apologia for the present than do Heidegger's own rumblings constitute a nostalgic retreat. The exposure, for example, of the structural frame — what Mies refers to at one point as the "unambiguous constructive appearance" of the skeleton[12] — could be interpreted less as a celebration than as an attempt in fact to register, acknowledge, even unmask technological order, just as the unclosed or unbounded I-beams could be seen less as an affirmation of their harmonious self-sufficiency[13] than a gesture towards that which in itself resists or delimits framing or enclosure, the very unframability or incompletion of the frame and thus an internal opening to something other.

Similarly: the "modernist razing of the ground," rather than signifying an abstract erasure of local context or contours, is in fact not incompatible with a certain "regional inflection"[14] (as in, for example, the Toronto towers, where a terracing consistent with the "natural" topography of the original shoreline is no doubt evident), just as the stilts apparently raising the tower "off the ground" might be seen to signify not a weightless disembodiment or detachment but precisely the hinge or joint situating (but problematically, because in a disjointed or ungrounded fashion) the building in its context (which, as such, becomes less than self-evident or "proper").

Thus, too, it may be noted that the famous glass "skin," ostensibly introduced as an alternative to the cover-up of stone or concrete, was in fact rarely if ever intended (or used) to express full transparency or visibility: not in the 1922 skyscraper project, when it was, in any case, the reflective and aleatory — hence radically contextualizing — properties of the surface that were emphasized[15]; not in the dark, opaque (and even stonelike) glass of the Seagram or the Toronto-Dominion towers, against which the matte-black steel stands in muted, far from assertive, contrast; perhaps not even in the Barcelona Pavilion either, where the very transparency that might have overcome the difference between inside and outside,[16] thus signifying the simultaneous merging with and conquest of external "nature," manages somehow to do precisely the opposite.[17]

It is in this sense that Mies's repudiation of de Stijl[18] (or, for that matter, Kasimir Malevich[19]) can be interpreted less in terms of an anxiety of influence (or as a reaction to an all-too-hastily-designated "formalism") than as an effort to think the specificity of architecture as that which exceeds the static "painterly" — in the narrow sense — domain of the present, visible, or perceptible. It is temporality that is ultimately at stake here: "I never make a painting when I want to build a house . . ."[20] In this regard, Mies's somewhat flamboyant defense of the picture-window — "if you view nature through the glass walls of the Farnsworth House, it gains a more profound significance than if viewed from outside"[21] — is perhaps less to be indicted for its ocularcentric or "theoretical" ambitions than to be appreciated for a certain reticence or determination that "nature, too, shall live its own life."[22] This despite the phantasm of a "higher unity" that is to "bring together nature, houses, and human being,"[23] and despite every symptomatic appeal to the lexicon of, to speak Heideggerian, the *Zeit des Weltbildes.*

Conversely: Heidegger's insistence that we begin to think the "original Greek"[24] meaning of *techne* not as the mastery of an inertly available nature but as a form of *poeisis* or revealing (a meaning both obscured and presupposed by the modern "technological" epoch) in no way advocates a revival of that "brief but magnificent time,"[25] despite appearances and despite the (by now mercilessly lampooned) evocations of Greek temples and Black Forest huts. Heidegger argues, indeed, that such a revival (he includes here every neoclassicism) would express only the ideology of the modern (the argument essentially repeats Friedrich von Schiller's dialectic of the sentimental), betraying a historicist nostalgia for fixed beginnings, naturalizing the "origin," thus, as a mere "beginning," thereby reifying time as such. The famous "step back" critically engages the present: the "saving power" grows precisely in the "danger"[26]: to think "Greek" today is already, insists Heidegger, to think "more than Greek."[27]

And so on: in short, the waters are muddy and this compare-and-contrast exercise has already gone on far too long. Something more still needs to be said. If, for both Mies and Heidegger, technology in its modern, planetary development determines the present age in its entirety — a "fact" or "given," according to Mies,[28] a "sending" or "destiny" [*Geschick*], according to Heidegger, according to both thinkers, a conceptual and ideological mutation comparable in scope to any epochality (Heidegger), "historical movement" (Mies)[29], or (again, Mies) "world in itself"[30] — clearly neither celebration nor refusal is the issue. In this respect the official gestures — Mies's studied neutrality ("neither yes nor no"[31]), Heidegger's ambiguity ("a simultaneous yes and no"[32]) — are more or less parallel, whatever the specific determinations, inflections, or tone. In this sense as well, Mies's presentation of architecture as an *interpretation* of technology and Heidegger's demand to think the "*essence* of technology"[33] (according to some non-essentialist version of essence[34]) are rigorously congruent, as is the perception that somewhere in all this, "building" (in the broad sense) has a privileged role. If (for essentially economic reasons) architecture, of all the arts, seems most implicated in mass technology — thus in the same epoch Walter Benjamin was to write of a certain "hermaphroditic" or hybrid fusion if not indeed confusion between architecture and technology[35] —

it would by this same token bear the promise of a political engagement and edge. In 1950 Mies announces that consummated technology indeed "transcends into architecture," which thereby achieves its mission as the "real battleground of the spirit."[36] Heidegger, writing not long after of the need to "confront" technology by thinking its essence, remarks that such confrontation occurs in a place both "akin" to [verwandt] and "different" from technology — "art" in its originally "poetic" or "revealing" role.[37] Deferring the question of the precise place of architecture among the arts in Heidegger's kinship system (and passing over the genealogical disturbances suggested by Benjamin's image of hermaphroditism), I want to move on. Something more still needs to be said.

I can't now, and not only for reasons of time, fully elaborate on or account for Heidegger's strange silence if not outright dismissal of "modern art" — "in all its domains," as he was finally to put it[38] — a silence and dismissal not quite captured (or shrugged off[39]) by the ironic protestations of ignorance ("I am glad to be instructed"[40]), ill-humor or generalized despair ("only a god can save us"). Suffice it to say that if Heidegger's objection seems to focus above all on the international, if not indeed planetary, aspect of modernist artworks — their failure to ground, express or embody "the world of the people or the nation [Volk]"[41] — such an objection is not quite the same as, although not entirely different from, either Adolf Hitler's excoriation of "modern art" for its nomadic or metropolitan — "Jewish-Bolshevik" — detachment from the "popular base,"[42] or, for that matter, the "post-modernist" attacks on architectural modernism leveled in the 1970s in the name of local vernaculars or "regional" style.[43] Suffice it also to point to Heidegger's hesitation, vacillation, and official "indecision" regarding the "final truth" of Hegel's judgment regarding the so-called death of art, that is, the end of art's possibility as an "essential and necessary" site for the "setting-to-work" of truth (thus the end of art as a historical expression, i.e. a manifestation of Being's historicity as such).[44] If technoscience in its global dimension would have effaced, by displacing, the very possibility of a truly regional or "popular" (which is not to say necessarily populist) artwork (henceforth marking every appeal to the "people" as at the very least regressive if not downright racist), Heidegger concedes, and indeed it is more than a concession, that "modern art" in fact corresponds to the most extreme exigency of the "modern age."

He leaves open, then, whether in an age in which "astronautics and nuclear physics" has reduced Being to a Nietzschean vapor — "almost nothing," as Heidegger will eventually put it[45] — art might retain or reclaim its prior "founding" (which is not to say foundational) role. I will only pause here to consider[46] whether for Heidegger the very impossibility of modern art might not equally express just its most acute possibility: I am referring to the peculiar nonreferentiality or what Heidegger calls "objectlessness" (not to be confused with self-referentiality) of the modernist work.[47]

Something more still needs to be said. I had promised to talk of "almost nothing," and not just for the sake of all-too-easy one-liners: that is, of the almost nothing that might connect Mies and Heidegger today. "Almost nothing" (like "less is more") is, of course, one of those eminently quotable "sayings," a case of pure citationality (to my knowledge Mies never actually wrote these words): a kind of ad-talk almost invented for the repartee it was inevitably to inspire. "Less is more" (Philip Johnson), "less is nothing" (Sybil Moholy-Nagy), "almost nothing is too much" (Lewis Mumford), "less is a bore" (Robert Venturi), "more is not less" (Robert Venturi) — one could no doubt continue the series — sheer supplementarity without origin: by such reproductive strategies "modernism" as such is retroactively, here as elsewhere, born.

Heidegger too, of course, spoke of nothing, and loquaciously (his critics thought they were being very witty to notice this): specifically, of (the) nothing that marks both the opening and the limit of thought as such. In 1929, the year Mies will have seen erected his famous pavilion in Barcelona (a building in which, he is to insist, "no objects were to be exhibited — nothing"[48]), Heidegger delivers his inaugural lecture at Freiburg University, a lecture that both defines (the) nothing as the slippage or superfluity of extant entities and assigns to human existence its ambiguous place as "placeholder" — if "place" still is thinkable here — of the nothing. For Heidegger, "nothing" names the site of Being's withdrawal, abstention, or oblivion: its recession from what presents itself as any present being. Being is equivalent to "nothing" for Heidegger, not (as Hegel had argued in his *Logic*) due to a common abstraction or Zen-like indetermination, but as the highly determinate "nihilation" or distance from the order of self-present beings. "Nothing" marks simultaneously both the limits of representation (in that it exceeds every object) and — indeed for this very reason — the opening or "draw" (or attraction) of thought as such. Thus, Being is defined simultaneously as both loss (retreat or recession) and as excess ("transcendence") — if you like, a "less" that is "more." In their orientation "beyond" present entities (and "toward" that excess that is Being as such), human beings are assigned to be "placeholders" or "lieutenants" [*Platzhalter*][49] of (the) Nothing.[50] Thus "openness" — simultaneously "dis-closure" [*Erschlossenheit*] and "resoluteness" [*Entschlossenheit*] — both defines and orients human existence, a "clearing" that, because already recessed or occluded, is of course far from clear. Such a clearing already implicates humanity in the sacrificial economy of loss and surplus: as Heidegger remarks in the *Letter on Humanism,* humanity "loses nothing" in the loss of subjective control or certainty, gaining ultimately in fact the "essential poverty of the shepherd." [51]

I'll refrain from engaging in vague and impressionistic appreciations of Miesian silence, hesitation, and open spaces, or to evoke considerations of a zero-hour, zero-degree *Zeitgeist* of loss, negativity, or absent gods. I'll resist too the inevitable temptation to intone the familiar rosary of dwelling-building-and-thinking, that is, the Heideggerian topos *par excellence* (the *topos* of place or *topos* as such). If it is tempting to argue that Mies presents or exerts a point of pressure or resistance to Heidegger's (global) diagnosis of (global) technology as the final expression of (global) metaphysics — an "opening" free equally of nostalgia and of utopian escape — such speculations are not exactly now to the point. Whatever the specific determinations of Miesian "openness" (and I'd like simply to point to the peculiar differentiation of this openness), the precise philosophical (not to mention ideological) connections remain, perhaps inevitably, obscure. Something more, then, needs to be said.

I want to close here with three questions, all related, intended as much to pare down or close off the hyperbolic nature of the preceding as to open up a direction for future thought. The issue, once again, is almost nothing. If I appear, in what follows, to mingle or cross Heideggerian and Miesian discourse, it's less through a conviction of their ultimate twinship or kinship than because I'm not sure to whom, ultimately, these questions are aimed. I'll be very brief.

*First question.* What would it mean to think "openness" apart from transparency? That is: beyond the phantasm of universal accessibility, which, as always, can only function ideologically as both a substitute and (thus) a screen for a prior foreclosure uncritically assumed?

*Second question.* What would it mean to think of a "clearing" apart from the pristine innocence of a new beginning? That is: beyond the illusion of a *tabula rasa* or blank check indifferently redeemed by the first buyer?

*Third question.* What would it mean to think "less is more" apart from the compensatory logic defining Enlightenment rationality, that is, the logic of instrumentality and exchange? Such a logic is far more persistent than one might think. What Friedrich Nietzsche excoriated as the slave logic of the *qui perd gagne,* Hegel had already identified as the driving ideology not only of Enlightenment but equally (and most insidiously) of its most persistent and outspoken antagonists. It is one step from the crude instrumentality that would maximize profits (one interpretation of Mies's predilection for prefab) to the more sublimated formulations that find nobility in simplicity (a banality frequently attributed to Mies), or even to the various "sublime" renderings to the effect that imagination's pain is reason's gain (I am referring to a certain elaboration of the currently fashionable theme of the Kantian sublime). To think "less is more" in a non-sublimated, even, perhaps, non-sublime fashion would signal a break or opening in what Georges Bataille identified as a closed economy (epitomized, of course, in modern capitalism in all its expressions). But that might be, ultimately, to think less (or more) than either Heidegger or Mies, either together or apart, would lead or enable us to think.

**Notes**

1. Cf. Reiner Schürmann, *Heidegger on Being and Acting: From Principles to Anarchy,* trans. Christine-Marie Gros (Bloomington: Indiana University Press, 1987), pp. 286f. and Rodolphe Gasché, "'Like the rose — without Why': Postmodern transcendentalism and practical philosophy," *diacritics* 19 (Fall/Winter 1989), p.101.

2. Martin Heidegger, "Nachwort zu: 'Was ist Metaphysik?',' in *Wegmarken* (Frankfurt am Main: Klostermann, 1967), p. 107.

3. Fritz Neumeyer, *The Artless Word: Mies van der Rohe on the Building Art,* trans. Mark Jarzombeck (Cambridge, Massachusetts: MIT Press, 1991).

4. Ludwig Mies van der Rohe (quoting Goethe), "Lecture Notes" (n.d.), in Neumeyer, p. 326. The remark is, curiously, a later addition to the manuscript that is then crossed out.

5. E.g., Mies van der Rohe, "Where Do We Go From Here?" (1960), in Neumeyer, p. 332.

6. Mies van der Rohe, "Building Art and the Will of the Epoch!" (1924), in Neumeyer, p. 245.

7. Cf. Heidegger, "Die Kunst und der Raum" (1969), in *Aus der Erfahrung des Denkens, Gesamtausgabe, Bd. 13* (Frankfurt am Main: Vittorio Klostermann, 1983), pp. 203–10.

8. Cf. Heidegger, "The Age of the World Picture," in *The Question Concerning Technology and Other Essays,* trans. William Lovitt (New York: Harper and Row, 1977), p. 135.

9. Heidegger traces the etymological link to the *buan, bhu, bheo* series (ultimately to "our word *bin,*" that is, "Being," in "Building Dwelling Thinking," in *Poetry, Language, Thought,* trans. Albert Hofstadter (New York: Harper and Row, 1971), pp. 146–48.

10. Mies van der Rohe, "The Preconditions of Architectural Work" (1928), in Neumeyer, p. 301.

11. Cf. Sybil Moholy-Nagy, "Has 'Less is More' Become 'Less is Nothing?'" in *Four*

*Great Makers of Modern Architecture* (New York: Columbia University School of Architecture, 1961).

12. Mies van der Rohe, "What Would Concrete, What Would Steel Be without Mirror Glass?" (1933), in Neumeyer, p. 314.

13. As William Jordy would have it. See "The Laconic Splendor of the Metal Frame: Ludwig Mies van der Rohe's 860 Lake Shore Drive Apartments and his Seagram Building," in *American Buildings and Their Architects: The Impact of European Modernism in the Mid-Twentieth Century,* ed. William Pierson (Garden City, New York: Doubleday, 1972), vol. 4, p. 243.

14. Kenneth Frampton, "Towards a Critical Regionalism: Six Points for an Architecture of Resistance," in *The Anti-aesthetic: Essays on Postmodern Culture,* ed. Hal Foster (Port Townsend, Washington: Bay Press, 1983), p. 27.

15. Mies van der Rohe, "Skyscrapers" (1922), in Neumeyer, p. 240. See also K. Michael Hays, "Critical Architecture: Between Culture and Form," *Perspecta* 21 (1984), p. 19; and Detlef Mertins, "Mies's Skyscraper 'Project': Towards the Redemption of Technical Structure," in this volume.

16. On the "modernist" unity of inside and outside, see, for example, Robert Venturi, *Complexity and Contradiction in Architecture* (Garden City, New York: Doubleday, 1966), Chapter 9, "Inside and Outside."

17. See in particular José Quetglas, "Fear of Glass: The Barcelona Pavilion," in *Architectureproduction,* ed. Beatriz Colomina (Princeton: Princeton Architectural Press, 1988), pp. 122–51, and Robin Evans, "Mies van der Rohe's Paradoxical Symmetries," *AA Files* vol. 19 (Spring 1990), pp. 56–68. The visual indeterminacy or non-self-identity of materials in this instance — glass appearing as stone, stone as glass, steel as light, water as mirror, and so on — indeed suggests, if anything, a Heideggerian sense of "earth" as the insistent materiality that, in the artwork, discloses itself precisely in its resistance to "penetration" or exposure. Such refusal would mark, for Heidegger, the very event of truth as the inaugural conflict of "clearing" and concealing: *Unverborgenheit.* See, with reference to the mutation of materials in Mies, K. Michael Hays, "Critical Architecture: Between Culture and Form," *Perspecta* 21 (1984), p. 24, as well as Kenneth Frampton, "Modernism and Tradition in the Works of Mies van der Rohe," in *Mies Reconsidered: His Career, Legacy, and Disciples,* ed. John Zukowsky (Chicago: Art Institute of Chicago, 1986), p. 37. With respect to Heidegger's determination of earth, see "Origin of the Work of Art," in *Poetry, Language, Thought,* pp. 47ff.

18. For Mies's rejection of the MOMA assimilation of Mies to Mondrian, see Peter Carter, *Mies van der Rohe at Work* (London: Pall Mall Press, 1974), p. 180.

19. See Peter Blake, "A Conversation with Mies," in *Four Great Makers of Modern Architecture: Gropius, Le Corbusier, Mies van der Rohe, Wright* (New York: Columbia University School of Architecture, 1963), pp. 101f., as well as Peter Blake, *The Master Builders: Le Corbusier, Mies van der Rohe, Frank Lloyd Wright* (New York: Norton, 1960), pp. 189f.

20. Quoted by Peter Carter, p. 180. See, in general, on this point, Caroline

Constant, "The Barcelona Pavilion as Landscape Garden: Modernity and the Picturesque," *AA Files,* vol. 20 (1991), pp. 46–54.

21. Christian Norberg-Schulz, "A Talk with Mies van der Rohe" (1958), in Neumeyer, p. 339.

22. Neumeyer, p. 339.

23. Neumeyer, p. 339.

24. Heidegger, "Building Dwelling Thinking," p. 159.

25. Heidegger, "The Question Concerning Technology," in *The Question Concerning Technology and Other Essays,* p. 34.

26. Heidegger, "The Question Concerning Technology," pp. 33f.

27. Heidegger, "Das Ende der Philosophie und die Aufgabe des Denkens," in *Zur Sache des Denkens* (Tübingen: Niemeyer, 1976), p. 79.

28. Mies van der Rohe, "The New Time" (1930), in Neumeyer, p. 309.

29. Mies van der Rohe, "Architecture and Technology" (1950), in Neumeyer, p. 324.

30. Mies van der Rohe, "Architecture and Technology," p. 324.

31. Mies van der Rohe, "The New Time," Neumeyer, p. 309. ("The new time is a fact; it exists whether we say yes or no to it. But it is neither better nor worse than any other time. It is a pure given and itself undifferentiated.... Even the changed economic and social conditions we will accept as facts. All these things go their fateful, value-blind way....")

32. Heidegger, *Gelassenheit* (Pfullingen: Günther Neske, 1982), p. 23.

33. Heidegger, "The Question Concerning Technology."

34. Heidegger, "On the Essence of Truth," translated by David Farrell Krell in *Basic Writings* (New York: Harper and Row, 1977), pp. 117–41.

35. Walter Benjamin, *Das Passagen-Werk,* hrsg. Rolf Tiedemann (Frankfurt: Suhrkamp, 1982), p. 222.

36. Mies van der Rohe, "Architecture and Technology" (1950), in Neumeyer, p. 324.

37. Heidegger, "The Question Concerning Technology," pp. 34f.

38. Heidegger, "La provenance de l'art et la destination de la pensée" (1967), translated into French by Jean-Louis Chrétien and Michèle Reifenrath, in *Martin Heidegger, Cahier de l'Herne,* vol. 11 (1983), pp. 84–92, at p. 87.

39. Heidegger, "'Only a God Can Save Us': The *Spiegel* Interview (1966)," in *Heidegger: The Man and the Thinker,* ed. Thomas Sheehan (Chicago: Precedent Publishing, 1981), pp. 45–67. When pressed by the interviewer regarding his summary evaluation of modern art as "destructive," Heidegger brusquely responds, "All right, cross it out" (p. 64).

40. Heidegger, "'Only a God Can Save Us.'"

41. Heidegger, "La provenance de l'art et la destination de la pensée," p. 87.

42. Hitler, Speech inaugurating the "Great Exhibition of German Art 1937" in *Die Kunst im Dritten Reich,* vol. I, pp. 7–8 (July–August 1937); trans. Ilse Falk in *Theories of Modern Art,* ed. Herschel B. Chipp (Berkeley, Los Angeles and London: University of

California Press, 1968), p. 476.

43. See here Jean-Joseph Goux's exemplary article, "Politics and Modern Art: Heidegger's Dilemma," in *diacritics* 19 (Fall–Winter, 1989), pp. 10–24.

44. Heidegger, "Epilogue" to "The Origin of the Work of Art," *Poetry, Language, Thought,* pp. 79ff.

45. Heidegger, "La provenance de l'art at la destination de la pensée," p. 91.

46. This question has been raised with great acuity by Jean-Joseph Goux (see n. 45 above).

46. In so far as the modern epoch distinguishes itself by the principle of pure "relationality" or order, Heidegger argues that both subject and object [*Gegenstand*] are subsumed (without reconciliation) within the "constancy" [*Ständigkeit*] of disposable "reserve" [*Bestand*]. (See "The Question Concerning Technology," p. 17, and "Science and Reflection," in *The Question Concerning Technology,* p. 173). In this sense, argues Heidegger, the terms of objectivification are simultaneously confirmed and erased — the subject-object relation "attains its most extreme dominance" ("Science and Reflection," p. 173) precisely where "objectlessness" [*Gegen-standlose*] as such comes to dominate (*Der Satz vom Grund* [Pfullingen: Neske, 1957], p. 65) — such that, in fact, the very condition or presupposition of objectivity (i.e. "standing," *Ständigkeit*) now, for the first time, comes to light. Such would be the revelatory and consummating potential of the *Gestell* as *Seinsgeschick.* In this context Heidegger introduces the theme of "modern" art, which he claims to be stripped of all "work" (that is, truth) character, and which is characterized by an "objectlessness" symptomatic of the ambiguity that is at stake (see *Satz vom Grund,* p. 66).

48. "Mies Speaks," interview with American Radio University in Berlin (1966), in *Architectural Review,* vol. 144, no. 862 (December, 1968), p. 451.

49. Note that *Dasein* is here said to be the holder of a *Platz* (neither an *Ort* nor a *Stelle*): already ambiguously positioned, therefore, between "dwelling" and the homelessness characteristic of the *Gestell.*

50. Heidegger, "What is Metaphysics?" in *Basic Writings,* ed. David Farrell Krell (New York: Harper and Row, 1977), p. 108.

51. Heidegger, "Letter on Humanism," in *Basic Writings,* p. 221.

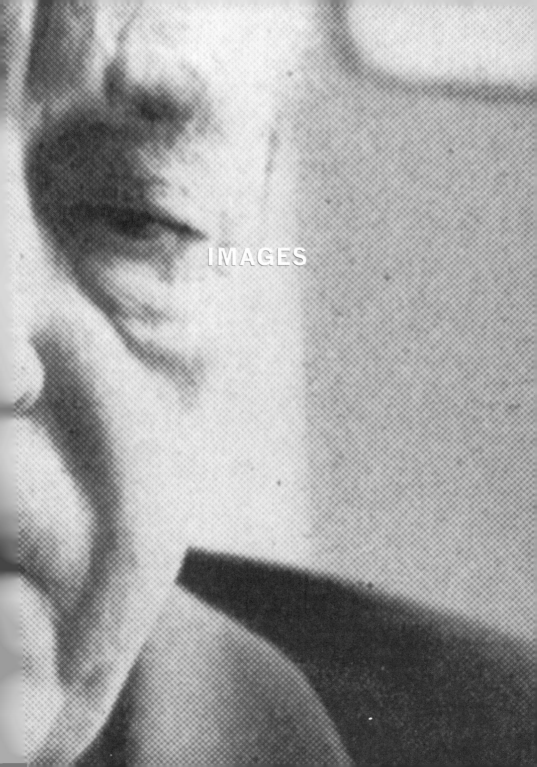

IMAGES

1. Photographs of Mies van der Rohe
and Lake Shore Drive Apartments in Chicago,
*LIFE,* March 18, 1957, pp. 66–67.
Photos Frank Schershel.

Images

## MIES NOT

*Beatriz Colomina*

It was the Spring of 1992 and I was busy finishing a book on Adolf Loos and Le Corbusier, which was taking very long because every time that I looked at the manuscript it threatened to explode in another point. I was there, trying to put the lid on that project, on that can of worms, which were rather like snakes trying to snare me back into the book, and then the telephone rang . . .

. . . It was Detlef Mertins inviting me to participate in this symposium, and I immediately started making noises about not being a Mies scholar, not having any particular expertise, not knowing anything other than what everybody knows . . . in other words, it would seem as if I were trying to get out of it. But Detlef had an answer to all of that: the conference was not meant to be scholarly; at least, not only. Rather, it was about the different ways that one could think of Mies van der Rohe today. Besides, other people who had been invited had no particular expertise in Mies either. There were even architects. And so I was reminded that I am also an archi-tect, at least on paper, and that architects (who knows why) are allowed to talk about architecture or anything else in a non-scholarly way. By the end of our conversation I had been persuaded to accept this invitation, now aware that all it would take was a change of hat. I did not need to act the historian part, and that was initially a relief (from the guilt of not knowing enough, of having only a "superficial" knowledge, the historian's guilt). Anyway, I told myself, "images" — the title of the session in which I was asked to participate — are essentially superficial. They are, first of all, surfaces. So why would I need depth?

As time passed, however, doubts crept back in (one does not engage in such cross-dressing exercises without some tension) and I would have withdrawn from the event if it was not that, all of a sudden, I was struck by the question: "Why not?" That is, "Why not Mies?" Why, in my travels through the roads of the modern movement, despite the multiple occasions on which I have found myself at crossroads leading to his work, have I never gotten off at the stop called "Mies"? And in the end, this question — prompted by the invitation — became sufficiently engaging to induce a little detour, to make me leave the familiar trajectories of Loos and Le Corbusier, in order to ask myself "Why not Mies?" Or the same question reversed: What is it about those themes that draw the historian into them? What about those that disinvite one? Passion is a necessary element of research, particularly of archival research. Why would anyone do it otherwise? Why drag oneself through the dark, dusty, interior space of the archive? And if this passion, which I have felt on so many other occasions, is not here for me when addressing Mies, the question becomes: What about Mies keeps me out?

The question continues to haunt me, strangely drawing me further and further into Mies's work. The more I wonder why I am on the outside, the more I find myself inside. A complication that was there from the beginning, because I like Mies's work, and I do not mean "like" here in the academic sense that the work speaks about this or that (although this is clearly the case), but in a more primary sense. It gives me pleasure, as does good food, for example. Living in the cracks of several cultures and languages, one becomes ridiculously aware of the different ways of expressing the same idea. Of the time I spent in Paris working in the archives of the Fondation Le Corbusier, I now remember the waiter's perennial question: *"Qu'est-ce que vous ferait plaisir?"* — literally, "What will give you pleasure?" — as distinct from "What would you like?," *"Cosa prendeno?" "Que van a tomar?,"* or even the more direct, if not brutal, *"Que quieren?"* ("What do you want?"). Many times I have thought about how these seemingly innocuous formulations influence what we end up ordering. "What do you want?" and "What would give you pleasure?" are, in the end, completely different questions.

So if I like Mies's architecture, if the work, the images give me pleasure, and if by now, at the end of a very long project (which could be described precisely in terms of images, the images of modern architecture, or modern architecture as image, as mass-media), I can see that this pleasure of the image is probably the driving force behind most of the work I have done so far, then the question "Why not Mies?" or "Why not Mies's images?" becomes ever more pressing. It is from this sense of uneasiness that this paper is produced, for a symposium with the name: *The Presence of Mies*, for a session number 6, called "Images."

But what does it really mean? The presence of Mies in images? The images of Mies's work? Mies's image? And in any case, what is it in these images that deters me from getting closer, from entering the private space of Mies's archives, of hand-written notes, of annotated books, of correspondence, of trial documents, of incriminating photographs, in short, the space of scholarly work? The pleasure of the historian is, after all, the (voyeuristic if not fetishistic) pleasure of the archive. But, I have remained at the door, outside, in the public space of the images of Mies made available to all of us, his public image: images of himself in photographs, writings (by or about him); images of his work, the multiple ways in which it has been represented to us, in photographs, collages, photomontages, drawings, exhibitions, essays, monographs, surveys, gramophone records, radio interviews, films, and so on. Of all of these images, I will start with the best known, the most publicized, the ones everybody has seen without even intending to look, has heard about even without bothering to read.

While I write these notes, Lou Reed sings about Andy Warhol on the radio. It is a song called "Images" from a compact disc all covered in velvet titled "Songs for Drella — A fiction," and it goes something like:

*Images*
I think images are worth repeating
Images repeated from a painting
Images taken from a painting
From a photo worth re-seeing
I love images worth repeating, project them upon the ceiling
Multiply them with silk screening
See them with a different feeling
Images/Images/Images/Images

Some say images have no feeling, I think there's a
deeper meaning
Mechanical precision or so it's seeming
Instigates a cooler feeling
I love multiplicity of screenings
Things born anew display new meanings
I think images are worth repeating and repeating
and repeating[1]

So what are the images of Mies, the repeated images? How is Mies repeated?

First, the image of the architect. In photographs, he appears enormous, a "massive man," an imposing physical presence, sometimes smoking his legendary cigar. He almost always looks down. The words that accompany these images always insist on how big he is and then quickly add that he is shy, reserved, phlegmatic, taciturn . . .[2] All of this as if trying to explain his posture, his refusal to address the camera. But, who knows why, all I can think about is that painful remark made by his daughter, Georgia, some 40 years later, that when "they" (Mies's children) used to visit him after his separation from Ada Brun, he would utter a barely audible "Hello," without even raising his head from the newspaper.[3] All I can think about is "What is he hiding from, behind the newspaper, behind the drawing?" After all, in almost every photograph he is looking down to a drawing, through a model, or even turning his back entirely to the camera.

Few writers fail to comment on his physical appearance, his "commanding presence," as somebody puts it. They always remark on his clothes as well. Not an incidental question; we can no longer separate clothing from modernity. But what is most curious about the common reading of the image of Mies — his physical image — is how easily it slips into the reading of his work, so as if to make them into one. Take, for example, James Johnson Sweeny, a longtime friend of Mies who wrote this tribute to him in 1969, a few days after his death:

> Standing here in Crown Hall, with its scale that so appealed to Mies, I like to remember the first time I saw Mies van der Rohe and the impressions I had. It was in the Spring of 1933. I had admired an apartment interior he had designed for Philip Johnson . . . in New York. I was on my way to Europe and Germany on a business trip. Philip Johnson suggested that I call on Mies. I wrote him. He invited me to his office. When my wife and I entered, we both saw at once the answer to a question which had been troubling us for some time: Why was the Barcelona seat so wide? As we opened the door we realized. Mies was seated on one and it just comfortably accommodated his breadth.
>
> Perhaps "amply" would be a more accurate word than comfortably. For we recognized something ample about Mies himself at first glimpse — a quality which seemed related to everything about him, everything he admired, everything he did. The suit he was wearing was ample — well cut to be sure, but easy on him — and of a sober rich material. The cigars he offered me, and smoked, one after another, were likewise "ample" – and of the finest Havana leaf. The glass and chromium steel table near which he was seated, which we had always thought strangely high in proportion to its width, now looked perfectly in scale with its designer. Even on the first visit, I realized Mies' love of space, scale and quality of material.[4]

Likewise, Peter Blake uses a photograph of Mies (fig. 2) to open his words of homage. "The Master of Structure," and writes: "His clothes are extremely elegant; most of his suits were tailored by Knize...." And here, even if Blake does not refer to it, the informed reader is already thinking of Loos, who also bought his suits at Knize and even designed their shops. In any case, Blake continues:

> He is, indeed, something of a dandy in a subdued way: there is generally a very soft, very expensive handkerchief trailing out of his breast pocket, and he obviously likes fine quality in all his personal belongings.
>
> Yet there is nothing dandified about his features: his head looks as if it had been chiseled out of a block of granite; his face, infinitely lined, has the massively aristocratic look of a wealthy Dutch burgher by Rembrandt....
>
> No one seeing this large and impressive figure would suspect that Mies ... was born the son of a rather humble mason and stone cutter.... [who] when he is at ease — generally late in the evening, with a group of friends — likes to talk about the days when he learned to put brick on brick. "Now a brick that's really *something*," he will say, with his infectious smile. "That's really *building*. Not paper architecture."[5]

Do you see the line of thought here? Tailored clothes, minimal decoration, chiseled head, granite block, infinite lines, son of a stonemason, basic materials but with the look of richness, even an aristocratic look, a richness of simple materials then, brick, stone ... that's real building, not paper architecture. I am all for associations of ideas. There are always only associations. But what exactly is going on here?

To start with a detail, taking the least conspicuous of the jumps made here — from stone to brick — we could simply point to something that did not escape even the devoted Blake, namely, that "there is some doubt as to how many bricks Mies ever laid one on top of the other, for his father was a *stone*mason,"[6] not a bricklayer. But in their zeal to establish the origins of Mies's architecture — and by extension of good architecture in general — in craftsmanship, in tectonics, in building details, in some fundamental reality, most historians forget what they are talking about. For a stonemason would never touch a brick. The way they work is fundamentally different. This is not simply a small detail, and, anyway, supposedly for Mies, "God is in the details." If all of Mies's authority rests on his origins in stonemasonry, no detail could be more important.

This slip structures almost all readings of Mies. Even when Richard Padovan attempts to undo the "canonical" interpretation, the monolithic image that he identifies as having been "built up and consolidated, as ideas and whole phrases were virtually lifted from one work of homage to the next,"[7] in this very moment he unconsciously lifts the idea of the stonemason. He writes: "It is true that Mies's buildings of the 1920s are distinguished

2. Portrait of Mies van der Rohe from Peter Blake,
*The Master Builders: Le Corbusier, Mies van der Rohe,
Frank Lloyd Wright* (1961).

from those of his contemporaries ... by their unmodish, dateless quality and their greater sense of materials and craftsmanship. But the one-sided, *granite image* of the great architect as an enduring and monolithic symbol of universality and perfection has been made meaningless by repetition; and today a fresh approach is needed if we are to renew our understanding of him."[8] Needless to say, I can't agree more with this statement, and yet, here again, in the moment of announcing a new, fresher look at Mies, where did Padovan get the reference to granite, if not from the same sources he is criticizing? Somehow the "solid" image of Mies slips back in. We are no longer simply talking about an image of granite, it is a "granite image" deployed by historians to sustain a particular ideological reality.

It is hard to find any account of Mies that does not make a big deal out of his being the son of a stonemason and of his supposed apprenticeship in the workshop of his father. Yet there is even some doubt about how much Mies actually worked in his father's atelier. In an interview with his grandson, Dirk Lohan, in 1968, he was asked: "When you were very young, were you obliged to help in the family atelier?" To which he answered:

> I did it for the fun of it. And always when we had vacations. I especially remember that on All Souls Day, when so many people wanted new monuments for the graves, our whole family pitched in. I did the lettering on the stones, my brother did the carving, and my sisters put the finishing touches on them, the gold leaf, and all that. I don't think we added very much to the process, but it probably was a little better for it.[9]

Lettering, and later drafting, are obviously the talents that Mies exhibited at an early age and the ones that earned him his first paying jobs. Strange how these remarkable qualities of the young Mies, which can be clearly established historically, do not interest the historians so much, perhaps because they will start to see that the "master of structure" was first a "graphic artist," something that does not go so well with the solid (if not petrified) image that we have of Mies. Instead, brick is invoked, using Mies's words as a prop: "All education must begin with the practical side of life."[10] With the brick, hastily adds the historian. And while it is true that Mies apprenticed as a bricklayer to a local builder, he was never paid for his work, and his tasks included, from his own account, bringing hot water to the workers: "We had to go out and get boiling water for the carpenters framing in the roof.... They used the water to make coffee. And if we didn't get the water fast enough, they would throw one of their sharp axes after us to make us hurry up."[11] But when, after a year of apprenticeship, Mies requested to be put on wages, he was not hired. So, one may safely conclude that he was not particularly good at that work. Yet he did not have any trouble finding a job as a draftsman. At the age of fifteen Mies landed his first job, at a firm in Aachen (Max Fischer) that specialized in stucco decorations for building interiors:

> We had huge drawing boards that went from floor to ceiling and stood vertically against the wall. You couldn't lean on or against them; you had to stand squarely in front of them and draw not just by turning your hand but by swinging your whole arm. We made drawings the size of an entire quarter of a room ceiling, which we could then send on to the modelmakers. I did this every day for two years. Even now I can draw cartouches with my eyes closed.... I worked in all historic styles, plus modern. All conceivable ornaments.[12]

His drawing abilities alone (no degree was required) were also to gain Mies his first job in Berlin, in the city building offices of Rixdorf, where he was assigned the detail design of the neo-Gothic wall paneling for the new Town Hall. With this departure, Mies turned his back on the past, never to look back again. But this break was not simply from place; he also disowned his social origins. He left behind not simply Aachen and the world of the "ateliers," but also a complex system of beliefs that are sustained by the mentality of that *modus operandi*. Mies's father, according to Franz Schulze, did not believe that his sons should go to *Gymnasium* because it was beyond their social class; as the children of a craftsman, they should attend vocational school. This is the reason behind Mies's education in apprenticeship. His "origins" are all within the restrictive world of craft. So why do architectural historians feel the need to glorify such social immobility? Why the urge to return him to the very scene he fought so hard to leave? An urge so strong as to lead them to distort history, the very task they have undertaken to carry out, as when an established historian writes: "No doubt, Mies learned to work with brick from his father." No doubt? Leave aside for the moment the almost surreal thought of learning brickwork from a *stone*mason. There is no history without doubt.

The privileging of working-class, craft origins is yet another case of the generic appeal to authenticity, reality, materiality, unconscious truths, and so on that one finds throughout critical and historical discourse. The craftsman's supposedly unmediated proximity to materials gives an aura of authenticity, of simple direct truth. And certainly this is consistent with the standard claim that the simplicity of Mies's forms exudes some fundamental, if not eternal, truth. (David Spaeth, for example, writes: "Over the years that I have studied Mies's work ... I have come to hold it in ever greater respect because it is concerned with *eternal values,* with *eternal verities.*"[13])

The humble brick, then, is a figure for the poetry and truth that emerges when the most basic elements are assembled in the most direct way. But does Mies really use humble materials? Not only are his suits made of a "sober rich material" and his cigar of the "finest Havana leaf," but his buildings are made of the most expensive stones, the most expensive fabrics: Algerian onyx, Swedish linen, Indonesian mahogany, Macassar ebony, Roman travertine, Tinian marble and so on.[14] While the historians go on and on about Mies's humble origins, Mies insistently keeps his distance from them. According to Sandra Honey, "while the German social housing programme was keeping most radical architects fully occupied, Mies concentrated on building up his private practice. . . . [He] employed only one or two draughtsmen [but] was fashionable in appearance: his suits were made from the best fabrics by the best tailors, his shoes were handmade for him in England and he sported an immaculate Homburg . . . the white silk linings of which were reputed to be spotless. . . . He enjoyed good food, good wine, and good company." And when he took over the Bauhaus in Dessau, he employed a butler in his house, who was "always dressed in a dark suit with white gloves. . . . Mies himself was always immaculately turned out, in a plain, well-cut suit of a dark fabric."[15] So much for humbleness.

But what is with the brick, anyway? Perhaps no other citation of Mies has enjoyed more academic acclaim than: "Architecture begins when two bricks are carefully put together." First of all, this is about the dumbest definition of architecture I have ever heard. Second, I have my doubts about its veracity since he never used the word "architecture," preferring the German word *Baukunst* — literally "building art" — and insisted that "'Bau' is construction and 'Kunst' just a refinement of that and nothing more."[16] In fact, one can argue that the very opposition between architecture and building is itself a kind of class opposition: the high art of architecture versus the craft of building. It is surprising, then, that the historians who romanticize Mies's supposed craft origins reinstate the elite concept of architecture in the very moment of eulogizing those humble origins. In an interview in *House and Garden,* in 1947, Mies goes as far as saying, "I desire the absence of architecture and I practice the art of building," seemingly supporting all the historians' efforts to associate him with the truth of materials, but throwing their concept of architecture out the window. Even if we replace "architecture" with "building art," returning now to Mies's famous statement, to say that the building art starts when two bricks are put together sounds to me like saying that the weaving art starts when two threads are interlaced. That is, you can get rid of the word "art" and the whole thing makes much more sense. But it is not that the historian wants to establish the origins of Mies's idea of architecture in the weaving of bricks, as when Adolf Loos follows Gottfried Semper in identifying architecture with textile (incidentally, that would be a far more promising line of inquiry). What is curious here is how many historians and critics of the modern movement seem to be turned on by craftsmanship, paradoxically the very thing that the modern movement was turning away from.[17] The fact that Mies was the son of a stonemason and apprenticed in several crafts is invoked (as with Loos, whose father was also a stonemason) to give free rein to a series of extremely suspect assumptions about what good architecture is: tectonics, precise building details, attention to materials, and so on. The litany continues ad nauseam. Blake, for example, proclaims: "'Discipline' — this has been the watchword of Mies's life and work. Discipline, order, clarity, truth."[18] Well, maybe it is because I grew up in a dictatorial ultra-Catholic regime, the Spain of Franco, but when I hear these words I want to run the other way. And on my way out, I am reminded, again by association of ideas, of the surprising statement made by Mies in the 1950s, that "in the next ten years the best architecture will come from Spain." True, there were good architects in the Spain of those years, some working in a manner not so distant from that of Mies. But he could not possibly have made this statement independently of the political conditions of that country in those years. In the Spain of Franco, Mies may have seen his dream realized: working for a totalitarian regime without renouncing the idiom of modern architecture, something that had proved impossible in Germany. So, perhaps I had very good reasons for not getting off at the stop marked "Mies." But the nausea, I discovered in the meantime, is not just mine.

Surely what is most significant about Mies's origins (as with Loos's) is that, the workshop of his father notwithstanding (and presumably with it a sure way of making a living), he left. And when interviewed about this moment, his departure, by his grandson, Dirk Lohan, in 1968 (one year before his death), he comes up with the elaborate story of how "because he had not been able to procure himself a [first-] class ticket," he got sick and vomited practically all the way from Aachen to Berlin, first through the window of the train, then at the stop in Cologne, and when he finally arrives in Berlin he gets in a cab and again gets sick and vomits and has to get out of the cab, vomits yet again on the sidewalk, and finally gets to his destination by taking a tram.[19] Bizarre story, of vomit! And it gets very detailed. He says, and one should note that this remark is made some sixty-three years after the fact: "Around 8:15 the train started up again, and at 8:16, I opened the window, stuck my head out, and threw up."[20] Astonishing precision, railway precision; shock precision, one might even say. At first I was taken by his matter-of-fact assertion that all of this had happened because he did not have a first-class ticket. I told myself, or maybe the historian in me did, that perhaps we no longer associate trains with motion-sickness, just as we hardly think about it any more with planes, and so for a while I embarked on a side-track research into the pathology of early train travelling. (A fascinating story. Nothing in research is more gratifying than these unexpected, off-track journeys, which in the end give you just a cryptic footnote, if anything at all.) Many disorders were attributed to early train travel. The idea of modernity cannot be separated from the idea of illness. Strained eyes, for example: the landscape shooting past the window caused the traveller to lose eyesight, it was believed, in the same way that cinema was later believed to do, and people with weak eyes were advised not to go to the movies. (From film, the eye pathology moved to television, and today we have the same situation repeating itself with computers and video games.) If modernity is tied to new forms of vision and perception, perhaps it is not surprising to encounter around each new technology that makes a new form of vision possible the greatest resistance in the form of illness. The train was clearly such a technology. But it is not just a question of vision. Many other disorders were associated with early train travel: bodily fatigue, strain of the muscles, deafening noise, psychological stresses of various kinds, tremors, rapid aging of commuters, and so on. Everything, it would seem, could be blamed on the train in these early days, everything but nausea. So that, returning after this little detour to Mies's strange story of vomit, all I can think about, all I can ask myself, the only thing left to ask, is: "What is he trying to get rid of?"

Mies "threw up" his origins. After all, he wanted a first-class ticket. It is naïve or ideological to suggest that Mies simply followed his father. On the contrary, he rejected his father. He even rejected his father's name. In 1913, after his breakup with Behrens, he opened his own studio and changed his name to Miës van der Rohe, adding his mother's family name "Rohe" to his own with the Dutch preposition "van." According to Sandra Honey, "things Dutch ran high in Germany at the time." Other critics have suggested that he was hoping it would ring close to "von," with its aristo-cratic overtones. In any case, he clearly renounced his father's name.

He even added the umlaut to the "e" of Mies, so that the word would be pronounced in two syllables. "Mies" in German means "awkward, nasty, miserable, poor, seedy, out of sorts, bad or wretched."[21] He clearly did not want any of these attributes associated with his work. He defaced his father's name.

Mies's knowledge of building materials may well be attributed to his upbringing, but to invoke his father as the foundation of his architecture is simply to remain within the patriarchal structure of the architectural profession, rather than to clarify Mies's practice. Indeed, the only role of this gesture may be to give Mies the role of father (no matter how horrific a father he was in his personal life). Not by chance, this tradition of architectural writing that is obsessed with origins is the same one that ends up speaking of the architect as a "master." You will remember the title of Peter Blake's book, *The Master Builders,* where he puts together his vision of Wright, Le Corbusier, and Mies. What is shocking is not so much that Blake could not find a more appropriate label in 1960, but the success of the label and its blind adoption by the presumably more enlightened critics and historians of the end of the twentieth century.

Ironically enough, on that one point the guest of honor is much more enlightened than the somewhat too-solicitous critics paying homage to him:

> As I was born in an old family of stonemasons, I am very familiar with hand craftsmanship. . . . My receptiveness to the beauty of handwork does not prevent me from recognizing that handicrafts as a form of economic production are lost. The few real craftsmen still alive in Germany are rarities whose work can be acquired only by very rich people. What really matters is something totally different. Our needs have assumed such proportions that they can no longer be met with methods of craftsmanship. . . . Let us keep in mind that all these theories about hand craftsmanship have been composed by aesthetes under the beam of an electric lamp. They enter upon their propaganda mission on paper that has been produced by machines, printed by machines, and bound by machines.[22]

Considering the little that Mies wrote (it can all be read in an afternoon), it is amazing that the critics of the "son-of-the-stonemason" school have passed through this passage without seeing it. Their blindness is only justified inasmuch as they would have had to recognize themselves as those very confused aesthetes under the electric lamp. Perhaps they need a new bulb.

And, of course, those are the same critics who "forget" to explain how we got to know Mies in the first place. Anybody with the most cursory knowledge of Mies would recognize that his place in architectural history, his role as so-called "founder" of the modern movement, was established through a series of five projects, none of them actually built (or even buildable — they were not developed at that level), that he made public through exhibitions and publications during the first half of the 1920s. So much for "no paper architecture"! I am referring, of course, to the two Glass Skyscrapers of 1921 and 1922, the Reinforced Concrete Office Building of 1923, and the Concrete and Brick Country Houses of 1923 and 1924. These projects should be considered together with the publicity apparatus that not only supported but clearly produced them.

The first Glass Skyscraper was Mies's entry into the Friedrichstrasse competition of January 1922 and was exhibited in the Berlin City Hall. Soon Mies developed another version that was exhibited at the annual Berlin Art Exhibition (Grosse Berliner Kunstausstellung) in 1922. Both versions were then published in a long list of journals, both avant-garde and professional, including *Frühlicht* in 1922, *G* in 1924 (fig. 3), *Journal of the American Institute of Architects* in 1923, *Merz* in 1924 (fig. 4), *Wasmuths Monatshefte für Baukunst* in 1925, *L'Architecture Vivante* in 1925, just to talk about the first three years. The glass skyscrapers were also included in many books on modern architecture written during the 1920s, including Walter Gropius's *Internationale Architektur* (1925), Gustav Platz's *Die Baukunst der neusten Zeit* (1927), and Walter Curt Behrendt's *Der Sieg des neuen Baustils* (1927). The concrete office building made its public appearance simultaneously in the Berlin Art Exhibition of 1923 and in an issue of *G*. After the Berlin exhibition, it was shown, together with the Glass Skyscraper, at the Internationale Architekturasstellung at the Bauhaus in Weimar. And in the fall of the same year, Theo van Doesburg invited Mies to exhibit these two projects in the De Stijl exhibition in the Galerie L'Effort Moderne in Paris. (Mies was actually the only non-Dutch architect invited to participate.) The Concrete Country House project was exhibited in the same Berlin Art Exhibition where Mies had presented the Concrete Office Building, and was published in *G* 2, and so on.

Mies's first writings were also produced in relation to these projects. His first article, "Hochhäusser," ("Skyscrapers") was published in *Frühlicht*. Here, on the occasion of the Friedrichstrasse competition, Mies wrote an article on high buildings, to accompany the two versions of his glass skyscrapers, that states: "The structural concept is the essential foundation of the artistic design . . ." But, as Tegethoff has pointed out, "neither the Friedrichstrasse plan nor the published version of the curvilinear plan gives any indication whatever of the structural system."[23] Nevertheless, these plans and photographs would appear in the long list of journals both German and foreign, both avant-garde and professional, that I have referred to, even if some of the professional journals use the illustrations to massacre the building from a technical point of view, as when the *Journal of the American Institute of Architects* in 1923 calls Mies's Glass Skyscraper, "Nude Building falling down stairs." Mies's subsequent articles were again written to accompany his projects: "Bürohaus" was published in the first issue of *G* together with the Concrete Office Building, and "Bauen" ("Building") written with Hans Richter, the editor of *G*, appeared framing the Concrete Country House in the second issue (fig. 5).

In fact, Mies wrote a total of seven articles in these years. He clearly had

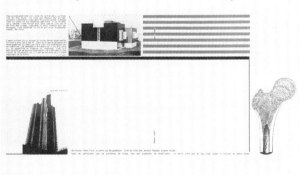

3 & 4. Mies van der Rohe,
Glass Skyscraper of 1922 as published on the
title page of G, no. 3, June 1924 and as
attributed to Nies van der Rohe in Kurt
Schwitters's magazine *Merz*, no. 8–9 (1924).

a keen sense of publicity. Even his change of name should be considered an act of publicity, as was his joining the Novembergruppe in 1922 and the Werkbund in 1923. By the mid-1920s, Mies had secured for himself a strong position within Germany's leading artistic and architectural associations: the Werkbund, the Novembergruppe, the B.D.A, and der Ring.

What the theorist of the "son-of-a-stonemason" school for the most part tends to obscure is Mies's role as publicist and propagandist: the fact that he not only contributed to G, but also supported the journal financially; that he did not simply belong to the Novembergruppe, but headed the architectural section from 1921 to 1925 and, in this capacity, directed four exhibitions, in which four of his five famous projects were included;[24] and that the commission to build the apartment house block of the Weissen-hofsiedlung of 1925–1927, was "given to him by the Werkbund for his skills as a publicist of modernism," as Richard Pommer pointed out, "rather than as a proponent of housing").[25] And therefore, if we are to engage in a pseudo-psychological analysis of character, in parallel to the theories of the "son-of-a-stonemason" school, we will probably conclude that he was a very ambitious person, not a humble craftsman but one who understood the power of the media and exploited it, using it as his voice. Mies may have been a man of few words (as the historians like to insist), but he was "speaking" all the time. He was using the media as a loudspeaker. In these terms, his famous "less is more" (attributed to Mies by Philip Johnson[26]) is true at least in the sense that never has so little said by an architect reached such a large audience.

It was these five projects, these five paper architectures, together with the publicity apparatus enveloping them, that first made Mies into a historical figure. The projects that he had built so far (and that he would continue to develop during the same years) would have taken him nowhere. Sure, some historians may object that the Riehl house of 1907 had already been noted by a critic. And, indeed, the house was published in *Moderne Bauformen* and in *Innen Dekoration.* But between the somewhat modest articles covering this house in 1910 and his own article in G in 1921, presenting the glass skyscraper, nothing else of Mies's work was published.

Should we attribute this silence to the blindness of architectural critics of his time, as some historians seem to imply? Here again Mies's attitude is clear. In the early 1920s he destroyed the drawings of most of his work prior to that time, thereby constructing a very precise "image" of himself, one from which all incoherences, all *faux pas,* were erased.[27] (Here the parallelism with Loos, who destroyed all the documents from his projects when he left Vienna for Paris in 1922, may be more to the point than the fact that they were both sons of stonemasons.) And even in 1947 Mies did not allow Philip Johnson to publish most of his early work in the monograph that Johnson was preparing that would constitute the first book on Mies. "Not enough of a statement," Mies is supposed to have said about the drawings of some early project that Johnson wanted to include. And when, thirty years later, Johnson is asked in an interview, "How would you do the book today?" he answers: "Most of all I would look into . . . the suddenness with which Mies went from what he had been doing to the glass skyscraper of 1921," and he utters something about "Expressionism, the feeling of a defeated Berlin, the character of the Novembergruppe," and other — to my ear — lateral issues.

A far more convincing clue to Mies's sudden change of direction was provided by Sandra Honey when she wrote that the breaking point (in Mies's early career) came when Walter Gropius refused to exhibit Mies's project for the Kröller-Müller house in his 1919 Exhibition for Unknown Architects.[28] According to Mies, Gropius said: "We can't exhibit it, we are looking for something completely different."[29] In light of this rejection, we can see that the Friedrichstrasse competition of January 1922 did not simply give Mies the opportunity to exhibit his first modern project; the Glass Skyscraper was "modern" precisely *because* it was produced for that context.

This project becomes an illustration of something that I have been arguing for some years now: modern architecture becomes "modern" not simply by using glass, steel, or reinforced concrete as it is usually understood, but by engaging with the media: with publications, competitions, exhibitions, etc. With Mies this is literally the case. What had been a series of rather conservative projects realized for "real" clients (the Riehl house, the Perls house, the Kröller-Müller house, the Urbig house) became in the context of the Friedrichstrasse competition, of *G*, of *Frühlicht* and so on, a series of manifestos of modern architecture.

Not only that, but in Mies you can see, perhaps as in no other architect of the modern movement, a true case of schizophrenia between his "published" projects and those developed for his clients. Still, however, in the 1920s, at the same time that he was developing his most radical projects, Mies could build such conservative houses as the Eichstädt House in a suburb of Berlin (1922) (fig. 6) and the Mosler House in Potsdam (1924) (fig. 7). Can we blame these projects on the conservative taste of Mies's clients? Once again, not so easily. Mosler was a banker and his house is said to reflect his taste. But when in 1924 the art historian and constructivist artist, Walter Dexel, who was very much interested in and supportive of modern architecture, commissioned Mies to do a house for him, Mies blew it. He was unable to come up with the modern house his client had desired. He gave one excuse after another. The deadline was repeatedly postponed.

5. Mies van der Rohe,
"Building," as published in G, no. 2
(September 1923).

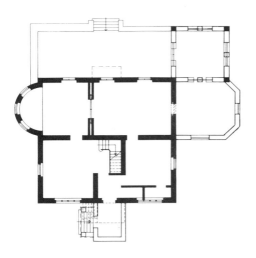

6. Mies van der Rohe,
Eichstädt House, 1920–21, Berlin-Zehlendorf.
Ground floor plan. Redrawn Sandra Honey.

7. Mies van der Rohe,
Mosler House, 1924–26,
Potsdam-Neubabelsberg. Exterior.

And in the end Dexel gave the project to another architect.[30] It was precisely the very knowledge of traditional construction, which his critics now worship, that got in Mies's way. In fact, it was not until 1927 that he was able to break with tradition, when he managed to put up non-loadbearing walls in his apartment building at the Weissenhofsiedlung. For a long time, then, there was an enormous gap between the flowing architecture of Mies's published projects and his struggle to find the appropriate techniques to produce these effects in built form. For many years he was literally trying to catch up with his publications. Perhaps that is why he worked so hard to produce a sense of realism in the representation of his projects, as, for example, in the photomontage of the Glass Skyscraper with cars flying by on the Friedrichstrasse. Ironically, it was his technical sophistication with the image, which may be related to his original graphic ability, that allowed him to become an apprentice of the latest technologies.

In what I have said so far, I hope to have made it clear that I am more interested in how Mies came to be such a gigantic figure in the history of modern architecture than in the gigantism of his physical figure.

And so, when I see the picture of Mies shaking hands with the King of Spain (Alfonso XIII) inside the Barcelona Pavilion (fig. 8), I see, of course, his legendary "presence" and how well-dressed he is, as Blake and others would say. But I also see how much at ease he seems to be (he who is reported to be an extremely shy person) and I cannot stop myself from thinking: How did he get his commission? As if the ease with which he holds himself before the King will hold a clue to the rather official commission of representing Germany in Barcelona. And when I realized, as Bonta points out, that the Barcelona Pavilion was seen by "nobody," I too am very interested in how it managed to become such an icon in the history of modern architecture. And, in the end, is it not obvious, even in the case of Mies, that the modern movement has little to do with authenticity, with truth to construction and materials, with details... and everything to do with reproduction and publicity. Even if this publicity is about authenticity.

And if it was really "authentic," shouldn't we then be joining the ranks of what I will call here, for the sake of the argument, the "Where's the beef?" kind of critic in architecture? I am referring to those scandalized by the fact that Le Corbusier's buildings leak, or that after he theorizes the ready-made furniture object, the Maple chairs in the L'Esprit Nouveau Pavilion were custom-made because the originals did not fit through the door, and so on. Or, specifically about Mies, shouldn't we complain that the Barcelona and Tugendhat chairs were, in the end, handmade, even if they were presented as industrial?[31] Or that the walls of the Barcelona Pavilion were in the end load-bearing, even if Mies claims that it was there, in the pavilion, that he

8. Mies van der Rohe shaking hands with King
Alfonso de Borbón of Spain, at the opening of
the German pavilion ("Barcelona Pavilion") in the
1929 International Exposition in Barcelona.
Photo José Maria Sagarra

first realized the independence of wall from supporting structure (leaving alone the fact that the principle had been announced five years earlier by Le Corbusier[32], and the practice was long in place in American steel frame structures)? It is here that we find the common reading of Mies more paradoxical. After all those hang-ups with Mies and "authenticity," we are asked to take yet one more leap and realize that "what counts" in Mies's buildings is not how they are really built, but what they "look like." What counts, then, is their image, their photographic image.

The work of Mies became known almost exclusively through photography and the printed media. This presupposes a transformation of the site of architectural production, displaced from the construction site into the seemingly immaterial sites of publications, exhibitions, competitions, journals. Paradoxically, these are more ephemeral media and yet in many ways more permanent: they secure a place for an architecture in History, a historical space (designed not just by the historians and critics but also by the architects themselves who deployed these media).

To rethink Mies's work will mean to rethink the architecture of that space. This is not a small task. Generations of historians have been trained to guard it. It is precisely this ideologically defined space that I have not wished to enter up to now. This symposium has forced me to consider how I would enter it (and I have not been able to leave it since then). I can only conclude by pointing out the direction my thinking is taking, rather, is taking me, research being something one is not so much in control of.

**1.** If modern architecture is actually produced within the discursive space of exhibitions, catalogues, books, architectural magazines, competitions, photographs, world's fairs, journalism, museums, art galleries, conferences, architectural schools, and so on, then Mies's work is such a beautiful example of this new state of affairs, almost a text-book illustration, a cata-logue of all the new contexts of production. Think again about what made him famous: the five projects of the early twenties (which never existed outside of their publication), the Barcelona Pavilion (a temporary building in a fair, that "nobody" saw but still became such an icon of modern architec-ture); the House for a Bachelor (again, a pavilion, this time inside a building, for the Berlin Exhibition of 1931); organizing the Weissenhofsiedlung exhibition; the directorship of the Bauhaus ... Should we go on? At the very least we will have to think about how he got his American clients through Johnson and the MoMA. And exactly what effect did the exhibition of his work in the MoMA and the book by Johnson have on his reputation? And what confluence of forces produced the retrospective canonization of the pavilion in the late 1950s. And even today, in 1992, what brings us to this conference? To what extent are we actively producing Mies, keeping him present, maintaining rather than analyzing "The Presence of Mies"?

So the first point is that we have to read Mies's architecture in these contexts and not just in that of the building site. Architecture does not start when two bricks are put together, but when these two bricks, one way or another, enter the space of architectural discourse.

**2.** If modern architecture is produced within the space of publications, photographs, exhibitions, etc., then the second point that one can make is that this space is for the most part two-dimensional, and at a certain point architecture somehow internalizes that space, that flatness (fig. 9). In Mies you can start seeing that with the Barcelona Pavilion, the Tugendhat House, the House for a Bachelor, and other projects. Traditionally Mies's architecture is described in terms of flowing, three-dimensional space, but in fact the architecture is organized by two-dimensional frames. The space is not simply contained by the walls.

**3.** A third, not unrelated, point is that architecture is not simply something represented, but is a way of representing. The building itself should be understood in the same terms as drawings, photographs, writings, films, advertisements, and so on, not only because these are the media in which we often encounter it, but because the building is a mechanism of representation in its own right. It is a "construction" in all the senses of the word. This means, among other things, that the building is not simply represented in images but is a mechanism for producing images.

Mies's houses can be understood as frames for a view; more precisely, frames that construct a view. Mies once wrote "I cut openings into walls where I need them for view or illumination." But here, as in most of his writings, nothing could be further from his architecture. Mies's windows are almost never holes in a wall. The walls are no longer solid planes punctured by windows, but what Le Corbusier would call "walls of light." That is, the walls have been dematerialized, thinned down with new building technologies and replaced by extended windows, lines of glass whose view defines the space. The non-transparent walls of the house now float in the space rather than produce it. Seeing is a primordial activity of the modern house. The house is no more than a device to see the world, a mechanism of viewing. Shelter, separation from the outside, is provided by the window's ability to turn the threatening world outside the house into a reassuring picture. The inhabitant is enveloped, wrapped, protected by the pictures. These are not simply neutral views of the outside world. The world is at once turned into an outside and interrogated, intensified, transformed by being framed.

9. Mies van der Rohe,
Resor House, 1933,
Jackson Hole, Wyoming, (project).
Photomontage of the view from the interior.

PABELLON DEL SUMINISTRO DE ELECTRICIDAD
EN ALEMANIA

10 & 11. Mies van der Rohe,
Pavilion of the International Utilities and Heavy
Equipment Industries,
1929 International Exposition, Barcelona.
Exterior and interior.

As Mies puts it, "When one looks at Nature through the glass walls of the Farnsworth House it takes on a deeper significance than when one stands outside. More is asked for from Nature, because it becomes part of a greater whole."[33]

**4.** An entirely different mechanism for the production of space is at work here. Mies's architecture is all about constructing a horizon. The first symptom of this is that all of the projects, even the skyscrapers, are so insistently horizontal. But more than this, each image of them is dominated by the horizon line. I am not referring here to the horizontal symmetries of Mies's architecture, which, as Robin Evans has pointed out, profoundly stabilize the asymmetry of the plans. Rather, I am referring to the way in which the horizon line defines space. If Mies's projects are frames for a view, what these projects frame is a horizon. It is not just that they frame an existing horizon, rather the frame is a mechanism for producing a horizon. This can be seen for instance in those projects in which Mies literally marks the horizon line across the window. It is even more clear when there are no windows at all, as in the project for the Convention Center in Chicago (1953–54) where, in the collage of the interior, the heads of people seem to construct a horizon (see Baird, fig.1); or in the Electrical Industry Pavilion (fig. 10 & 11), a less well known building for the 1929 International Exposition in Barcelona where large-scale photographs were projected onto the windowless walls, creating in Fritz Neumeyer's words, "a three-dimensional panorama that seemed to open the space towards an imaginary *horizon* and made one forget its walls."[34] The horizon in its original Greek sense means enclosure. While Mies's architecture is solely constructed with two-dimensional frames, what these frames project is an enclosure defined by a horizon. Indeed, the space of Mies's architecture is no more than this constructed horizon.

To rethink Mies will be to rethink that line. To do so would be to show that Mies neither stands against the restless mobility of images with an architecture of eternal values, nor participates fully in that mobility. Rather, he uses that very mobility to define space. So perhaps it would indeed be worth my while to get off at the stop marked "Mies."

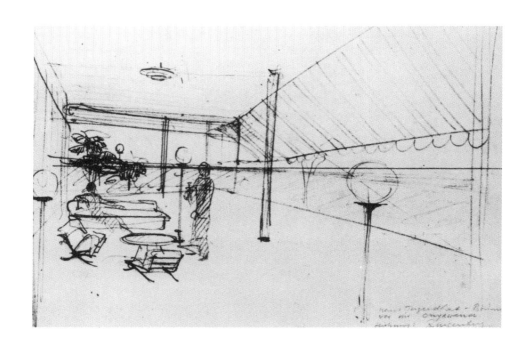

12. Mies van der Rohe,
Tugendhat House, 1928–1930
Bruno, Czechoslovakia.
Sketch of the large window.

## Notes

1. "Images," written and performed by Lou Reed and John Cale on "Songs for Drella — A Fiction," 1990, New York, Shire Records.

2. See for example, Peter Blake, *The Master Builders: Le Corbusier, Mies van der Rohe, Frank Lloyd Wright* (New York: Alfred. A. Knopf, 1961), p. 153ff. "Unapproachable, taciturn and cryptic," writes Graeme Shankland in "Architect of 'the Clear and reasonable,'" *The Listener*, October 15, 1959. And according to Peter Smithson, "He has a banker's calm and a love of orderliness and quiet, built into him." See his "For Mies van der Rohe on his 80th birthday," first published in *Bauen and Wohnen*, May 1966, and reprinted in Alison and Peter Smithson, *The Heroic Period of Modern Architecture* (New York: Rizzoli, 1981), p. 61.

3. Georgia van der Rohe, personal conversation with Elaine S. Hochman, May 10, 1973. Quoted in Elaine Hochman, *Architects of Fortune: Mies van der Rohe and the Third Reich* (New York: Weidenfeld & Nicolson, 1989), p. 57.

4. James Johnson Sweeny, tribute to Mies van der Rohe, October 25, 1969, reprinted in Peter Carter, *Mies van der Rohe at Work* (New York and Washington: Praeger Publishers, 1979), pp. 183–84. The text continues to insist on the parallelism between Mies's figure and architecture: "And thirty-three years later I was reminded of that first sight of Mies, when one evening after museum hours, looking for him, I happened into his Cullinan Hall of the Museum of Fine Arts in Houston and found him alone in that sparsely hung, white gallery — 100 feet by 95 feet with a ceiling 32 feet high — once again on a Barcelona seat, again smoking a similar cigar, quietly studying the space he had so sensitively proportioned."

5. Blake, pp. 153–55.

6. Blake, p. 155.

7. Richard Padovan, "Mies van der Rohe Reinterpreted," *UIA International Architect*, 3 (1984), p. 39. (Emphasis added).

8. Padovan, p. 39.

9. Franz Schulze, *Mies van der Rohe, A Critical Biography* (Chicago and London: The University of Chicago Press, 1985), p. 12.

10. Mies van der Rohe, from inauguration speech at IIT, 1938. Quoted in Blake, p. 155.

11. Blake, p. 155.

12. Dirk Lohan interview with Ludwig Mies van der Rohe (Chicago, summer, 1968). Typescript in Mies van der Rohe Archive, Museum of Modern Art, New York. Quoted in Schulze, pp. 15-16.

13. David Spaeth, "Ludwig Mies van der Rohe: A Biographical Essay," in *Mies Reconsidered: His Career, Legacy, and Disciples* (New York: The Art Institute of Chicago and Rizzoli International, 1986), p. 13.

14. "Onyx is a precious material. Mies was asked if it did not give the pavilion a rarefied character: 'I can't follow that sort of reasoning. People say: it's aristocratic; it

isn't democratic. Rubbish, to me it is all a question of values, and I try to do things as well as I can.'" In "Mies Speaks," *Architectural Review* December 1968, p. 452.

15. Sandra Honey, "Mies in Germany," in *Mies van der Rohe: European Works* (London: Academy Editions), p. 18, and "Mies at the Bauhaus," *Architectural Association Quarterly,* vol. 10, n. 1, 1978, p. 53.

16. Peter Carter, "Mies van der Rohe: An Appreciation on the Occasion, this Month, of his 75th Birthday," *Architectural Design* 31, vol. XXXI, March 1961, p. 96.

17. In fact, Mies was the only "progressive" German architect who used brick in the 1920s. His contemporaries refused to do so because of its handicrafts connotations. But Mies appreciated that it was a structural material that did not need to be concealed. He repeatedly said that it was through Berlage that he had developed his interest in brick.

18. Blake, p. 155.

19. Dirk Lohan, interview with Mies van der Rohe, Chicago, Summer, 1968. Typescript in Mies van der Rohe Archive, Museum of Modern Art, New York: "Wahrscheinlich, weil ich keine . . . klasse billet nahm. . . ." ("Probably because I did not have a . . . class ticket. . . ."). I am assuming here the blank space in the transcript could only have meant first class. Incidentally the pathology of early train travel does not account for different symptoms in first- and second- class passengers.

20. Dirk Lohan interview with Mies van der Rohe, p. 19. Quoted in Schulze, p. 3.

21. Sandra Honey, "Mies in Germany," p. 14 and 25 (note 14). David Spaeth, "Ludwig Mies van der Rohe: A Biographical Essay," in *Mies Reconsidered,* p. 15.

22. Mies van der Rohe, "Baukunst and Zeitwille," *Der Querschnitt* 4, n.1 (1924), pp. 31–32. English translation in Fritz Neumeyer, *The Artless Word: Mies van der Rohe on the Building Art* (Cambridge and London: MIT Press, 1991), translated by Mark Jarzombek, p. 246.

23. Wolf Tegethoff, "From Obscurity to Maturity," in *Mies van der Rohe, Critical Essays,* p. 43.

24. Philip Johnson, *Mies van der Rohe* (New York: The Museum of Modern Art, 1947), p. 22.

25. Richard Pommer, "Mies van der Rohe and the Political Ideology of the Modern Movement in Architecture," in *Mies van der Rohe: Critical Essays,* p. 107. See also, Richard Pommer and Christian F. Otto, *Weissenhof 1927 and the Modern Movement in Architecture* (Chicago and London: The University of Chicago Press, 1991).

26. Johnson, p. 49.

27. "At some point in late 1925 or early 1926, Mies directed his assistant Sergius Ruegenberg to climb to the attic of his studio at Am Karlsbad 24 and destroy all the old plans and drawings that had been stored there." Wolf Tegethoff, "From Obscurity to Maturity," in *Mies van der Rohe,* Critical Essays, p. 33.

28. Sandra Honey, "Who and What Inspired Mies van der Rohe in Germany," *Architectural Design* 3/4, 1979, p. 99; and "Mies in Germany," p. 16.

29. Mies van der Rohe in an interview with Ulrich Conrads, Berlin 1966 (recorded on a L.P. album, "Mies in Berlin," Bauwelt Archiv 1). Quoted by Sandra Honey, "Mies in Germany," p. 16.

30. Wolf Tegethoff, "From Obscurity to Maturity," in *Mies van der Rohe, Critical Essays*, pp. 57–58.

31. David Spaeth, Mies van der Rohe, p. 76.

32. Cf. Robin Evans, "Mies van der Rohe's Paradoxical Symmetries," *AA Files* 19. As Robin Evans notes: "It is difficult to understand why this realization of 1929 should so often be cited, as if Mies had achieved some completely new insight." (p. 68, n. 13.)

33. Christian Norberg-Schulz, "Talks with Mies van der Rohe," *L'Architecture d'aujourd'hui*, 29, n. 79, September 1958, p. 100.

34. Neumeyer, p. 226.

Note: This text was first given at the symposium "The Presence of Mies" and then elaborated as part of the "Preston Thomas Memorial Lectures" that Beatriz Colomina gave at Cornell University in the Fall of 1993.

1. Laughs.

Images

## WHAT'S SO FUNNY:
## MODERN JOKES AND MODERN ARCHITECTURE

*Brian Boigon*

Modern Architecture and Modern Jokery are two subjects that have yet to be joined. However, the techniques of their respective representations are surprisingly similar. "What's so Funny" traces the spatiality of the punchline as it is characterized by the modern architecture of the stand-up comedian. My presentation is meant only to introduce the problem of *the joke in space* and to begin its excursions into the fine art of modernist deceit. I suggest here that although "it is what it is,"[1] both Modern Architecture and the Modern Joke display their sordid past(s) when called to the foreground by real time.

And finally let me add that jokes and architecture have a brilliant *Einfalt*[2] in an early work by Lilly Reich and Ludwig Mies van der Rohe: the Silk and Velvet Café at the 1927 Exposition de la Mode in Berlin. We witness in their project the efficiency of the curtain and its theatrical presences. It is this work that introduces modernity to the burlesque principles of the curtain.

### A Short History of the Twentieth Century in Point Form

1844    The first pre-mixed tube of paint
1900    Henri Bergson publishes *Laughter: An Essay on the Meaning of the Comic*
1905    The first public commercial cinema houses
1905    Sigmund Freud publishes *Jokes and Their Relation to the Unconscious* (the first English edition was released in North America in 1916)
1908    Peter Behrens designs the Turbine Hall of the AEG factories in Berlin

| 1910 | The first mass-produced tube of toothpaste |
| 1911 | Walter Gropius and Adolf Meyer design the Fagus-Werk Shoe Factory |
| 1920 | The first radio broadcast intended for home reception |
| 1921 | Ludwig Mies van der Rohe designs his infamous Glass Skyscraper office building for the Friedrichstrasse competition in Berlin |
| 1948 | 75% of American households have a television |
| 1991 | 38 million Super Mario games have been sold in North America |
| 1992 | The last airing of Johnny Carson's Tonight Show |
| 1993 | 36 million Sony Walkmans have been sold worldwide |

## What's so Funny?

Little Red Riding Hood goes into the forest, but this time she is hiding a .44 magnum in her basket of goodies. The Wolf follows her into the woods and grabs her from behind. "Now that I've got you, I'm going to fuck you until dawn," he growls. But Little Red Riding Hood pulls out the .44 magnum, holds it to his head and announces calmly, "No you're not. You're going to eat me like the story said."[3]

Now, not everyone will share in the laughter of this joke. Little Red Riding Hood and the Wolf are still privy to the same level of sexual violence, making the power shift from Wolf to Red a dubious improvement on the original. However, the former was a fable for the ears of tired children, and the latter is an adult *touché* that compresses the fable against the joke. If you had not heard the story first when you were a child, the second time would be of little value. The seduction of a "gender taboo" makes the second story into a joke.

The re-tale is what makes a mere story into a hilarious joke. It is this component of historical compression that gives the joker a modern face. Jokes, by their very construction, are meant to present the past as the present.

## A Word about Jokes, Bewilderment and Illumination

In his book on jokes and the unconscious, Freud once defined a joke as a *playful* judgment. Jokes have had the long-standing ability to find similarity between dissimilar things. One could also say that joking is the ability to combine, with surprising speed, several ideas that are in fact alien to one another.

Freud goes on to suggest that the use of bewilderment and illumination in the following joke is almost a classic principle in jokery: "A poor lottery agent boasts that the Baron Rothschild had treated him quite as his equal — quite 'famillionairely.'"

2. James Brown teaching a few steps to the godfather of late-night talk shows in 1967.

3. Mies at home.

4. Ed Sullivan doing the really big show . . . 1966

"Miss Jenkins, would you please bring a round object into my office?"

5. What is this? What does it do? What's funny about it?

6. Partition by Stanley Kubrick.

7. "Miss Jenkins, would you please bring a round object into my office!"

Here the word acts as a vehicle for the joke. It appears at first to be simply a word wrongly constructed, something bewildering. The comic effect is produced by the solution of this bewilderment, by understanding the word. The first stage of enlightenment — recognizing that the word means both "rich" and "familiar" — is followed by a second stage in which the listener realizes that this meaningless word has bewildered us and has then shown us its true meaning. Theodor Lipps suggested that it is only this second illumination, this discovery that the word that is meaningless by normal linguistic usage has been responsible for the whole conundrum, that produces the comic effect. In other words, the complex experience of being both bewildered and then illuminated produces laughter.

### Invincible Jokes

According to Theodor Lipps, a joke — or in our case — architecture — "says what it has to say, not always in few words, but in too few words. It may even actually say what it has to say by not saying it." The premise of this paper is not specifically Miesian; rather, it originates from Modern Architecture at large and its relationship to Modern Jokes. I report not as an historian, but as a newscaster who will soon jeopardize his job by speaking candidly and with personal innuendo about topics that he knows have been sanctioned unjokable and perhaps even unlaughable: Mies van der Rohe and the Adventures of Modern Architecture.

My proposition is simple if not at the very least funny. Modernist Jokery and Modernist Architecture share the same temporal and spatial field. They share the same historical episode of anti-ornamentalism and suffer equally from the new problem of transparency brought on by the introduction of the architecture of the curtain wall and, in the case of popular theater, the incorporation of the stage skirt in front of the curtain as part of the performance stage itself. For example, vaudeville theater perfected the use of the MC stage act in which a speaker-comedian appears in front of the stage curtain, introduces himself or herself and delivers a candid monologue confiding in, and sometimes even interacting with, the audience directly. This new breach of the curtain may perhaps signify the dissolution of certain theatrical devices, but for the purpose of my presentation it signals the emergence of the profession of stand-up comedy and, in effect, stand-up space.[4]

Comedy in front of the curtain — existential monologue — no mosquito net, no costume, no ornament, and definitely no visual illusion. As we have all seen on television, this curtain wall for the stand-up comic has remained one of the few historical codes left on stage by all the networks. More importantly, the curtain has been assigned a highly mobile and even nomadic life on stage. For example, Ed Sullivan liked the vaudeville version of his curtain to be tight up against him. Ed's producers kept his candid personality in the foreground by blending Ed's suit with the curtain itself. I could suggest that Ed was just one big curtain — one big surface — no outside inside, just Big Daddy bringing home the toys for the whole family.

Johnny Carson's curtain was set quite far back from the front of the camera/stage. His set-up gave the impression that television was the stage of live truth. Carson gave the curtain wall a new spatial presence that empowered the foreground to erase the background; no more back stage, only front stage, only real-time events and the theater of the real — golf, music, sidekicks, and panoramic photomurals.

Mies had kept his curtains far back as well. That is to say, Mies had his options for settling the free walls anywhere inside his transparent grid. Mies kept his sense of humor away from the front of the stage. He tended to make his jokes in the privacy of a sound-proof box.

I understand that Mies was not exactly a barrel of laughs in plan, section, and elevation. The only Mies joke that I know is the one in which he comes home after a hard day at the office and sees that someone has moved the furniture. He exclaims, "Just when I learned how to make ends meet, some-body moves the ends."

A Modern Joke is born out of the same generalized code as Modern Architecture.

In particular, stand-up comedy parallels the emergence of Modern space. However, it was not until the late advancements of modernity and technology that the joke and architecture intersected. In fact, one had to wait until the advent of television in the home to truly see the effects of a bare-bones delivery in front of a network curtain. The progression toward the dissolution of the stage into the proscenium is signaled by several theatrical maneuvers in front of the camera. First, costume that characterizes a time other than its own vanished (no longer being necessary), and second, a joker's delivery was no longer compounded by the rhetoric of metaphorical prose and was replaced by the one-liner. Say what you want to say, to whom you want to say it, any way you want and "everything is the same except the composition."[5]

Without the traditional masking devices of costume, building, and light, a more subtle game of comedy and architecture had to take place. The stage set for this game was premised on the illusion of live (to tape) broadcasting, the concealment of any structural engineering on the set, camera angle, and most importantly, caricature — the exaggeration or distortion of form to express content. I am speaking here of both the caricature of bodies and buildings. In the case of the latter, one is presented with an endless origami architecture — ceaselessly unfolding its burlesque spaces and curtains to the audience in a seamless camera feed of stationary angles and zooms. This is not an architecture of the dolly, but rather of the stationary.

**The Bank Joke**

Since the curtain wall was first introduced, architecture was presented with the internal problem of screening or masking transparency in space, that is, transparency floating between the curtain wall galls and a service core like a plasmatic gas. Mies handled the transparency problem in the Toronto-Dominion Bank Pavilion by the simple modeling of partitions. Banks just can't embrace the consequences of full-tilt transparency, since if they did, well ... who would want to see all their money hanging out to dry in a glass vault? Mies's use of transparency and counter-transparency creates the paradox of a perpetual display of everything and nothing — and nothing and everything.

What does this have to do with Modern Jokes? First, the Modern Joke is constituted by the blurring of bewilderment and illusion caused by precisely the same paradoxes of the curtain wall — now you see it — to the partition — now you don't. Second, the Modern Joker is a comedian who no longer hides behind a theater of narrative, but rather stands up and speaks in real time. What stands, then, between the stand-up comic and the crowd? Caricature stands between us and them. Pee-Wee Herman stood between us and Pee-Wee's own wee-wee. Rodney Dangerfield's self-loathing stood between us and ... "I used to wake up feeling sorry for myself until one morning I woke up and my dog had committed suicide."

By removing one layer of opacity, another surely emerges. Second surfaces, or the deep surface partition, were never meant to be exposed to the elemental semiotics of windows and doors. "Like, hey, we were Mindanao our own business and then the next thing you know, someone rips our face off and says, 'Show us your corridors.'" No wonder that the partition has been contorted into a fetish lifestyle. Modernity introduced partitions that in turn became caricatures of themselves. Caricature distorts form with content. Modern Architecture does just the same: it distorts its form with its content. Lips are not lips but giant elevator doors ready to ...

**The Water Cooler**

I am very pleased that we are conducting this symposium on Mies in Viljo Revell's Toronto City Hall (1958–65). It gives me my first opportunity to speak inside a real flying saucer. Toronto is one of those Sci-Fi aspiring cities that probably thought it was getting Isaac Asimov's design and was shocked to discover that it was not his, but went ahead with it anyway.

While our politicians were busy lobbying for one shot at close encounters, Canadian bankers were busy building Cartesian shapes that represented credit power. Those were the days before sexual harassment laws, before water coolers turned out not to be just water coolers and jokes not to be just jokes but linguistic conundrums filled with steamy innuendoes of sexism, racism, and grade two satire. It is hard to imagine a water cooler without the echo of a bad joke. "Jokes produce freedom and freedom produces jokes."[6] Some of the Modernists would have agreed that good architecture could do the same as a good joke. For example, the water cooler (and later the drinking fountain, and then later again the spring water cooler) was first introduced into the Modern office space as an appliance.

In fact, perhaps the only significant changes in the public spaces that emerged within the Modern workplace were those established by the introduction of the built-in drinking fountain. The development of the free plan produced an overwhelming sense of placelessness for office workers, perhaps even worklessness, as evidenced by the social intensity that inhabits coolers, photocopiers, and other communal office appliances.

## Are We Having Fun Yet?

The adventures of Modern Architecture have been marked at least once by a glass curtain wall skyscraper. More specifically by the non-loadbearing transparency and the introduction of a subsidiary set of opaquing devices: partitions, counters, and venetian blinds. The adventures of Modern humor have been marked first by the radio-partition, cinema-counter, and television-venetian blind.

Each new (entertainment) technology prescribes a whole new set of relations to masking and unmasking illusion. Here, I do believe that architecture is a kind of entertainment. "Sometimes reality is too complex to explain, so fiction interprets it."[7] Roland Barthes used to say that in order to have narrative one must have distance. In order to have jokes work, one must have humor close by — that is, close by but hidden. In order to have Modernity work, one must have its meanings close by. Face it, the Ten Commandments are not supposed to be multiple choice. But, hey, listen to your conscience, even though you've been told never to take advice from a stranger.

8. Here's Johnny . . .

9. "Portrait of Bureaucrat's Ass,"
Klaus Staeck, 1974.

10. Less is More.

## The Vampire Joke

Two vampires are talking to one another, and one says, "Hey let's go suck some blood outta some poodles at the kennel," and the other one says, "Hell no, Bob, we can't do that." "Why not, Avery?" "Well, because, Bob, poodles are the most evolved creatures on Earth and if we alter their morphogenetic evolution, I fear that the human race may never catch up and thereby never reach the level of poodle consciousness. Don't forget, Bob, before sending his findings to the Center for Advanced Evolution, Darwin erased the poodle from his ape charts. Everybody knows that modern man was a poodle first, then a dolphin who turned into a gorilla when he hit land, and then finally evolved to what he is today."

One cannot appreciate the techniques of joking without also identifying the phenomenon of laughter. Regina Barreca's book on women's strategic use of humor suggests that laughter is a necessary attribute of jokes, and that "laughter is always in need of a group." How can one explain the spontaneous laughter of a crowd? How could Modern Architecture make people laugh? Certainly we have produced, in this century alone, three of the most hilarious surfaces: the snap, crackle, and pop of the scopic field — the glass curtain wall *Snap* — the cinematic screen *Crackle* — the television monitor *Pop*.

I'll leave the smell of the cinema and TV for another time, and underline here that the development of the *curtain wall* was not simply parallel to the development of the modern joke but was even perhaps akin to the rise of the (stand-up) *free-standing comic*.

Modernity brought with it "the cult of the personality," the invention of stardom. Everybody knows that joke telling is an ancient art. And every period of history has jokers who are particular to it. But the stand-up comic was a new breed that did not adhere to the traditional masking inherent in satire or irony but arose out of the cinema and television and was later immortalized in Las Vegas. The stand-up comic gave us the everyday as if it were there to serve as material for laughter.

Jokes, as it were, could be found anywhere, any time. "Freedom produces jokes and jokes produce freedom." But like Modernity, while jokes expose a truth, they also conceal one: the impossibility of real time. Did you hear the one about the vampire who met a comedian and got into a jocular vein?[8]

## Notes

1. James Brown (date unknown).

2. Martin Heidegger uses the word *Einfalt* to refer to simplicity or, literally, onefoldedness.

3. Regina Barreca, *They Used to Call Me Snow White ... but I Drifted: Women's Strategic Use of Humor* (Harmondsworth: Penguin Books, 1992).

4. I suggest here that "stand-up space" is a kind of playful description of space which has suddenly become itself. It no longer has the filter of the symbolic to shield it from the UV of real time.

5. Gertrude Stein, *Composition as Explanation* (Oxford: Oxford University Press, 1926).

6. Jean Paul Richter, *Vorschule der Ästhetik* (Hamburg: F. Meiner, 1990).

7. Jean-Luc Godard, *Alphaville.*

8. "Morning Smile," *The Globe and Mail* (September 29, 1993).

1. Mies van der Rohe,
Seagram Building, 1954–58, New York.
Perspective sketch of the plaza.

Afterword

## ODYSSEUS AND THE OARSMEN,
## OR, MIES'S ABSTRACTION ONCE AGAIN

*K. Michael Hays*

"Art remains alive only through its social power to resist society; unless it reifies itself, it becomes a commodity. What it contributes to society is not some communication with the same but rather something more mediate — resistance. Resistance reproduces social development in aesthetic terms without directly imitating it. Radical modernism preserves the immanence of art by letting society into its precincts but only in dimmed form, as though it were a dream. If it refused to do so, it would dig its own grave."[1]

Take the 1922 skyscraper project, for example, Mies van der Rohe's first attempt at working through the determinate dialectic of resistance versus sheer immanence. On the one hand, the skyscraper's newly achieved optics of mechanical reproduction (as Detlef Mertins calls it) is a thorough encoding of post-war society's technical advances out of which Weimar culture was to be constructed. The vivid coordination of the reflective and refractive glass surface, the repetitive steel structural elements and floor plates, the contingent plan and aleatory volume, the technical form of the high-rise building itself (all of which must be understood as historically specific, contextually emergent forms) attest to architecture's social power of representation, to architecture's letting society into its precinct. And that same opticality makes its own kind of contribution to the contradictory experience of that society's development, which comprises almost equal measures of euphoria and anxiety, higher consciousness and alienation, and finds its principal location in Berlin.[2] Learning from expressionism's anguished stimulation of the object (itself a projection of subjective disturbances), Mies's glass curtain wall, alternately transparent, reflective, or refractive —

depending on light conditions and viewing positions — absorbs, mirrors, or distorts the immediate, constantly changing images of city life. The very body of the building contorts to assume the form demanded by the contingent configuration of the site and to register the circumstantial images of the context. But countering expressionism's subjectifying tendencies, the reiterative steel structure mimics the anonymous repetition of the assembly line and poses mechanization as another sort of contextual determinant.

Here I have imported the phenomenological reading mechanism of Rosalind Krauss to characterize this architecture's immersion in a contradictory particularity, but also its mimetic submission to the alienating, reified context in which it emerges (Krauss, p. 133). On the other side of Theodor Adorno's dialectic, however, the skyscraper demonstrates architecture's power of resistance through its autonomy, the independent material existence Ignasi de Solá-Morales Rubió insists upon (Solá-Morales Rubió, p. 154). For the other aspect of the project — most apparent in the thick, black, silent elevational drawing — strives toward an immediate materiality of the surface, attempting to oppose and negate the contextual status quo and assert itself as a radically intrusive, nonidentical object within an unsatisfactory social and physical fabric, an opaque refusal of the situation that was its sponsor. Mies seems eager here to escape the kinds of interiority bequeathed to aesthetic practice by the traditional bourgeois cultural values from which his early work had emerged — the map of prior experiences drawn by the cultivation of subjective refinements and aesthetic discriminations, the fetishization of experience as a kind of private property, the individualism that substitutes for the life and culture of groups. But he also wants to escape the "incomprehensible triviality" (as Martin Heidegger would say) of the social product. His later work would emphasize again and again its ambition to salvage the purity of high art from the encroachment of mass production, technological modernization, urbanization, in short, of modern mass culture and everyday life. But already in the skyscraper project — or at least in this one of its aspects, the elevational drawing seeming incompatible with the socially "reflective" model — Mies has reserved a dimension of antisociality and refusal (Mertins, fig. 2). *"Denn wahr is nur, was nicht in diese Welt passt,"* Adorno would say. Only what does not fit into this world is true.[3]

The two aspects of Mies's project are, then, the result of the encounter between these contradictory impulses: representation and resistance, submission and refusal, mimesis and expression (mimesis meaning objective dissonance in this case and expression the subjective attempt to transcribe it). I want to keep this dialectic of Mies's 1922 skyscraper project in the near background for some time (I will show later why I think dialectic rather than contradiction or ambiguity is the correct concept to cover Mies's work) for it is a dialectic that he will return to over thirty years later in the high-rise buildings of North America. With this, I offer my preliminary thesis: the abstraction of Mies's North American architecture arises out of a central tension in his overall architectural program, namely, that between the desire to desubjectify the aesthetic phenomena — to displace the subject-centered categories of experience, consciousness, interiority, and the like with the elementary bits and pieces of the object world itself — and the commitment to produce aesthetic experience — to maintain some last dimension of fully achieved engagement with form that the desubjectifying desire cannot wish to deny. What will happen under this strain is that Mies's aesthetic production will push back toward the ineffable limit condition of architectural form, to the silence, the abstraction that almost every analysis of Mies ends up declaring.

Fritz Neumeyer's central thesis regarding the reciprocal mediations between art and technology, gravitas and transparency, etc., is not incompatible with what I have claimed for the skyscraper project above. Neumeyer has already alerted us to the persistence of a dialectical structure in Mies's writings, the "double way to order"; rehearsing one of Mies's manuscripts from 1927, for example, Neumeyer notes "a regular two-step of opposites: life and form, inside and outside, unformed and overformed, nothing or appearances, what had been or what had been thought, how and what, classical and Gothic, constructivist or functionalist."[4] Neumeyer continues, interpreting Mies through his underlinings of Romano Guardini's 1925 *Der Gegensatz*: "This conflict of opposites was not resolvable by a redeeming formula. Life could not be thought as a 'synthesis of disparities' nor even as a whole the two sides of which are complementary 'parts'. It exists rather as an elemental form, a 'bound duality.'"[5]

What is more, the oscillations of this same structure should prove helpful in our pursuit, with Detlef Mertins, of Mies's "more than." For the limit condition of Mies's dialectic (called, for now, a bound duality) is for Neumeyer and Mertins (they are not alone) nothing less than art itself, and, as Mertins and Solá-Morales agree, the "working through" of that limit condition entails a reconceptualization of signification and subjectivity outside the domain of technical skill and magisterial intervention.

But I must be careful with my attributions, for talk of art in general (let's think of it with a capital A) must normally presuppose a primitive accumulation of the capital of aesthetic experience and allude to what you already know about art, must normally make appeals to greatness or the Idea or Spirit or something like this, and if you don't know about these things already, then no one can tell you. In matters of such art, some would say, there is only the experience itself or its absence. I would insist, however, (and will try to make the insistence specific shortly) that the aesthetic experience produced in Mies's architecture is different from essences or ideals or some hovering *Geist* waiting to be discovered and made palpable. It is rather an experience well-nigh unprecedented, a blocking together of the aesthetic and the anti-aesthetic: *le fait social mise-en-architecture*. Mies wrestles with the inescapable contradiction that anything that appears architecturally, thematized through the discipline's signs, risks falling to one side into the net of subjectifying discourse with all its placating aestheticism and visual commodification, and to the other side onto the scabrous surface of the ordinary where it is transformed into a similarly fetishized symptom of objective processes. And yet, architecture cannot abdicate its aesthetic vocation altogether without turning into the unformed; the capacity for representation, fictionality, and imagination is not a supplement to building art but rather its distinguishing feature. Such problems are historicized in Mies's work, they subtend the trajectory of his architectural program begun in 1922 to intersect with another skyscraper in the altogether different time and place of Park Avenue 1954–58 (the first of Mies's encounters with Canadian patronage), to which we can now turn.

The facts of the Seagram project are well known: Samuel Bronfman and Phyllis Lambert's desire for a building of solid patrician elegance that would rise above the mediocrity of steel and glass in Manhattan; the centrality of Mies's position in American architectural discourse of the 1950s; the axial, frontal "American" dialogue of the Seagram building with McKim, Mead, and White's Racquet and Tennis Club, the elementarist "European" play of volumes; and the negative dialogue of Seagram's pink granite plaza with the cavernous streets of New York.[6] I wish only to underscore one of the facts here: that the focus of Mies's attention seems to be, from the start, judging from the documents, the plaza itself, with the building surface understood as a kind of frame or support for that primary clearing in the deadening thickness of the Manhattan grid (fig. 1). The sketch of the plaza is the only drawing "in Mies's hand," as the archival curators say, that sketch and two dozen or so more of sculptures for the plaza.

Look at that sketch. Traces of Karl Friedrich Schinkel are there still, perhaps, attesting to this new architecture's noble heritage; the Crown Hall drawing of 1955 is there with its five bays and human figures drawn in and its "universal" space of the clear-span pavilion; the New National Gallery is somehow prefigured, with Alberto Giacometti replaced by Mies's own scribbles for sculpture. But mostly there is just the space of the plaza and the few props — edges, planes, and frames — needed for its definition. Neumeyer will want to see this as a staking out of a "space of contemplation," I suppose, with all the promise for subjective experience that notion holds out.

But it's hard for me to understand Mies's *Bilderverbot* as promising anything like experience in its older sense; it attests more to the utter fungibility of subject and object alike.

It is more correct to think of this sketch as Mies's attempt to pass beyond the contradictions of representation and resistance, or mimesis and expression, manifest in the two aspects of the 1922 skyscraper project — that is, the model's commitment to the context and the elevational drawing's inexorable autonomy—toward some vanishing point where something like the "space of appearance" (Baird through Arendt)[7] and "almost nothing" (Comay through Heidegger) are conjoined and architecture doggedly holds both together in order to deny that either is any longer actually possible by itself. To say it another way: architecture, of course, cannot eradicate appearance altogether (the untranslatable *Schein* being perhaps the better formulation for my purposes since it captures the aesthetic artifice or *illusion* of the appearance), cannot become nothing without destroying itself, turning into a reductive materialism, and leaving behind the unmediated symptoms of the unsatisfactory reality it hopes to change. But Mies regards with distrust any appearance since with that concept of fabricating a space in which the modern subject might actually emerge comes the nagging worry that what's driving the architectural representation (what's behind the appearance, so to speak) are just those social forces — instrumental technology, the market, the masses, *das Licht der Öffentlichkeit* — into whose service architecture is constantly being pressed. If architecture could do away with appearance, if every trace of reference could be emptied out of it, then perhaps it could just be what it really *is,* which is social nonetheless; and perhaps we could indeed contemplate *that,* were it not for the necessary illusions.

This simultaneous production of difference and integration with the social city, this impossible third term or "bound duality" is what the Seagram plaza as built tries to effect. It is a cut-out in the city, a literal nothing endowed nevertheless with a positive presence through its material and dimensional precision. What would become the most significant feature of the Seagram building, its curtain wall of glass and steel, is in the sketch notated by only a hasty, rhythmic zigzag of the pencil. Yet it is necessary that it be notated, for without this veil of matter-to-come there would be no architectural body to support the aesthetic and social effects, no idea to contemplate (if you still want that formulation), no evocation of any essential truth within the experience of modernity so framed.

Let us then jump quickly to that matter as it was built. And let me again appropriate Krauss's reading mechanism, now of Agnes Martin's minimalism, and apply it, as she allows we might, with little modification to the Seagram's surface. "First there is the close-to reading, in which one is engaged in the work's facture and drawing, in the details of its materiality in all their sparse precision (Krauss, p. 140)." Here the Seagram's famous I-section steel mullion is crucial; it is the nexus of meaning of the entire building surface: functional, factural, symbolic; utterly commonplace yet raised to representational status in the matrix that is the Seagram's surface; the primary mark out of which the surface's tissue of effects is produced. What is more, the I-section mullion can be construed as the final stage in a set of transformations from a purely technical, instrumental fragment to a new form that organizes the *visual exchange* between the work and its reader; that is to say, from the I-section's use as a load-bearing component in some hypothetical steel-frame building to its tectonic role in the trabeated frame and brick infill at IIT (where the I-section still functions as a structural support behind the glass line or embedded in the wall), to Seagram where the I-section, for one thing, stands as a synecdoche for the steel construction now pushed behind, but, by dissolving its factural identity into a mode of address, becomes strikingly more thing-like and *present* than ever.

So, in "a crucial second moment" of reading (still following Krauss) we move back a little until the facture of the architecture is taken over by its visuality, which is to say this logic of surface perception. The series of bronzed steel mullions now casts shadows on the bronze glass, erasing themselves as figures and the glass curtain wall as ground "into the continuous immediacy of a purely optical spread" (Krauss, p. 145). The modulations of the surface — the reticulated grid of welded mullions and panels — as tectonically thick as they are, cannot be read "deeply" like the agonized surface of the 1922 project, which still projects subjective disturbances and contextual dissonances onto the full body of the building. Rather, they can only be scanned for textural information; they are metal-marked calibrations of autonomous vision. Though they trace a manufacture and a certain skill, these marks signal precisely the renunciation of expression and of a controlling agency in favor of an immanent evenness of surface persisting from start to finish as if unencumbered by subjective intent. This, I take it, is Mies's abstraction, the effort to turn subjective experience into objectivized form and images but which now flow back into the space of experience thus left open.

It is helpful to consider the built wall of the Seagram building together with Mies's sketches for the sculptures, the wall seemingly come into existence fully conceptualized, with little intermediate development (I could find no developmental drawings in the archives), the sculptures churned out in variation after variation, then finally discarded (fig. 2, 3, 4). The sketches have a kind of hit-or-miss quality; they can be taken lightly, as if they were never meant to go into production, as if they had flowed from Mies's ruminations over the famous cigar and whiskey in the leisure time still allowed to the social mandarin back in his Chicago apartment. There is this implacable optical field of the building and the unsure plastic figure of the sculpture, the object found *already* and the object not-being-found. And the two make sense only as negations of one another. By 1958, it seems, if there is to be a figure at all, it will be that which the activity of architecting has excluded. The abstract field will displace the figurative object, put it in the back pages of the notebook or submerge it in the pools that finally appeared in the plaza in its stead, and then itself take on just enough of the aesthetic substance necessary to remain in experience at all.

One is reminded of Piet Mondrian who, while dancing to his favorite Broadway boogie-woogie, suddenly turned to his partner. "Let's sit down," he said, "I hear a melody." Now, perhaps Mies's abstraction harbors just this negativity of modernist refusal; perhaps Mies is just like all the others of the avant-garde, only more so. But I think there is more and we must now push beyond a phenomenological reading of surfaces. The Miesian desire to build "almost nothing" is at one with the "edified public life" that Baird detected, the "deliberate intention to heighten the consciousness of the passer-by in the historical particulars of his or her situation." (Baird, p. 163) If abstraction could finally dispose of any conciliatory melody, but in such a way that you could still dance to it, then architecture might discover some other means of signifying experience; it might put itself in a different sort of relation to the world, create an experience that culture had not yet invented or not yet banalized. "Almost nothing," indeed, because there is not much left to work on.

Abstraction is late modern architecture's way of working through the social fact, part of its "social power to resist society," to recall the formulation by Adorno with which I began. Manfredo Tafuri, in perhaps the most provocative and most elliptical interpretation of Mies's North American building, sees the abstraction of its surface — construed as an Adorno-like opposition filtered through Roland Barthes's "white writing" — as the last, desperate no-solution to the historical guilt of modern architecture. Tafuri:

> The "almost nothing" has become a "big glass" . . . reflecting images of the urban chaos that surrounds the timeless Miesian purity . . . in the neutral mirror that breaks the city web. In this, architecture arrives at the ultimate limits of its own possibilities. Like the last notes sounded by the Doctor Faustus of Thomas Mann, alienation, having become absolute, testifies uniquely to its own presence, separating itself from the world to declare the world's incurable malady.[8]

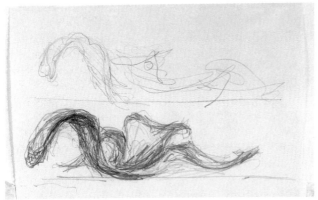

2, 3 & 4. Mies van der Rohe,
Seagram Building, 1954–58, New York.
Three study sketches of sculpture for the plaza.

For Tafuri, abstraction is a sign of formal closure and withdrawal in the face of overwhelming historical forces. Architectural abstraction is legitimate precisely because it reproduces the abstraction of the social system of exchange itself, putting the best face on the society's rationalization and planification of the subject, which ultimately disposes altogether with that inconvenience and reduces subjective choice to market desire. At the same time, Tafuri sees in Mies's work a wish to neutralize the social, which is not to say that it succeeded in doing so, or even that such a project makes any sense, for the social will still be found but, for Tafuri, *outside* the work.

I want to modify this slightly to find the social still inherent in the work. It is therefore important to historicize Mies's effort at Seagram and factor in the anthropological shock of the European mandarin in contact with the new North American democracy that is its social surround, and in particular with social practices that assured the destruction of the last remnants of surviving aristocratic forms, but came into being independently of the class struggle with an aristocratic *ancien régime,* as had been the case in the Old World. For American popular culture in the 1950s had, on its own, so to speak, become as technologically advanced as anything modernism could have hoped for — or better, there was a simultaneous leap forward both technologically and culturally in which these two developments were consciously linked, resulting in the emergence of what we now call media culture. It is here that we can focus Beatriz Colomina's concern with images on the task at hand. For in the 1950s, unlike in modernism's earlier stages, it was the *image* of mass production and consumption, and the logic of mass advertising and image-reception, that were foregrounded over the mechanical production techniques of the modern "masters." The logic of *image reception* began to displace that of *object production.*

The emergence just later of pop art is enough verification of this. And the work of Archigram, the Smithsons, and the Independent Group in Great Britain, and later Robert Venturi and Denise Scott Brown in the United States are only the most obvious examples of architecture's close involvement with consumer culture and mass advertising and the consequent challenge to the cherished modernist ideals of profundity and autonomy. During the years of the Seagram Building and just after, more intensely than any other time in modern history, architecture itself began to be seen as part of commodity culture in general. Not only does this mean that the aesthetic tastes of the new mass-cultural subject will be different in kind from those of the controlled and more comfortable identities of either the older aristocratic or bourgeois publics, it means ultimately the end of any doctrine of aesthetic universals or invariables, the tendency going even so far (as we now know from our postmodernist perspective) as to break up the very concept of the aesthetic unity and organicity of the work. It means that aesthetic self-referentiality begins to recede as a possible defense against mass culture.

The re-emerging consumer culture of the 1950s, with its newly devised strategies of advertising — the technique of large-scale color printing on outdoor billboards and the use of electric lighting for advertisement, both of a scale and pervasiveness not previously imaginable — changed the very nature of the experience of urban public space. For now visual reception challenged tactility, and the perception of architectural surfaces began to overtake the experience of urban space in the traditional sense. The extensive development of buildings on the outskirts of cities and the new distribution of services to suburban commercial zones made the control of the quality of urban space through traditional compositional, tectonic, and constructional means more and more difficult. Consequently a split was felt to open up between the world of quality building, in the European tradition of *bauen* or *Baukunst,* and the everyday world of the American popular environment; and this would later (with Venturi and others) become a fundamental split in architectural theory.

It is precisely the isolation, self-referentiality, and conceptual opacity of modernist abstraction that has been fixed on by historians and critics as the definitive characteristic of the resistant abstraction of modernism. But I want to suggest that when read through a logic of the surface — a perceptual logic we must now understand as having been given to us by mass society itself — self-referential or autonomous is too passive an adjective for Mies's abstraction. Abstraction in its fullest sense as a historically specific mode of organizing both subject and object comes into our perception in forms that are themselves produced by society, not by architecture alone. The experience of abstraction therefore belies architecture's autonomy, pinning that "inside" and that "appearance" (Mies) to its "outside" of American mass culture and the "nothingness" of reification itself.

I have already made the first of two relevant points about this particular abstraction: that in the Seagram project there is only a visual field so homogeneous, spread out, and intense that I have adopted the painting critic's nomenclature and called it optical. There is an aspect of the Seagram building that addresses itself to the eye alone, and the result is a new kind of architectural space and experience. But here I am attempting to interpret opticality not as an ontological threshold but rather as a specific cultural response. A second point is that Mies's use of the tower type as well as of the grid here amounts to the appropriation of found forms as if each were a ready-made. Given this second emphasis, the work thus actually shares with pop art and so-called pop architecture a common source — the newly awakened interest in ready-made units and systems — and, with that, makes problematic the conventional distinction between the ordinary, functionally and commercially derived object and the rarefied object of high art. And the development of the curtain wall generally is consistent with this dialectic of a ready-made system of enclosure and the production of unique objects for what amount to advertising purposes, or, in any case, objects that compare themselves to the surfaces of advertisement. Venturi's famous distinction between the self-referential duck of modernism — a building that speaks antagonistically but only of itself — and the decorated shed of pop — a building that compares itself to other surfaces of the everyday environment — this supposedly definitive and long-held distinction is utterly collapsed. The result is something like what art critics call a "handmade ready-made" — something that maintains the aspirations of modernism toward a visual logic derived from the qualities of materials and the nature of construction processes, but, at the same time, is not impervious to the gritty world of commercial culture that modernism, in its most famous moments, tried to refuse.

The particular experience of this "something," which is at once autonomous and porous, which "lets society into its precincts but only in dimmed form," which "reproduces social development in aesthetic terms without directly imitating it," is what many of the contributors to the present volume try to characterize — Mertins with "passibility," Neumeyer with the convergence of art and technology, Baird with the space of appearance, Solá-Morales with minimalism. And I can do no better than add one more attempt to the list, but one that gets more at the radical working through of the conjunction of the aesthetic and anti-aesthetic — of art with a capital A and advanced technical reification.

In the first chapter of *Dialectic of Enlightenment,* Adorno and Max Horkheimer replay the Sirens episode of the *Odyssey* as homologous struggles of class and aesthetic reception and read the experience of art as a series of cancellations and repressions — the colonization of pleasure by the commodity fetish (experience as the "after-image of the work process"),[9] the denial of happiness yet the holding out of its possible existence in some unrepeatable past, in short, the experience of art not as *bonheur* but rather only its *promise:*

> He knows only two possible ways to escape. One of them he prescribes for his men. He plugs their ears with wax, and they must row with all their strength. Whoever would survive must not hear the temptation of that which is unrepeatable, and he is able to survive only by being unable to hear it. Society has always made provision for that. The laborers must be fresh and concentrate as they look ahead, and

must ignore whatever lies to one side. They must doggedly sublimate in additional effort the drive that impels to diversion. And so they become practical. — The other possibility Odysseus, the seigneur who allows the others to labor for themselves, reserves to himself. He listens, but while bound impotently to the mast; the greater the temptation the more he has his bonds tightened — just as later the bourgeois would deny themselves happiness all the more doggedly as it drew closer to them with the growth of their own power. What Odysseus hears is without consequence for him; he is able only to nod his head as a sign to be set free from his bonds; but it is too late; his men, who do not listen, know only the song's danger but nothing of its beauty, and leave him at the mast in order to save him and themselves. They reproduce the oppressor's life together with their own, and the oppressor is no longer able to escape his social role. The bonds with which he has irremediably tied himself to practice, also keep the Sirens away from practice: their temptation is neutralized and becomes a mere object of contemplation — becomes art. The prisoner is present at a concert, an inactive eavesdropper like later concertgoers, and his spirited call for liberation fades like applause. Thus the enjoyment of art and manual labor break apart as the world of prehistory is left behind. The epic already contains the appropriate theory. The cultural material is in exact correlation to work done according to command; and both are grounded in the inescapable compulsion to social domination of nature. . . . Just as the capacity of representation is the measure of domination, and domination is the most powerful thing that can be represented in most performances, so the capacity of representation is the vehicle of progress and regression at one and the same time.[10]

What is produced here for Odysseus alone is nothing less than art itself. Yet, impotent in his bonds, he can only contemplate its contours of pure sound; his experience is utterly hollowed out. ("Not Italy is offered but evidence that it exists" is the famous phrase from the chapter, "The Culture Industry," that registers the same domination capacity of representation.[11]) The oarsmen, like Mies, like the rest of us, whatever closeness to materials and production we might salvage, can neither hear art's song nor delight in its labor but can only sense that we are missing out on something, das Unwiederbringliche, the genuine experience that can never be brought back from prehistory.

But it is important to insist on the thematic integration of what is presented in the quoted passage as two differentiated modes, for the encounters of Odysseus and the oarsmen are but two aspects of the same process, namely, abstraction as the historically emergent form of organizing experience. Karl Marx's painful lesson reappears in Adorno's retelling of the Homeric story, that the experience of the degree of an artwork's concreteness, density, and plenitude, or of its abstraction, dispersion, and impoverishment, ultimately derives from the concreteness or abstractness of the particular moment of society itself (however nonsynchronously it may be periodized). And in modernity, a unified and substantial center of experience can never be restored but only represented through modernism's abstraction. For Adorno, this has everything to do with mass production and the rationalization of the labor process — the equivalence imposed on every dimension of our world — for aesthetic reception itself is structured like the mode of production (even mental processes have been "Taylorized") and the experience of the products of "high" modernism and the Culture Industry alike is what we might call the reception *of* production at its most advanced.

But the crucial move of Adorno, and I am claiming of Mies as well, is to pose abstraction as at one and the same time the ultimate achievement of reification — the separation and neutralization of Odysseus's intellectual labor and the crew's manual labor being the precondition of abstract thought— and an historically new experience, the only possible experience adequate to everything we have lost in reification. Here I circle back to the epigraph with which I began: art must submit to reification in order to preserve the possibility of something more true. What results in the Seagram building is a series of transductions whereby abstraction changes its nature as it passes from the social to the aesthetic and back again. The plaza at Seagram is perhaps the first pulling back from the alienating life of the metropolis, and the assertion of the architectural surface as the support for that space is commensurate with that withdrawal. At this point, however, reification is borrowed back from the social in the form of the technical steel frame and the optics of mechanical reproduction; even more, the commodity form is made available and tangible in the volumetric ready-made of the high-rise building. Then, in a final moment of transfer, reification appears as the experience of abstraction. By designating itself as abstract, architecture acquires a means to escape that same status, to refuse to become a mere thing among things. Abstraction — the pure sound of the Sirens, the organizing absent presence — is the maximal limit of modern architecture. With it, Mies constructed an architectural object on the very edge of the category of architecture.

## Notes

1. Theodor Adorno, *Aesthetic Theory*, trans. C. Lenhardt (London: Routledge & Kegan Paul, 1984), pp. 321–22; translation modified.

2. In this context one cannot but invoke, by way of analogy to this presence of Mies, Georg Grosz's 1919 interpretation of the Friedrichstrasse and Georg Simmel's characterization of the city's mental life, both of which are enclosed by the same boundaries of time and place as Mies's architectural representation and both of which analyze what Adorno, following Simmel and Georg Lukács, called reification — that epistemic *anomie* resulting from the systematic fragmentation, quantification, and depletion of every realm of subjective experience.

3. Adorno, *Aesthetic Theory*, p. 86.

4. Fritz Neumeyer, *Mies van der Rohe: The Artless Word*, trans. Mark Jarzombek (Cambridge, Massachusetts: MIT Press, 1991), p. 197; Mies's manuscript is presented in Appendix I, p. 12.

5. Neumeyer, p. 200.

6. See Franze Schulze, *Mies van der Rohe: a Critical Biography* (Chicago: University of Chicago Press, 1985), pp. 270ff.

7. The locution of Arendt that Baird refers to in its context: "Action and speech create a space between the participants which can find its proper location almost any time and anywhere. It is the space of appearance in the widest sense of the word, namely, the space where I appear to others as others appear to me, where men exist not merely like other living or inanimate things but make their appearance explicitly." Hannah Arendt, *The Human Condition* (Chicago: University of Chicago Press, 1958), pp. 198–99.

8. Manfredo Tafuri and Francesco Dal Co, *Modern Architecture*, trans. Robert Erich Wolff (New York: Harry N. Abrams, 1979), p. 342.

9. Max Horkheimer and Theodor Adorno, *The Dialectic of Enlightenment*, (New York: Continuum, 1988), p. 137.

10. Horkheimer and Adorno, pp. 34–35.

11. "The new ideology has as its objects the world as such. It makes use of the worship of facts by no more than elevating a disagreeable existence into the world of facts in representing them meticulously. This transference makes existence itself a substitute for meaning and right. Whatever the camera reproduces is beautiful. The disappointment of the prospect that one might be the typist who wins the world trip is matched by the disappointing appearance of the accurately photographed areas which the voyage might include. Not Italy is offered, but evidence that it exists." (Horkheimer and Adorno, p. 148.)

# TORONTO-DOMINION CENTRE

Architects
Ludwig Mies van der Rohe, Design Consultant
John B. Parkin Associates and Bregman + Hamann, Associate Architects

Location
55 King Street West, Toronto, Ontario, Canada

Client
CEMP Investments Ltd. and the Toronto-Dominion Bank

Dates

| | | |
|---|---|---|
| 1962 | November | First public announcement of the Toronto-Dominion Centre project |
| 1963 | December | Architectural team commences work |
| 1964 | February | Ground breaking (stage one: 56 storey tower) |
| | November | Tower grillages in position (stage one) |
| 1965 | February | Erection of structural steel commences (stage one) |
| | July | Erection of steel cladding commences (stage one) |
| 1966 | April | Topping-off of tower (stage one) |
| | June | Erection of steel cladding completed (stage one) |
| | September | Ground breaking (stage three: 46 storey tower) |
| | November | Ground breaking (stage two: banking pavilion) |
| 1967 | February | Erection of structural steel commences (stage three) |
| | March | Tenants move into 56 storey tower (stage one) |
| | April | Erection of structural steel commences (stage two) |
| | September | Concourse open to the public (stage two) |
| | October | Concourse and Cinema open to public (stagetwo) |
| | November | Erection of structural steel complete (stage two) |
| | | "Conference of Tomorrow" held on the 54th floor |
| | December | Erection of steel cladding commences (stagethree) |
| 1968 | May | Official opening of Toronto-Dominion Centre |
| | July | Topping-off of tower (stage three) |
| | | Erection of steel cladding completed |
| 1969 | August | Tenants move into tower (stage three) |
| | | December Stage three 46 storey tower completion |

1. TDC under construction in early 1965.
Photo Toronto Star Syndicate.

Program
Area of site: 5½ acres
Area of site built upon: 2 acres
Area of site left as public space: 3½ acres
Permitted gross area above grade: site area x 12

*56-storey tower (Toronto-Dominion Bank Tower)*
Gross area above grade: 1,686,875 sq. ft.
Net leasable area: 1,311,000 sq. ft
Gross area of typical office floor: 30,250 sq. ft.
Structural bay: 30'–0" by 40'–0"
Typical floor to ceiling height: 9'–0"
Typical floor depth: 3'–0"
Ground floor lobby height: 26'–0"
Height of tower: 731'–0"
Population: 8,500

*46-storey tower (Royal Trust Tower)*
Gross area above grade: 1,180,812 sq. ft.
Net leasable area: 917,700 sq. ft.
Gross area of typical office floor: 26,530 sq. ft.
Structural bay: 30'–0" by 40'–0"
Typical floor to ceiling height: 9'–0"
Typical floor depth: 3'–0"
Ground floor lobby height: 26'–0"
Height of tower: 600'–0"
Population: 6,500

*Banking Pavilion (Main Branch, Toronto-Dominion Bank)*
Size: 150'–0" by 150'–0"
Gross area: 22,500 sq. ft.
Height of Pavilion: 30'–8
Floor to ceiling height: 25'–6"

*Shopping Concourse*
Net shop and restaurant area: 150,000 sq. ft. approximately

*Parking*
700 cars on two levels underground

Cost
$140,000,000 approximately

Structure
Steel frame and concrete foundations

Materials
Exposed steel painted matte black; black anodized aluminum; St. John gray granite; green Tinos marble; English brown oak; travertine; glass

Consultants
C.D. Carruthers and Wallace Consultant, Structural Engineers
H.H. Angus and Associates Ltd., Mechanical and Electrical Engineers
Edison Price, Lighting Consultant
R.B. Magee, Real Estate Consultant

Contractors
Pigott Construction Co. Ltd., General Contractor
Dominion Bridge Co. and Frankel Structural Steel Ltd., Steel Contractor
Crump Mechanical Contracting Ltd., Mechanical Contractor
Ainsworth Canada Ontario, Electrical Contractor

From *The Architects' Report* by Sidney Bregman, executive architect, TDC, November 1970

2. Model of TDC 54-storey tower montaged into
an aerial photograph of the site, c. 1963.

3. View across the north plaza towards
the Banking Pavilion and King Street, 1968.
Photo Panda.

4. Underground parking garage, 1968.
Photo Panda.

(next page)
5. View of south plaza.

6. A typical part of the underground shopping
concourse, 1968.
Photo Panda.

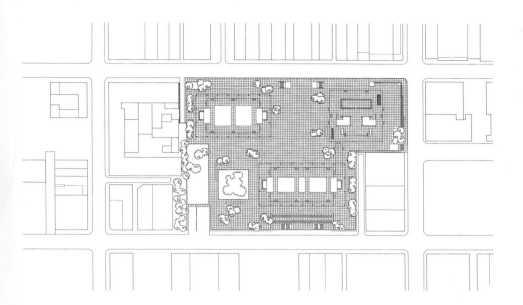

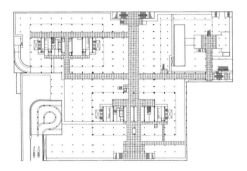

1. Site plan

2. Plan of the underground concourse.

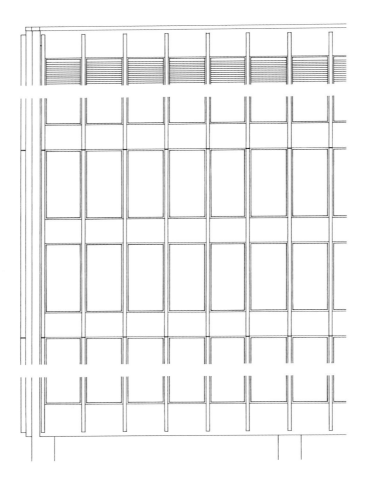

3. Detail elevation of the curtain wall.

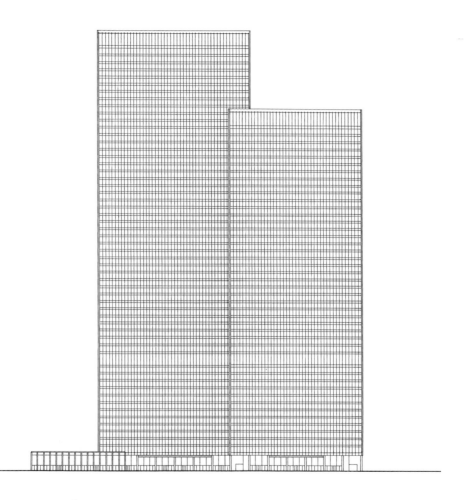

4. King Street (north) elevation.

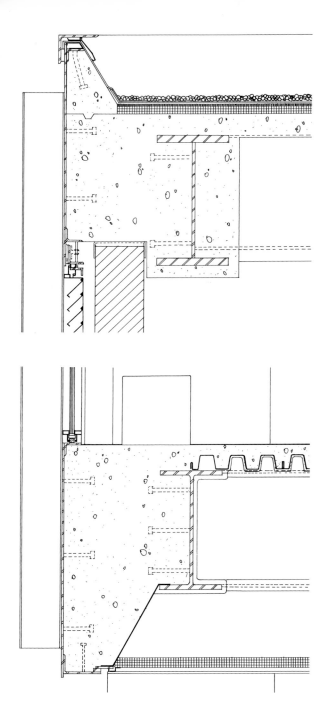

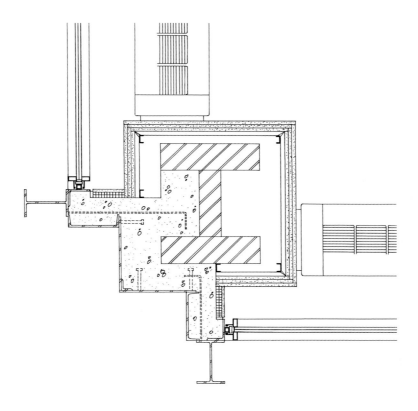

5. Typical detail section of the towers.

6. Typical detail plan at corner of the towers.

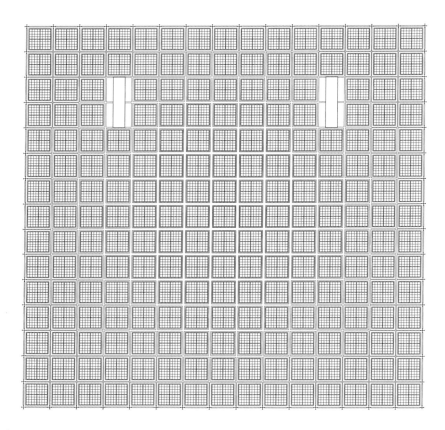

7. Reflected ceiling plan of the Banking Pavilion.

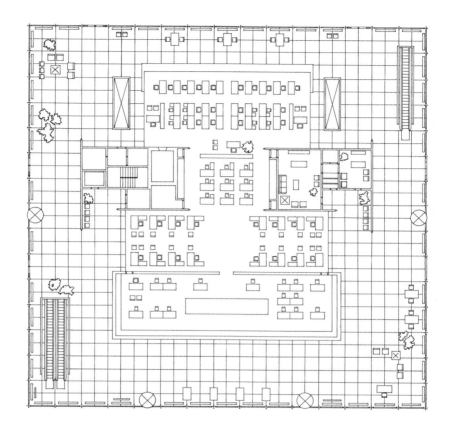

8. Plan of the Banking Pavilion.

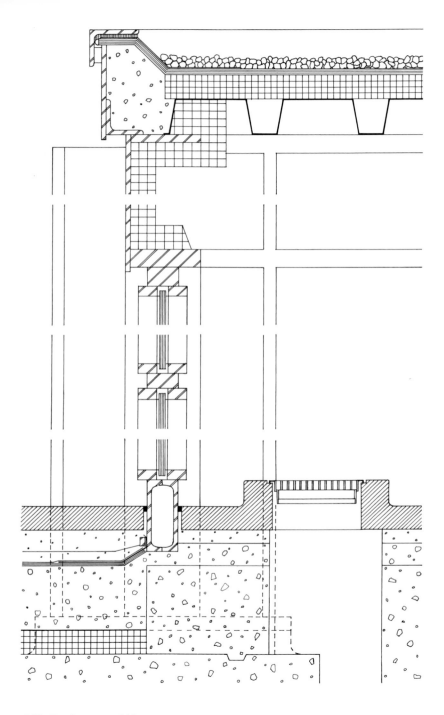

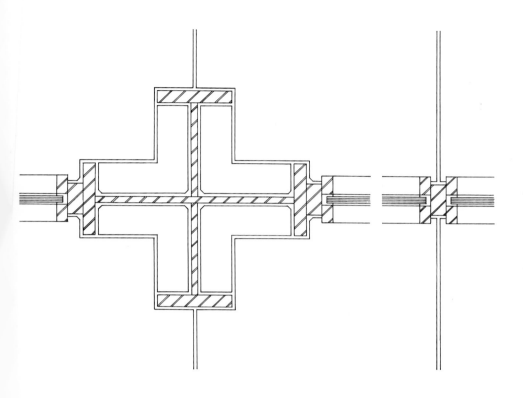

9. Typical detail section of the Banking Pavilion.

10. Typical detail plan of the cruciform columns of the Banking Pavilion.

# Contributors

**George Baird** is an architect, urban designer, and critic, and is professor of architecture at Harvard University's Graduate School of Design. He is the author of numerous essays on architecture, was co-editor of *Meaning in Architecture* (1969), and has just completed an extensive rereading of architectural modernism and postmodernism entitled *The Space of Appearance,* forthcoming from MIT Press.

**Brian Boigon** is an artist and theorist who teaches architecture at the University of Toronto. In addition to his artistic practice Boigon has written extensively, was editor of *Impulse,* author/producer of *Speed Reading Tokyo* (1989) and founding director of the *Culture Lab,* a symposium series that explores the convergence of cultural theory, art, architecture, and entertainment. The series is being published as *Culture Lab 1, 2,* and 3 by Princeton Architectural Press.

**Beatriz Colomina** is an architect, historian, and theorist who teaches in the School of Architecture at Princeton University. She has written extensively on questions of architecture and the modern institutions of representation, particularly the printed media, photography, advertising, film, and television. She is editor of *Architectureproduction* (1988) and *Sexuality and Space* (1992). Her book *Privacy and Publicity: Modern Architecture as Mass Media is forthcoming from MIT Press* (1994).

**Rebecca Comay** teaches philosophy and literary studies at the University of Toronto. She has published extensively on various aspects of modern French and German philosophy, literary studies and aesthetics. Her book on Hegel and Heidegger, entitled *On the Line; Reflections on the Bad Infinite* is forthcoming. She is also working on a book on Benjamin and Heidegger to be called *Pausing for Breath.*

**K. Michael Hays** is an architect, historian and theorist who teaches in the Graduate School of Design at Harvard University. He is the founding editor of the critical journal *Assemblage* which has become the leading forum for research in architecture in North America. Hays's essays on key figures of German modernism have appeared in numerous architectural journals. He is the author of *Modernism and the Posthumanist Subject: The Architecture of Hannes Meyer and Ludwig Hilberseimer* (1992).

**Dan Hoffman** directs the architecture program at the Cranbrook Academy of Arts, which has an exceptional record of experimental work in architecture. The results of Hoffman's provocative studio program are the subject of a forthcoming publication by Rizzoli International. Hoffman has exhibited and lectured widely.

**Rosalind Krauss** is Professor of Art History at Columbia University and a founding editor of the journal *October.* Her books include the seminal *Passages in Modern Sculpture* (1977), *The Originality of the Avant-Garde and Other Modernist Myths* (1985), *L'Amour Fou: Photography and Surrealism* (1985), and *The Optical Unconscious* (1993).

**Sanford Kwinter** is a theorist based in New York, co-editor of *Zone 1/2 The Contemporary City* (1986) and *Zone 6 Incorporations* (1992). In two forthcoming books, Kwinter discusses the role of time in modernist science and aesthetics, and the life sciences and their relation to twentieth-century history (MIT Press). He currently holds the Craig Francis Cullinan Chair at Rice University.

**Phyllis Lambert** is the President and Director of the Canadian Centre for Architecture in Montréal, whose extraordinary collection of architectural drawings, photographs, and books makes it one of the most important centers for architectural research in the world. She has been the Director of Planning of the Seagram Building (New York), the architect of the Saydie Bronfman Centre (Montréal), the design consultant for the CCA's own building, active in the preservation and scholarship of historical buildings and districts in Montréal, and the force behind the thought-provoking exhibitions and conferences of the CCA.

**Detlef Mertins** is an architect, historian, and critic teaching at the University of Toronto. He is co-curator of *Toronto Modern: Architecture 1945–1965* (1987) and curator-editor of *Metropolitan Mutations: The Architecture of Emerging Public Spaces* (1989). His work as professional advisor for the Kitchener City Hall Competition is documented in *Competing Visions* (1990). He is currently completing his dissertation, "Critical History and Architectural Modernity," at Princeton University.

**Fritz Neumeyer** is an architect, historian, and professor at the Technische Universität in Berlin. In addition to his numerous essays on German neo-classicism and modernism, he is the author of the landmark publication, *The Artless Word: Mies van der Rohe on the Building Art* (1991), in which he examines the formation of Mies's theoretical writings.

**Ben Nicholson** is an architect teaching design at the Illinois Institute of Technology. Nicholson's work, such as his *Appliance House* (1990), makes extensive use of photomontage and engages architecture in questions about technology, subjectivity, and the imagination.

**Ignasi de Solá-Morales Rubió** is an architect, theorist, historian, and professor in Barcelona, where he was one of the architects responsible for the reconstruction of Mies's 1929 Barcelona Pavilion. He is the author of *Minimalist Architecture in Barcelona,* which presents the renewal of modernism in that city, and has written extensively on architectural history and theory in both European and North American journals.

# Illustration Credits

Every effort has been made to trace the copyright ownership of the illustrations used in this volume. In some cases that has not proven possible and we would welcome the opportunity to include any omissions in future editions. We are grateful to the many organizations and individuals who have cooperated so readily in giving their permission to reproduce photographs and drawings.

## Introduction
Courtesy Detlef Mertins and Peter MacCallum.

## Lambert
Fig. 1: Collection Canadian Centre for Architecture, Montréal. PHTR1993:0007. Donation of Parnassus Foundation © George A. Tice.
Figs. 2, 7, 8, 10, 12: Mies van der Rohe Archive, The Museum of Modern Art, New York. Neg. nos. HB 21451-C (fig. 2), HB 33358-C (fig. 7), L.369-1 (fig. 8), F.1477-19 (fig. 10), HB 32147-A (fig.12).
Figs. 2, 8, and 10 were gifts of the architect.
Fig. 3: Ezra Stoller © Esto. Neg. no. 41T.3.
Figs. 4, 5, 6: Bregman + Hamann Architects, Toronto.
Figs. 9, 13: Toronto-Dominion Bank, Archives Department.
Fig. 11: Chicago Historical Society. Neg. HB-23513-L.

## Mertins
Fig. 1: Toronto-Dominion Bank, Archives Department. 77-239-18.
Fig. 2: Mies van der Rohe Archive, The Museum of Modern Art, New York. Gift of the architect.
Fig. 3: Karl-Ernst Osthaus Archiv, Hagen KÜ. 319/11/26.
Fig. 4: Reproduced from G, no. 5–6, April 1926 (Berlin), p. 134. Courtesy Der Kern Verlag, Munich.
Fig. 5: Photograph courtesy Mies van der Rohe Archive, The Museum of Modern Art, New York.
Fig. 6: Berlinische Galerie, Museum für Moderne Kunst Photographie und Architektur, Berlin, and VG Bild-Kunst.
Fig. 7: *Bauhaus Photography* (Cambridge, Massachusetts & London, England: MIT Press, 1985), p. 194.
Fig. 8: Toronto-Dominion Bank, Archives Department. 77-248-2.

Fig. 9: Steven Evans Photography.
Fig. 10: Kunsthistorisches Institut Frei Universität, Berlin.
Fig. 11: László Moholy-Nagy, *Painting-Photography-Film* (London: Lund Humphries, 1969), p. 130.
Fig. 12: *1910–1930 Zwanzig Jahre Weltgeschichte in 700 Bildern* (Berlin: Transmare Verlag, 1931), p. 244.

## Neumeyer
Figs. 1, 2, 4, 6, 7, 8: Fritz Neumeyer.
Fig. 3: AEG Archiv, Berlin.
Figs. 5, 9: Hedrich-Blessing, Chicago.

## Kwinter
Fig. 1. F. A. Kekulé, *Lehrbuch der organischen Chemie* (Erlangen: Ferdinand and Enke, 1861–87)
Figs. 4, 5: Rudolf Laban, *Choreutics* (London: MacDonald & Evans Ltd., 1966).
Fig. 3: Redrawn by Donald Chong.
Fig. 6, 7, 8, 9, 10: Joseph Needham, *Order and Life* (Cambridge: MIT Press, 1968).

## Hoffman
Figs. 3, 4, 7, 11: Photograph courtesy Mies van der Rohe Archive, The Museum of Modern Art, New York.
Fig. 5: Mies van der Rohe Archive, The Museum of Modern Art, New York. Gift of the architect.
Figs. 1, 2, 3, 6, 8, 9, 10, 12: Dan Hoffman.

## Nicholson
Figs. 1–6: Ben Nicholson.

## Krauss
Fig. 1: Hubert Damisch, *Théorie du /nuage/* (Paris: Éditions du Seuil, Paris, 1972), p. 167.
Figs. 2–4: The Pace Gallery, 32 E 57th Street, New York.

## Solá-Morales

Fig. 1: Steven Evans Photography.

## Baird

Fig. 1: Toronto-Dominion Bank, Archives Department, 77-252-38 W 239-20.
Fig. 2: Mies van der Rohe Archive, The Museum of Modern Art, New York. Gift of the architect.
Fig. 3: Photograph courtesy Mies van der Rohe Archive, The Museum of Modern Art, New York.
Fig. 4: Mies van der Rohe Archive, The Museum of Modern Art, New York. Gift of the architect.
Fig. 5: Peter Carter, *Mies van der Rohe at Work* (Washington: Praeger, 1972)
Fig. 6: Fritz Neumeyer, *The Artless Word: Mies van der Rohe on the Building Art* (Cambridge, Massachusetts & London, England: MIT Press, 1991), p. 234. Courtesy MIT Press.
Fig. 7: Panda Photography and Norr Partnership Limited, Architects Engineers.
Fig. 8: Leon Krier.
Figs. 9, 10: Toronto-Dominion Bank, Archives Department, 77-239-20, 77-241-6.

## Comay

Fig. 1: Redrawn by Donald Chong.

## Colomina

Fig. 1: *LIFE*, March 18, 1957.
Fig. 2: Peter Blake, *The Master Builders: Le Corbusier, Mies van der Rohe, Frank Lloyd Wright* (New York: Alfred A. Knopf, 1961). Courtesy Harold Ober Assoc.
Figs. 3, 5: G, no. 3, June 1924; no. 2, September 1923 (Munich: Der Kern Verlag, 1986)
Fig. 4: El Lissitzky and Kurt Schwitters, *Merz*, no. 8–9, (1924). Yale University Art Gallery. Gift of the Katherine S. Dreier Estate.
Fig. 6: Academy Editions.
Fig. 7: *Festschrift der Firma Henmann Schäler* (Berlin, 1930).
Fig. 8: *On Dieño,* n.73, Courtesy family Sagarro.
Figs. 9, 10: Mies van der Rohe Archive, The Museum of Modern Art, New York.
Fig. 11: Building Centre Trust.

## Boigon

Fig. 1: Preston Blair, *Animation* (California: Walter Foster Art Books, date unknown).
Fig. 2: *People Weekly,* June 10, 1991.
Fig. 3: *National Geographic.* From an advertisement for Polaroid Land Camera, date and year unknown, c. 1960s.
Fig. 4: *People Weekly,* Summer 1989.
Fig. 5: Whatzit coloring card, Cardz Distribution Inc. 1983, TM and © 1993 Hanna-Barbera Productions, Inc.
Fig. 6: 2001, Stanley Kubrick, date unknown.
Fig. 7: Source unknown.
Fig. 8: *People Weekly,* December 1967. Photo by Art Selby 1967.
Fig. 9: Courtesy Klaus Staeck © 1974.
Fig. 10: Smilby. *The Punch Cartoon Album.* (London: Grafton and Co., 1990).

## Hays

Figs. 1, 2, 3, 4: Mies van der Rohe Archive, The Museum of Modern Art, New York. Gift of the architect.

## Toronto-Dominion Centre

Fig. 1 & 2: Toronto-Dominion Bank, Archives Department, 77-240-1; 77-238-30.
Figs. 3, 4, 5, 6: Panda Photography and Norr Partnership Limited, Architects Engineers.
Figs. 7–15: Redrawn by Donald Chong, Dathe Wong, and Elaine Dydik (after Peter Carter).

Edited by Detlef Mertins
Designed at Bruce Mau Design Inc.
with Nigel Smith
Typeset in Monotype News Gothic
by Archetype
Printed and bound in Canada
by Friesen Printers